Poor Kids in a Rich Country

Poor Kids in a Rich Country

America's Children in Comparative Perspective

Lee Rainwater and Timothy M. Smeeding

Russell Sage Foundation • New York

The Russell Sage Foundation

The Russell Sage Foundation, one of the oldest of America's general purpose foundations, was established in 1907 by Mrs. Margaret Olivia Sage for "the improvement of social and living conditions in the United States." The Foundation seeks to fulfill this mandate by fostering the development and dissemination of knowledge about the country's political, social, and economic problems. While the Foundation endeavors to assure the accuracy and objectivity of each book it publishes, the conclusions and interpretations in Russell Sage Foundation publications are those of the authors and not of the Foundation, its Trustees, or its staff. Publication by Russell Sage, therefore, does not imply Foundation endorsement.

Library of Congress Cataloging-in-Publication Data

Rainwater, Lee
    Poor kids in a rich country : America's children in comparative perspective / Lee Rainwater and Timothy M. Smeeding.
        p. cm.
    Includes bibliographical references and index.
    ISBN 0-87154-702-3
    1. Poor children—United States. 2. Aid to families with dependent children programs—United States. 3. Income maintenance programs—United States. 4. Poverty—United States. 5. Child welfare—United States. 6. Poor children—Europe. 7. Aid to families with dependent children programs—Europe. 8. Income Maintenance programs—Europe. 9. Poverty—Europe. 10. Child welfare—Europe. I. Smeeding, Timothy M. II. Title.
    HV741.R33 2003
    362.7'086'9420973—dc21   2003047050

The paper used in this publication meets the minimum requirements of American National Standard for Information Sciences—Permanence of Paper for Printed Library Materials. ANSI Z39.48-1992.
Text design by Suzanne Nichols

RUSSELL SAGE FOUNDATION
112 East 64th Street, New York, New York 10021
10 9 8 7 6 5 4 3 2 1

About the Authors

LEE RAINWATER is professor of sociology emeritus at Harvard University and research director of the Luxembourg Income Study.

TIMOTHY M. SMEEDING is the Maxwell Professor of Public Policy at the Maxwell School of Syracuse University and overall director of the Luxembourg Income Study.

Contents

About the Authors   v

Preface   ix

Introduction   Taking the Definition of Poverty Seriously   1

PART I   *CHILD POVERTY AND INEQUALITY AT THE END OF THE TWENTIETH CENTURY*

Chapter 1   Child Poverty in Rich Countries in the 1990s: An Overview   17

Chapter 2   Patterns of Child Economic Well-Being   32

Chapter 3   Child Poverty and Population: Is Demography Destiny?   49

Chapter 4   Periods of Poverty: How Long Are Children Poor?   57

Chapter 5   Income Packaging: Market Income and the State   68

Chapter 6   Child Poverty and Income Packaging in Two-Parent Families   79

Chapter 7   Child Poverty and Income Packaging in Single-Mother Families   109

Chapter 8   Is There Hope for America's Low-Income Children?   132

PART II   *CHOICE AND METHOD IN RESEARCH ON POVERTY*

Chapter 9   Establishing a Poverty Line   145

Chapter 10   Establishing Equivalent Family Income   167

Chapter 11   Whence the Poverty Standard— Nations or Communities?   183

Appendix A   The Luxembourg Income Study Project   211

Appendix B   The U.S. State Database and Regional   213
              Combinations in Other Countries in the
              Luxembourg Income Study

Appendix C   From Relative Income to Real Income   216

Appendix D   Reweighting to Assess the Impact of   228
              Demography Versus Income Packaging

Notes   239

References   242

Index   253

Preface

THIS BOOK REPORTS some of the results of a continuing project begun some twenty years ago on the comparative study of economic advantage and disadvantage in North America, parts of Europe, and Australia. We have two goals and two overlapping audiences.

Our first goal is to report findings concerning American child poverty in comparison with the situation in European countries as well as in our neighbor Canada and Australia. We have done this in a nontechnical way in hopes of making the findings accessible to interested readers without burdening them with the kind of detail and methodological depth that specialists require. This is the narrative of part I of the book. We end part I with a discussion of some of the policy implications of our study. We hope readers will see other policy implications, depending on their own interests and experience. If we have done our job well, the reader will come away with a better understanding of how children fare in the United States and of the other possibilities in advanced democracies like ours.

In part II, we pursue a second goal with a more specialized audience in mind. Many social scientists, economists, political scientist, sociologists, and journalists are studying poverty issues and trying to do something about them. Whatever particular aspect of poverty they address in their own work, they are necessarily concerned with the fundamental conceptualizations of poverty and economic disadvantage that we had to address in designing the study reported in part I. This second part takes up three essential questions that those who study economic well-being must answer (consciously or tacitly) in their work and consider in making use of the work of others. It describes a method for making choices about the measurement of economic well-being derived from our comparative studies over the years. The interested reader will find there the guidelines we have developed in making concrete research decisions to follow out our central understanding: matters of resource distribution are not simply questions of what people can consume materially but rather questions of the kind of lives they can live—that is, of social participation and social identity. These guidelines should be of use to others in making choices in their own work and in evaluating other work.

In preparing this study for publication, our first debt is to those who have been members of the staff of the Luxembourg Income Study over the past twenty years. Their good humor, intelligent attention to detail, and hard work have made it possible to compare the countries we have studied with unusual ease. Cheri Minton carried out numerous computer tasks to facilitate the analysis of LIS data, and her models have been well followed by our current staff.

The LIS project has been supported from its inception by the Luxembourg government, which, under the leadership of two prime ministers, Jacques Santer and Jean-Claude Juncker, has provided us with a home base as well as funding to round out our multinational support network. We are also grateful for support in the form of data provision and funding by the nearly thirty member countries of the LIS project. Funds for this particular study have come from the Russell Sage Foundation, the Center for Advanced Study in the Behavioral Sciences, and the Ford Foundation.

We are most appreciative of the editorial work on the first draft of this study by Cindy Buck, who greatly improved the accessibility of the findings to the reader. Two anonymous readers provided many suggestions that have improved our presentation. We are also grateful to the staff at the Center for Policy Research at the Maxwell School of Syracuse University: Martha Bonney, Kim Desmond, Mary Santy, and Kati Foley, who made numerous checks of references, charts, graphs, and tables for which we are especially grateful. And finally, we thank Suzanne Nichols for shepherding the manuscripts through the editing process.

— Introduction —

Taking the Definition of Poverty Seriously

F OR SOME FORTY years now, poverty has been a central and self-conscious concern in American society. The War on Poverty, officially launched in 1964 by President Lyndon B. Johnson, spawned a large research establishment and literature (Johnson 1964). As analysts have dug into this large issue, it has proved fruitful to investigate the special circumstances and dynamics of different groups of the poor, particularly the notably dependent populations of the elderly and children. This book is about the economic well-being of the latter group. It examines American children from a particular perspective, that of their fates in comparison with the fates of children in other rich nations.

For much of the time since the War on Poverty was launched, poverty warriors have proceeded as if this effort were a new enterprise in American society, a project designed to eradicate the vestiges of poverty left after rapid economic growth in the post–World War II period. More recently, however, several excellent historical studies of the way American society has dealt with economic marginality and disadvantages have emphasized the continuity of issues and strategies in the War on Poverty with previous social welfare politics and policy (Ruggles 1990; Katz 1986, 1989; Patterson 1981).

Understanding poverty is, of course, more than a political project, and postwar America's concern about it has deep roots. The recognition, dating from the eighteenth century, that economic growth does not eradicate poverty may be relatively modern, but concern over the impact on society of large classes of poor people predates the development of economic strategies for

1

dealing with it. Indeed, poverty has been a subject of concern, debate, moralizing, and controversy throughout written history. Many would say today as in biblical times: "The poor shall never cease out of this land."

Economic and political strategies counter such fatalism by raising quantifiable questions, such as: How large is the class of the poor? Even though it is a rare society that would assert that it has no poor people, there may still be important differences among societies in how many they include in counting their poor. Surely it is important to count the number of poor people in a society, since we judge societies very differently when we discover that in some there are a great many poor people and in others only a few.

Comparing the situation of American children in low-income families with their counterparts in some other rich countries gives us a powerful perspective on the contexts and patterns of child poverty in the United States in the 1990s. This book examines patterns of child poverty in the United States and in fourteen other countries: twelve are in Western Europe—Belgium, Denmark, Finland, France, Germany, Italy, the Netherlands, Norway, Spain, Sweden, Switzerland, and the United Kingdom—and two are the Commonwealth nations of Australia and Canada. The surveys on which our analysis is based are from the Luxembourg Income Study (LIS), a database available to social scientists throughout the world that contains nearly one hundred income surveys (see appendix A). The fourteen countries chosen for comparison are those with surveys we judge to have the most complete and comparable coverage of income sources and demographic variables.

In this introduction, we discuss ways in which we can think about poverty as a characteristic of some people's life situation. We start, however, by discussing how we came to focus on children.

THE IMPORTANCE OF STUDYING CHILD DEPRIVATION

Families with children—or very often just children and their mothers—have been one dominant focus of writing about poverty and disadvantage in the long history of poverty studies beginning in the nineteenth century (Katz 1986; Skocpol 1992, 1995). The situation of children is one of three perennial concerns in both scholarly and political literature about poverty. (The other two are the adequacy of unskilled laborers' wages and the economic insecurity of the elderly.) Because children are dependent and vulnerable, it has seemed natural for socially minded people—ministers, charity workers, educators, social and medical professionals, and ordinary citizens—to be concerned about those children who live in families that do not seem to have enough to meet their children's needs. This interest is reinforced by the suspicion that children who are deprived as they grow up will have serious problems as adults and indeed may well make problems for others as they mature. In recent times this concern about the effects in adulthood of growing up poor has burgeoned into a substantial research enterprise (Haveman and Wolfe 1994; Duncan and Brooks-Gunn 1997a, b; Corcoran 2002).

A broad range of public policies has been promoted to respond to the problem of children in poverty in North America and Europe. Family and child policy initiatives have been a standard, if not the most costly, focus of social protection strategies in many countries (Kamerman and Kahn 1995, 1997). Studies to assess the effectiveness of these policies require measurement of the rates of child poverty and the impact on those rates of particular social programs, as well as the impact of the group of family policy programs as a whole. Comparison of poverty rates across countries with varying patterns of wage inequality and varying social programs provides an ideal testing ground for assessing the effectiveness of different policies and the impact of contextual factors on policy effects. This book provides a broad assessment of the success of efforts to combat child poverty in the United States as compared to such initiatives in other rich countries. And it provides a baseline for following the evolution of children's well-being in this new century. This assessment tells us where we stand now and suggests where we could go by examining the situation of children in other countries.

Both ordinary citizens' worry over the plight of poor kids and the policy analysts' and politicians' need for better understanding as a guide to policy have been intensified in the last decade by dramatic changes in family forms and relations and in patterns of the life course. As debated by many people, experts and ordinary citizens alike, there have been profound changes over the past half-century in the way American family roles, relations, and living arrangements throughout the life course are organized. Parallel changes seem to have occurred in most European societies. Ron J. Lesthaeghe (2002) has recently observed that "Western European and consequently also North American demographic systems of the past were characterized by long celibacy, late marriage and the dominance of the nuclear family. New households were neolocal and could only be established if economic independence was obtained. This 'Malthusian' system with 'prudent marriage' is an alien form of social organization to other societies and cultures."

Lesthaeghe goes on to suggest that this system was strengthened by the adoption of family limitation as the key to the first "demographic transition" of declining family size. Now, he argues, we are seeing a second "demographic transition" characterized by "increased divorce, again later marriage but insertion of periods of premarital cohabitation, marked postponement of parenthood, procreation within cohabiting unions, declining remarriage but increasing postmarital cohabitation or other forms of living arrangements, and persistence of sub-replacement fertility."

These changes, mostly regarded as the result of the preferences and choices of adults, have uncertain effects on children. Our particular concern is with the impact on the economic well-being of children. Continuing studies such as this are necessary if we are to understand the consequences of this second demographic transition (which must also be examined in the context of the evolution of so-called globalization as it affects the economic resources of families in different countries).

SOCIAL AND ECONOMIC CONCEPTS OF POVERTY

A concern with the size of the poverty class leads us to a broader question: What does it mean to be poor in a rich society? More specifically, what does it mean for a family, and particularly its children, to live in a state of poverty within a prosperous society?

To begin to answer these questions, we must look at poverty in the context of its opposite, plenty. As members of modern societies, we use a wide range of goods and services to effect our participation in social relations and to create and sustain our sense of social identity. The mainstream standard of living defines the "average American"; family resources that fall sufficiently short of the mainstream define deprivation, precarious subsistence, exclusion—in short, poverty. Our common cultural understanding is that we cannot play our social roles or participate meaningfully in our communities without the basic material resources necessary to carry out our activities (Parsons and Smelser 1956; Sen 1992). One way or another, each of us has to "get a living" in order to "have a life." The roles and activities that define participation are age-graded—child, teenager, young adult, mature adult, senior citizen—but for any one age these common cultural understandings allow people to pass judgment on their own rank and that of others in a continuum from destitution to unseemly affluence, based on what kind of participation they can effect.

In highly stratified societies, the economic resources available to individuals and families vary greatly. As members of these societies, we develop a lively sense of the implications of different levels of resources—that is, we see that experiences of plenty or of deprivation often seem to be critical in determining which other members of society we choose to interact with and the kinds of social participation that are feasible for us. In short, if we do not look at poverty as one aspect of socioeconomic inequality in modern societies, we are missing its essential nature.

Whatever we see from our own perspective—be it the low average income of some regions or nations, the economic deprivation of individuals with low income, or the political challenges encountered by policymakers—any correct study of poverty must proceed from a sociologically grounded understanding of the interpenetration of material and social well-being in modern societies. It must also recognize the particular degree of socioeconomic inequality in the social stratification system of each society.

The definition of poverty adopted by the European Council of Ministers in 1984 reflects such a concept of poverty. The European Union (EU) member countries now ground their approaches to poverty in an understanding of the nature of social stratification in prosperous industrial and postindustrial societies such as their own: "The poor shall be taken to mean persons, families, and groups of persons whose resources (material, cultural, and societal) are so limited as to exclude them from the minimum acceptable way of life in the member state in which they live" (European Commission 1985).

By contrast, writings about poverty in the United States tend not to focus so sharply on social exclusion but rather on the characteristics of the poor themselves. As Michael Katz (1989) argues, Americans have always been deeply preoccupied with the distinction between the undeserving and the deserving poor. (This concern has also been characteristic of Britain and its Anglo-Saxon Commonwealth nations.) In the United States the struggle to define the poor in these terms has been centered most recently in the welfare reform controversy, which has resulted in the abolition of the program Aid to Families with Dependent Children (AFDC). The undeserving-deserving dichotomy has now produced a welfare program, Temporary Assistance for Needy Families (TANF), whose premise was characterized by Senator Daniel P. Moynihan (1996, C7) at its passage as the idea that "the behavior of certain adults can be changed by making the lives of their children as wretched as possible."

The various U.S. wars on poverty, unlike those of some continental European countries, have usually targeted the situation of the very worst-off in society; American policymakers have long been more troubled by the situation of the lower class than by the broader situation of the working class (Korpi 1980). This concern has reinforced the emphasis in U.S. social welfare programs on developing means-tested mechanisms for meeting income needs rather than on ensuring social security. Historically Americans have seemed to find the individual problems of those who are "unable or unwilling to work" more compelling than the economic problems of unemployment, underemployment, and low wages.

Within this orientation, two perspectives contend in American characterizations of poverty. One sees economic status—that is, people's command over goods and services (Ruggles 1990; Citro and Michael 1995)—as the defining and sufficient indicator of being poor. The other perspective is more broadly concerned with people's socioeconomic situation. It was the latter kind of sociological concern that dominated the elite interest in poverty in the 1960s and launched the War on Poverty. Michael Harrington's *The Other America: Poverty in the United States,* first published in 1962, is generally credited with putting poverty on the agenda of the administration of President John F. Kennedy. Harrington combined his own experience as a writer about the American working class with much sociological research during the 1950s on the inner city, juvenile delinquency, and slums. For Harrington (1962, 18), there was

> a language of the poor, a psychology of the poor, a worldview of the poor. To be impoverished is to be an internal alien, to grow up in a culture that is radically different from the one that dominates society. . . . [The poor] need an American Dickens to record the smell and texture and quality of their lives. The cycles and trends, the massive forces, must be seen as affecting persons who talk and think differently.

As the War on Poverty progressed, the definition of both the nature of poverty and the goals of the War narrowed from this broad socioeconomic description of the poor to one centered on individuals' command over goods and services. To some extent such narrowing is inevitable when efforts to count the poor are undertaken. Nevertheless, it remains a perennial source of debate about poverty: Do we take the social or the strictly economic view of poverty? And however we answer that question, we must then ask another: Do we define poverty as an absolute condition or, especially in prosperous societies, a relative one?

When the Kennedy administration began to plan the War on Poverty in the early 1960s, government statisticians needed a standard by which to count the poor. The official U.S. poverty line, often called the Orshansky index after the government economist who developed it, grew out of this need (Orshansky 1965; see Fisher 1992). At its core was a definition of the minimum food budget required by a family. Given a minimum food budget, a minimum income was calculated that would provide this food budget and, by assumption, a minimum subsistence level of other necessary goods and services. This official poverty line is a so-called absolute poverty line: it refers to a particular basket of goods that just barely meets the needs of an individual or family, and because need is not assumed to change over time, the basket does not change, although its price must be adjusted for changes in costs. On the face of it, at least from a historical perspective, this assumption is ludicrous—the subsistence basket of today would have been regarded as one of plenty a century ago. The government statisticians involved in poverty analysis certainly expected that the official line would be updated from time to time. In the end, however, because of the potential political and budgetary impacts of a changing poverty line, each effort to increase the line to take into account rising standards of living was rejected by the government (see Fisher 1992, 1995). After an exhaustive review of the decades of discussion of poverty measurement in the federal government, Gordon Fisher (1995, 76) concluded:

> In addition, the fact that proposals to raise the poverty thresholds in real terms were rejected—leaving in place an official poverty line that had been made absolute—tended to serve as a further barrier to retention of the knowledge of the income elasticity of the poverty line. When the current official poverty line—the only poverty line that more and more people had ever been aware of—was made absolute, and remained so, it became more difficult for many people to realize (and less likely that they would investigate history to find out) that the basic pattern both in this country and in other countries is for poverty lines to rise in real terms as the real income of the general population rises.

The official poverty line has played a more central role in policy analysis in this country than in other countries. Most countries do, however, count low-income groups by using some kind of a poverty line, even if it is an implicit one. But no other country has adhered to the same poverty line for four decades; most update their standard annually or every few years. A few countries, such as Sweden and Canada, define a minimum income standard—known as the existence minimum—then link various social benefits to that line. Researchers can quantify the poor by counting those below the level of the existence minimum. More recently, the European Community has begun to count on a regular basis the population below a relative poverty line defined as half (or sometimes 60 percent) of the median after-tax income. In the United Kingdom and Germany, researchers have counted the poor by using the minimum income standards implicit in social assistance benefit levels.

SOCIAL MEASUREMENT OF POVERTY

Although the U.S. official poverty line is considered an absolute one, in fact no one has ever argued that it is unchangeable. It is understood that there is a historic component to the definition of a minimum standard of living; for instance, the U.S. poverty line would obviously be a line of affluence in many other parts of the world. Even so, some argue that it is possible to establish, for the time being, an absolute standard, and that it is unnecessary to adjust the poverty line regularly for increases (or decreases) in average incomes. At the core of the definition of an absolute poverty line such as the Orshansky index, however, is a hazily recognized contradiction—poverty is actually relative, but for now we will define it as unchanging in real terms (see also Smeeding, Rainwater, and Burtless 2001).

The more experience countries have with absolute poverty definitions, the more obvious becomes the absurdity of the rationale for them. Not surprisingly, attempts have been made to revise poverty lines so as to avoid this underlying absurdity. Any such effort requires that poverty lines be adjusted to reflect changes in living standards—an approach that has been exhaustively pursued, for example, by a committee of the U.S. National Research Council (Citro and Michael 1995).

The debate on the merits of absolute versus relative definitions of poverty has obscured the more fundamental difference between economic and social definitions of poverty. An economic measure of poverty determines the income needed to provide a minimum level of consumption of goods and services and implicitly assigns a given level of utility or satisfaction to the output of consumption. Researchers taking this approach make no effort to measure utility or satisfaction directly; after all, doing so would bring up subjective factors with no recognized relevance to the public policy issues involved.

A social measure of poverty is concerned ultimately not with consumption but with social activities and participation. Researchers with this orientation do not look at the problem of poverty in relatively affluent societies as one of low consumption per se but focus instead on the social and personal consequences of poor individuals' inability to consume at more than an extremely modest level. Without a requisite level of goods and services, individuals cannot act and participate as full members of their society, and it is this participation in social activities that confers utility, not consumption. While such a view is mainly identified with sociological (and anthropological) traditions, a few economists have adopted its insights by focusing on consumption as an intermediate activity—that is, as an input to social activities that in turn confer utility (Duesenberry 1949; Lancaster 1971; Sen 1992).

Denton Vaughan (1993, 22–23) provides an excellent description of the social meaning of poverty in contemporary societies:

> In the complex, largely urban, and industrial and service societies of the post–World War II United States, Canada, and Western Europe, the poverty problem stems from the existence of substantial population subgroups whose members lack the material resources required to perform—except with the greatest difficulty—roles in the central societal domains of family, work, and citizenship as defined by the mainstream members of society and as generally accepted by members of the low income groups themselves. [Members] have a relatively well-developed sense of the material resources associated with different levels in the material status hierarchy. It is this sense that permits the individual to judge the difference between a good salary and a poor one, a nice car and a bare bones econo-box, or a decent apartment and a slum tenement, and more generally to assess his or her location in the overall stratification system.

As Vaughan makes clear, we identify someone as poor by not only looking at social conditions but taking into account related social identities and meanings—those associated with both the poor person and, even more, the other members of society who hold that person responsible for his own social position. Such an identification is thus often said to be a subjective exercise on the part of the social scientist, one that involves making a value judgment. Amartya Sen (1981, 17) has responded to this charge in a very direct way:

> The view that "poverty is a value judgment" has recently been presented forcefully by many authors. . . . The exercise [of defining poverty] would, then, seem to be primarily a subjective one, unleashing one's personal morals on the statistics of deprivation. I would like to argue against this approach. . . . There is a difference between saying that the exercise *is itself* a prescriptive one and saying that the exercise must *take note* of the

prescriptions made by members of the community. To describe a prevailing prescription is an act of description, not prescription. For the person studying and measuring poverty, the conventions of society are matters of fact (what *are* the contemporary standards?), and not issues of morality or of subjective search.

With Sen, we would suggest that the first task of the poverty researcher is to discover the contemporary social standard of what constitutes poverty. However imprecise, that standard is every bit as much a social fact as a kinship relation or a political party preference, and like the myriad other social facts we use each day to orient ourselves in our societies, it can be determined by standard social science methods. The researcher can discover with more or less precision how small an income is perceived as so low that any individual or family bringing in such an amount should be regarded as poor—and therefore *is* poor in the sense of being unable to participate in ordinary societal activities. In attempting to determine contemporary standards for defining poverty, the researcher can construct, in effect, a societal poverty line—a line not to be confused with a government's explicit or tacit poverty line.

THE PLAN OF THIS BOOK

An overview of U.S. child poverty compared with child poverty in the fourteen other rich countries for which we have the most comparable data is presented in chapter 1. To sample a broader range of the comparison possibilities, chapter 1 also briefly discusses poverty rates among twenty-five other rich and not-so-rich nations. Chapter 2 analyzes the impact of income inequality on the child poverty rates of different countries. An obvious question with respect to poverty statistics is the effect of population characteristics, the subject of chapter 3. A brief foray into longitudinal analysis is the focus of chapter 4, which supplements chapter 2's analysis of income inequality by examining how long children live in poverty in the United States and in Germany. (Comparable data were available for these two countries only.)

In chapter 5, we introduce the subject that is central to the remainder of part I: income packaging and the role of different forms of income in alleviating child poverty. Chapter 6 focuses on the role of income packaging in accounting for the poverty rates of children in two-parent families, and chapter 7 considers income packaging in single-mother families. Finally, chapter 8 explores some of the implications of our findings for public policy in the United States.

We develop in part II the evidence and rationale for the choices we have made to answer the question: What *are* the contemporary standards for measuring poverty? In much poverty research, these choices are quickly passed over by using conventional definitions whose rationales either have never been explicated or are lost in the haze of earlier times. For example, virtually all of the vast literature on poverty in the United States uses the rough-and-ready statistical construct of the official poverty line without establishing a clear conceptual underpinning in sociology or economics or social science generally. We have attempted in part II to avoid this shortcoming ourselves by setting out the rationales for our measurement choices and describing their grounding in empirical social science and theory.

The most crucial of a number of choices we had to make was defining a poverty line. Three kinds of decisions went into drawing this line for each country, the first two of which are addressed in chapter 9. What definition of income should we use? Money income before tax or after tax? Should we include cashlike resources like food stamps or free rent? What about services provided to family members at no or reduced cost, such as health care? The second choice we faced was deciding finally how to assess the minimum level of living and draw the societal poverty line. We review the evidence that conceptions of poverty as relative to mainstream affluence have not changed significantly over the twentieth century.

Chapter 10 looks at the third question we had to answer: What is the effect of family composition on the level of living? How, if at all, is a family's income to be adjusted for differences in the material resources it needs and the societal activities in which it engages as a function of its composition—that is, its size, the number of adults, the number of children, and the ages of all its members? This adjustment to income is called equivalent income—after the adjustment, families are considered to have incomes that are *equivalent* in purchasing power.

Chapter 11 is concerned with one last factor in determining contemporary standards of poverty: the difference it makes if we take local communities rather than nations as the social unit within which a poor living standard is defined. Practical considerations forced us to use a national poverty line for this study, and we consider that a shortcoming of the study (and practically all others). In this chapter, we explore what difference a definition of community at the subnational level can make.

The authors hope that together these substantive and methodological excursions will help the reader to gain a fuller understanding of how economic inequality in the United States impacts families with children and what exact patterns of income acquisition account for the high and rising American child poverty rate over the past few decades—a rate that stands in contrast to the much lower and more stable rates in most of the rich countries with which we compare the United States. This analysis provides an empirical grounding for the consideration of policies to make it easier for working parents to earn a decent living while raising their children—policies such as parental leave, childcare support, increased income supports for working poor families, and a more socially oriented education policy. In fact, we conclude that America has high child poverty because we choose to have it—not because we cannot do anything about it. Other nations make different choices and get different results. In contrast to the Bush administration's rhetoric, we choose to leave a large fraction of America's children behind and the comparative analyses we present here inform us by how much.

Part I

Child Poverty and Inequality at the End of the Twentieth Century

—— Chapter 1 ——

Child Poverty in Rich Countries in the 1990s: An Overview

IT SHOULD BE evident from the discussion in the introduction to this book that although poverty analyses make use of a poverty line, there is no hard and fast qualitative difference between being poor and not being poor. Participating meaningfully in one's society is not an all-or-nothing ability. The contemporary social standards for what constitutes poverty or near-poverty or mainstream living are nodes along a continuum of affluence. When we use family income as an index of material well-being, we can conveniently rank people along a continuum from very low income to very high income. The poverty line, and our counts of those below it, are snapshots of part of that continuum that facilitate comparison—among groups, over time, among nations. Behind this simplification lies the complex reality of people's daily activity of converting their material resources into some sort of social participation. We want to count the poor as those for whom there must be a great struggle to thus convert their meager resources.

Child poverty is rare in neither the United States nor the other countries to which we compare it, although we will see large differences among those countries in the proportion of their children who are poor. Coincidentally, around the end of the twentieth century there were roughly the same number of children in the United States and the twelve European countries—around seventy-two million. But we find that as many as fourteen million American children are poor compared with some seven million poor children in our comparison European countries. Both are large numbers, but the United States certainly has a larger child poverty problem than this group of European countries.

THE POVERTY MEASURE

In defining a poverty line, we must establish indicators of the various aspects of economic well-being. How do we index the economic resources of families, the needs of the family as a function of who its members are, and the standard of living against which we compare a family's resources? The resources are those of the family as a unit. That unit may be headed by an unmarried person or by a married or cohabiting couple.[1]

The data available in the Luxembourg Income Study database allow us to index economic resources by the after-tax family income. In that income we include the money the family receives from earnings, assets, and transfers, and some "near-cash" income in such forms as food stamps, housing allowances, and tax credits like the Earned Income Tax Credit (EITC). Because of difficulty in measuring their incidence and their value, we cannot include important noncash resources available to some families—for example, private and public health insurance or mortgage subsidies. Especially important for this study, we cannot consider the resource of publicly provided child care, which is both in-kind transfer income and a facilitator of labor force participation. Similarly, we are not able to take into account tax expenditures, which are important for considering the distribution of pretax income.

We divide after-tax income by a need factor based on the number of persons in the family and the age of the head. The result is equivalent income, which we take as an index of dissimilar families' ability to maintain a given level of economic well-being. Obviously, the more people there are in the family, the more resources it needs to maintain a given level of well-being. But because there are economies of scale, need does not increase proportionately with size. We have also found evidence that social need increases with the age of the family head to a point in middle age and then declines, so we also adjust for age of head. (For a discussion of equivalence issues and the derivation of the equivalence factor used in this study, see chapter 10.)

For an index to the mainstream standard of living in the fifteen countries we are analyzing, we calculate the median equivalent after-tax income of the individuals in each country. For the poverty line we take one-half of that median. We count the economic well-being of families as the ratio of their incomes to the median. We count families and individuals as poor when their equivalent income is less than half of the national median. (See the discussion in chapter 9 for background on these choices.)

This choice of the national median as the mainstream standard is a compromise that bows to the problem of small sample sizes. A more realistic mainstream standard would take account of differences in income levels in different parts of a nation. When people evaluate the social meanings of income, they think in terms of the standard of living of the people in their own communities. It is that standard that influences their social definitions of who is well off, who is average, who is just getting along, and who is poor. Only if the community averages are more or less the same across the nation is the national median a really good guide to mainstream standards. Some of our countries have sample sizes of just a few thousand, however, and our results would have very large margins of error if we tried to define regional as opposed to national poverty lines. Our use of the national median is a conventional albeit a next-best solution to the problem of defining community standards. (Chapter 11 reports an experiment with regional poverty lines in the United States and a few of our comparison countries.)

It will also be helpful in the following analysis to look at the income groupings of children's families: high (one and a half times the median), middle (around the median), marginal or low (two-thirds of the median), and below the poverty line (half of the median). Some examples will give an indication of what these income classes represent in the United States. We label as high-income those persons living in a family of four (with a head forty-five years of age) whose 1997 after-tax family income was $66,700 or higher. A family with an income of $44,455 is exactly in the middle, and individuals are defined as low-income if their family income was below $29,600. The U.S. LIS poverty line in 1997 is drawn at $22,227 a year. This compares with the official U.S. poverty line in 1997 of $16,050. (For information on U.S. poverty guidelines, their construction, and their rationale, see U.S. Department of Health and Human Services [various years].)

TABLE 1.1 **LIS Poverty Lines for the United States, 1997**

Size of Household	Annual Income
One person	$14,000
Two persons	17,600
Three persons	20,200
Four persons	22,200
Five persons	23,900
Six persons	25,400

Source: Authors' calculations, using data from the Luxembourg Income Study.

To give an idea of where poverty starts, table 1.1 shows the approximate U.S. LIS poverty lines in the 1997 data for families of different sizes (all with a head age forty-five).

Table 1.2 shows the median equivalent incomes in each country after the family size and age adjustments, as described earlier. In the analysis that follows, persons are categorized in different income classes depending on where they stand in relation to their national median equivalent income.

TABLE 1.2 **Median Equivalent Income in Fifteen Countries in the 1990s**

Country	Year	Median Equivalent Income	Currency
Australia	1994	24,450	Australian dollars
Belgium	1997	764,561	Belgian francs
Canada	1997	30,074	Canadian dollars
Denmark	1992	166,949	Danish kroner
Finland	1995	105,868	Finnish markkaa
France	1994	121,955	French francs
Germany	1994	37,779	Deutsche mark
Italy	1995	24,515,000	Italian lire
Netherlands	1994	37,523	Dutch guilders
Norway	1995	203,980	Norwegian kroner
Spain	1990	1,234,723	Spanish pesetas
Sweden	1995	168,664	Swedish kronor
Switzerland	1992	52,718	Swiss francs
United Kingdom	1995	11,697	U.K. pounds
United States	1997	28,005	U.S. dollars

Source: Authors' calculations, using data from the Luxembourg Income Study.
Note: Amounts are given in national currency units.

POVERTY RATES OF ALL CHILDREN

Looking first at child poverty rates in the fifteen countries (see figure 1.1), we find that the United States had an extremely high poverty rate in 1997 of 20.3 percent. (Somewhat fortuitously, the official poverty rate of children was 19.9 percent in 1997. But see

FIGURE 1.1 Child Poverty Rates in Fifteen Countries in the 1990s

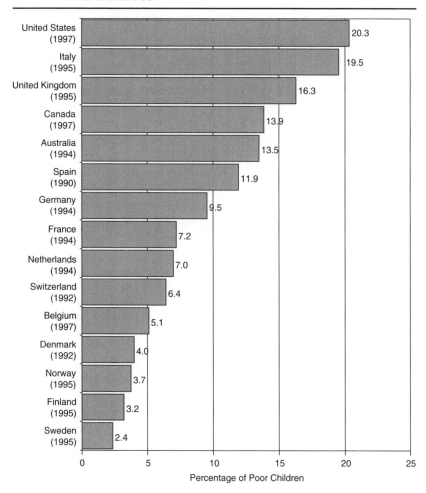

Percentage of Poor Children

Source: Authors' calculations, using data from the Luxembourg Income Study.

the discussion in the next section on trends in child poverty.) In other words, 20.3 percent of all American children lived in families with equivalent incomes below one-half of the median equivalent income. These are incomes so low that these children and others in their family were not able to participate enough in community activities to be perceived, by both themselves and others, as regular members of society.

Italy had the second-highest child poverty rate at just below 20 percent, followed closely by the United Kingdom at 16.3 percent. (In the tables and figures that follow in this and later chapters, we have listed countries by rank order from high to low, or low to high, to facilitate understanding of the pattern across countries.) The two Commonwealth nations, Canada and Australia, have rather high rates at more than 13.9 percent and 13.5 percent, respectively. At 11.9 percent, Spain's child poverty rate is almost as high.

The child poverty rates in the rest of the countries, starting with Germany, are all below 10 percent. France has a rate of approximately 7 percent, as does the Netherlands. Switzerland follows at 6.4 percent. The rest of the countries have very low rates of around 5 percent or less. Very low rates of child poverty prevail in the four Nordic countries.

In short, the poverty rate of American children is over four times as high as that of children in northern Europe. The contrast with the rate in the United Kingdom is almost as dramatic—British children suffer a poverty rate over three times as high as that of the northern European countries.

What are the odds of escaping poverty in these different countries? Answering that question, we see even starker contrasts. An American child has a slightly less than four-to-one chance of escaping poverty, and the odds are about the same for an Italian or British child. In contrast, a Nordic child has a twenty-five-to-one chance or better of escaping poverty. These children's chances of not remaining poor are six or more times greater than those of an American child, and around five times greater than those of a British child.

CHILD POVERTY RATES IN
TWENTY-FIVE COUNTRIES

If we broaden our focus to all of the countries for which LIS data exist, we find no wider range in poverty rates, but some interesting possibilities for comparison do emerge when we consider the child poverty rate for the most recent years for each country (see table 1.3). Two Western European countries—Austria and Luxembourg—fit neatly into the group of northern continental countries with rates under 5 percent. Ireland's high child poverty rate of 12 percent, on the other hand, is about the same as Spain's, Australia's, and Canada's, but not as high as the 16.3 percent rate in the United Kingdom.

Many people would choose not to include data from five Eastern European countries under the rubric of rich nations, but we should keep in mind that their standards of living are not much lower than those of Western Europe some forty years ago. By world standards, they certainly are rich nations.

The most interesting observation to be made about these five Eastern European countries is that the range in child poverty in these countries is as great as it is in the countries of Western Europe. In fact, of all the twenty-five countries, the two with the very lowest child poverty rates are the Czech Republic and Slovakia. Their rates are even about the same as those of Sweden and Finland. Hungary and Poland appear in the middle of the range with rates somewhat higher than France's but lower than Spain's. At 23.2 percent, the child poverty rate in Russia is higher even than in the United States. (Of course, the situation in the Eastern European countries has been unstable in the post-Communist period, and many suspect that poverty has increased in some of these countries.)

Data are available for two other countries, Israel and Taiwan. With rates not too different from the German poverty rate but lower than those of the two Commonwealth nations, the United Kingdom, and the United States, these countries have generally higher rates than most European countries.

Thus, broadening our scope from fifteen to twenty-five countries tells us that, within the range of economic development that these countries represent, there is little relationship between a country's prosperity and its child poverty rate. The Western European countries with very low poverty rates have gross domestic products close to three times those of the Czech Republic and Slovakia, yet their poverty rates are not very different. Spain and Ireland have twice the real GDP of Poland, but the three countries have very similar poverty rates. The United Kingdom, Italy, the United States, and Russia represent an enormous range in GDP, yet these four all have very high poverty rates.

TABLE 1.3 Trends in Child Poverty in Twenty-Five Countries, 1970 to 1997

Nation	Year of Survey	Before 1971	1972 to 1975	1976 to 1981	1982 to 1985	1986 to 1988	1989 to 1993	1994 to 1997
United States	1969, 1974, 1979, 1986, 1991, 1997	13.1%	17.3%	18.5%	—	22.9%	21.5%	22.7% ≥ 20.3%
Western Europe								
Austria	1987	—	—	—	—	4.8	—	—
Belgium	1985, 1988, 1992, 1997	—	—	—	3.4%	3.1	3.8	5.1
Denmark	1987, 1992	—	—	—	—	5.3	4.0	—
Finland	1987, 1991, 1995	—	—	—	—	2.9	2.5	3.2
France	1979, 1984a, 1984b, 1989, 1994	—	—	6.3	6.5/8.6c	—	7.5	7.2
Germany (West)[a]	1973, 1978, 1983/1984, 1989, 1994	—	4.0	3.2	4.8/6.4d	—	4.4	8.7
Ireland	1987	—	—	—	—	12.0	—	—
Italy	1986, 1991, 1995	—	—	—	—	10.8	9.6	19.5
Luxembourg	1985, 1991, 1994	—	—	—	4.1	—	3.6	4.6
Netherlands[b]	1983, 1987, 1991, 1994	—	—	—	2.5	3.6	4.1	7.0
Norway	1979, 1986, 1991, 1995	—	—	3.8	—	3.8	4.6	3.7
Spain	1980, 1990	—	—	12.3	—	—	11.9	—

	Years							
Sweden	1967, 1975, 1981, 1987, 1992, 1995	3.5	1.9	3.9	—	3.0	2.7	2.4
Switzerland	1982, 1992	—	—	—	3.3	—	6.4	6.7
United Kingdom	1969, 1974, 1979, 1986, 1991, 1995	5.3	7.0	8.5	—	9.9	16.7	16.3
Eastern Europe								
Czech Republic	1992	—	—	—	—	—	3.4	—
Hungary	1991, 1994	—	—	—	—	—	9.5	10.1
Poland	1986, 1992, 1995	—	—	—	—	10.6	9.0	12.7
Russia	1992, 1995	—	—	—	—	—	19.9	23.2
Slovakia	1992	—	—	—	—	—	3.2	—
Other								
Australia	1981, 1985, 1989, 1994	15.2	—	14.0	13.1	—	14.0	13.5
Canada	1971, 1975, 1981, 1987, 1991, 1994, 1997	—	14.6	13.9	—	13.6	13.5	13.1≥ 13.9
Israel	1979, 1986, 1992, 1997	—	—	8.2	—	11.1	10.6	11.3
Taiwan	1986, 1991	—	—	—	—	5.8	9.9	—

Source: Authors' calculations, using data from the Luxembourg Income Study.

Notes: LIS has annual data for the United States from 1994 to 1997. The child poverty rates for these years are as follows: 1994, 22.7; 1995, 20.1; 1996, 19.9; 1997, 20.3.

a. For comparison, the 1994 rate for West Germany is given in this table. Elsewhere in the text the rates are for all of Germany. There is a survey change in Germany from 1983 to 1984 and after.

b. There are significant changes in the Dutch data that are likely to affect the comparability from year to year.

c. The two figures represent poverty rates in the 1984a and 1984b surveys.

d. The two figures represent poverty rates in the 1983 and 1984 surveys.

If we focus on just the fifteen countries of primary interest, we find that the correlation between GDP per capita and poverty rates is effectively zero. As suggested by the broader scope, there is simply no association between a country's wealth and the inequality of its equivalent income distribution. National riches and national child poverty are neither positively nor negatively associated.

CHILD POVERTY VERSUS ELDER POVERTY

The lack of correlation between a nation's wealth and its child poverty rate raises a question: Is there something different about the cross-national pattern of poverty among children compared with the pattern for other persons? Since many working-age individuals are parents, we would not expect to find much difference in the pattern of poverty rates for working-age adults and children. In fact, there is likely to be some such difference because adults without children may have different poverty rates from those with children, and poverty rates for large families may differ from those for small families. Such differences do make for some differences in the poverty rates of children and working-age adults, but these differences turn out to be rather small.

There is another large group of individuals, however, who may fare very differently from children. The elderly seldom have minor children at home, and their income sources are quite different from those of working-age adults. To sharpen our understanding of poverty among children, we briefly compare the situations of elders (persons sixty-five years of age and over) with those of children in these fifteen countries.

Figure 1.2 plots the poverty rates for children and elders. The diagonal line indicates equal poverty rates for the two groups. Countries above the line have higher rates for elders than for children, and the reverse is true for countries below the line. We find three countries with high rates for both groups. In the United States elder and child poverty rates are both 20 percent.[2]

In the United Kingdom the elder rate is about the same, at 15 percent, as the child rate of 16 percent. In Australia the child rate of 14 percent is less than half the elder rate of 31 percent. Despite the similarities in child poverty between the two Commonwealth nations, in Canada the elder rate (5 percent) is much lower, one-sixth that of Australia. Indeed, Canadian elder poverty is lower than in all the other countries except Sweden.

FIGURE 1.2 **Poverty Rates of Elders and Children in Fifteen Countries in the 1990s**

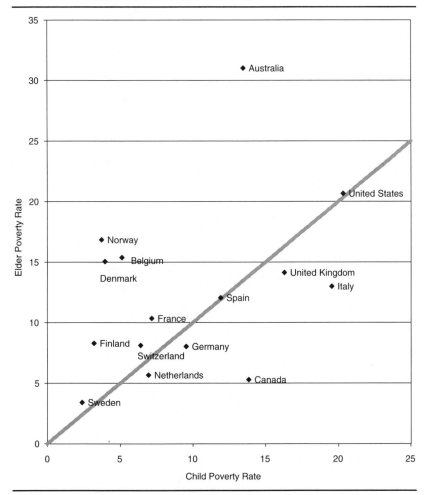

Source: Authors' calculations, using data from the Luxembourg Income Study.
Note: The diagonal line represents equal child and adult poverty rates. The survey year for each country can be found in figure 1.1 and table 1.2.

The correlation between the two rates over the fifteen nations is only 0.37. Six countries have rather large differences between the two rates, and in nine the child and elder rates are fairly similar, ranging from low poverty rates for both groups in six countries to increasing rates for both in Spain, the United Kingdom, and the United States.

Interestingly, the countries with child poverty rates of under 10 percent vary all over the place in elder poverty. In general, the elder rate is higher than the child rate in these countries, but there are variations in how much—from one point in the other direction in Germany and the Netherlands to over ten points for Denmark, Norway, and Belgium. If we wanted to understand elder poverty, we would probably move in rather different theoretical directions from where we need to go to understand child poverty. Note, for example, that although the American child poverty rate is over five times that of Norway, the elder poverty rate is only slightly higher than Norway's, or that while the United Kingdom and Italy have child poverty rates three or more times those of Norway, Belgium, and Denmark, all five countries share elder poverty rates near 15 percent.

TRENDS IN CHILD POVERTY

The results examined so far give us a snapshot of child poverty rates in the 1990s that depicts most prominently the very large differences among countries. Has it always been thus? Have these differences been stable over time, or are some countries experiencing increasing or decreasing rates?

To answer these questions, it would be desirable to have solid evidence gleaned from regular surveys over several decades for many countries. Unfortunately, there is no such database, and it is unlikely that such a database could even exist for periods before the 1970s. However, the LIS database does have data from 1970 on for a few countries, and for more countries since the 1980s. Thus, we have observations for some countries over a twenty-five-year period and for others over periods up to fifteen years. Because we have sometimes had to use different surveys at different points in time, and because sometimes the same survey has changed its methodology from one time to another, we can feel fully confident of a change only when there is a clear trend across more than two surveys, and preferably across more than three. When there is a jump solely from one period to the next, we have weak evidence of a change. Among other problems, the survey may be different, or the same survey may have undergone significant changes in methodology.

Reexamining table 1.3, we find *no country* in which the child poverty rate has declined significantly. In most countries there seems to be considerable stability in the child poverty rate. Two countries, however, have experienced large increases in child poverty. In the United States we find a steady increase from 1969 (13.1 percent) through 1986 (22.9 percent) and then a leveling off—to 22.7 percent in 1994 and 20.3 percent in 1997. Child poverty, in short, increased by more than 50 percent in the United States over the last quarter-century. Official U.S. child poverty has shown a decline from a high close to 23 percent in 1993 to a little above 16 percent in the new century. LIS figures show no such decline, suggesting that perhaps there are increasing numbers of children just above the official poverty line but below the LIS line. (For historical child poverty tables, see U.S. Department of Commerce, various years.)

It is interesting to note that even though the rate of American child poverty around 1970 was a little lower than Canada's rate, it rapidly surpassed Canada's in the 1970s, and the difference between the two countries continued to grow until the mid-1980s. By the mid-1990s the odds of a Canadian child avoiding poverty were almost twice as great as the odds for a child in the United States.

We must temper our conclusions for the United Kingdom. Although the survey is the same in all years, the rules and procedures for calculating disposable income may well have changed over the twenty-five years since 1969, and therefore we cannot be sure that the six surveys are exactly comparable. Even so, it is highly unlikely that the changes we observe are not fairly close to what actually happened. It would appear that since 1969 there has been a steady increase in child poverty in the United Kingdom, from around 5 percent to the most recent observation of 16 percent. In the United Kingdom, then, child poverty seems to have tripled. In the early 1970s the child poverty rate in the United States was two and a half times that of the United Kingdom, but by the 1990s it was only one-quarter higher.

We can assume for almost all of the countries for which we have sufficient data that the levels of child poverty are quite stable characteristics of their societies. Only for the United States and the United Kingdom do we have clear evidence of major change in the economic well-being of children. The United Kingdom has moved from being a country with low child poverty to one with a very high rate. Likewise, the child poverty rate in the United States has gone from high to very high. In contrast, four countries with moderately high child poverty rates—Spain, Israel, Australia, and Canada—have shown no significant increases or decreases.

Thus, the picture of child poverty in rich countries in the latter part of the twentieth century is largely static. Although we find marked increases in three countries, there are no countries in which there has been a significant decrease in the proportion of children experiencing the social exclusion attendant on living in a family with a low income. The effects of income-producing and redistributing institutions on children seem not to have changed in an important way anywhere except in the United States, the United Kingdom, and Italy.

A NOTE ON RACE AND ETHNICITY

A reader might be puzzled to find in the following chapters no discussion of the relation of patterns of race and ethnicity to poverty and income distribution in the countries studied. Clearly, ethnicity is a strong correlate of economic disadvantage in the United States and in some other countries. But in a cross-national context its status as a "cause" is ambiguous.

It is difficult to define ethnicity across countries in any way that one might call comparable. No other country has the history of slavery, de jure segregation, and continuing discrimination that one finds in the United States. The countries in our study have much smaller minority populations than the United States—on the order of 10 percent or less compared with one-third. Each country has a different history of methods for counting minorities, and thus there are many pitfalls to any attempt to define a group that is comparable to an American "race" or "ethnic group." For example, France categorizes by citizenship; thus, people of North African heritage who were born in France or are naturalized cannot be considered separately from those of French background. And finally, some of the LIS surveys used do not provide any information on nationality.

Since the American sample is large, we can confidently report its child poverty rates by ethnicity (see table 1.4). We find the rates for blacks and Hispanics about three times that for whites, in line with expectations. Given the lack of comparability among the other countries, we need to examine them one by one, and our conclusions must be quite tentative given the small sample sizes.

The Australian data provide data on world region of origin. Some 90 percent of Australians are of European origin, and the balance are of origins spread all over the world. Australian children of

TABLE 1.4 U.S. Child Poverty Rate, by Ethnicity, 1997

	Percentage in Poverty	Percentage of Total Population
White	12.4%	65.3%
Black	37.7	15.6
Hispanic	36.8	14.6
Native American–Eskimo	32.5	0.9
Asian–Pacific Islander	20.8	3.6
Total	20.3	100.0

Source: Authors' calculations, using data from the Luxembourg Income Study.

North African, Mideastern, and Southeast Asian origins seem to have elevated rates of child poverty. Canada has a similar history, but we cannot say anything about the situation of immigrants since the data distinguish only between English, French, and "others," the last category having slightly higher child poverty rates.

Ninety-five percent of the Belgian sample are of European origin. The "other" category (principally Moroccan and Turkish) has an elevated poverty rate of 23 percent.

In Denmark and Sweden over 90 percent of children are of those countries and have child poverty rates of 4 and 2 percent, respectively. The "other" children come from a very wide range of countries, so it is not possible to identify a particular disadvantaged group. Others as a group do have slightly higher child poverty rates: 11 percent in Denmark and 7 percent in Sweden.

In France there is a fairly large minority group (about 5 percent of children) composed of North Africans, with a few sub-Saharan Africans. The latter group and Algerians and Tunisians seem particularly disadvantaged, with a child poverty rate around 23 percent compared with the rate among the French-born of only 6 percent. Moroccan children are somewhat less likely to be poor (13 percent).

These are the only countries for which we have some form of ethnicity variable. There is no useful information on ethnicity in the surveys for Finland, Germany, Italy, the Netherlands, Norway, Spain, Switzerland, and the United Kingdom.

Our very rough conclusion is that while in most (or perhaps all) countries recent arrivals have elevated child poverty rates compared with rates for natives, these differences nowhere approach those in the United States between minorities and whites. And it is not clear that the differences that do exist are likely to persist over the decades in the same way they have in the United States.

—— Chapter 2 ——

Patterns of Child
Economic Well-Being

THE PREVIOUS CHAPTER outlined the broad picture of child poverty
in the fifteen countries of interest. Now we can turn our attention to the need to understand poverty as one aspect of the overall
inequality in economic well-being in a society. From the perspective of income distribution, we can think specifically in terms of
income classes ranging from extreme poverty to great riches. The
three income groupings described in chapter 1—high, middle, and
marginal or low—can be subdivided more finely into seven income
classes:

*High-income (more than one and a half times the median equiva-
lent income)*

1. Very rich: More than three times the median

2. Rich: More than twice the median

3. Prosperous: More than one and a half times the median

*Middle-income (between two-thirds and one and a half times the
median)*

4. Between two-thirds and one and a half times the median

Marginal income (less than two-thirds of the median)

5. Near poverty: Less than two-thirds of the median

6. Poverty: Less than half of the median

7. Extreme poverty: Less than one-third of the median

FIGURE 2.1 **Marginal-, Middle-, and High-Income Children in Fifteen Countries in the 1990s**

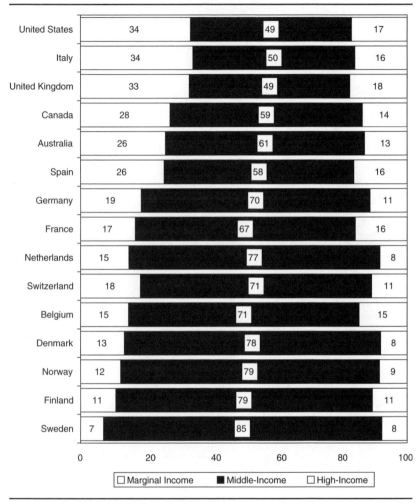

Country	Marginal Income	Middle-Income	High-Income
United States	34	49	17
Italy	34	50	16
United Kingdom	33	49	18
Canada	28	59	14
Australia	26	61	13
Spain	26	58	16
Germany	19	70	11
France	17	67	16
Netherlands	15	77	8
Switzerland	18	71	11
Belgium	15	71	15
Denmark	13	78	8
Norway	12	79	9
Finland	11	79	11
Sweden	7	85	8

□ Marginal Income   ■ Middle-Income   □ High-Income

Source: Authors' calculations, using data from the Luxembourg Income Study.
Note: The survey year for each country can be found in figure 1.1 and table 1.2.

Although the income classes into which we have divided the income distribution are arbitrary, they allow one to grasp the significance of differences in distribution more intuitively than would an overall measure of distribution. Figure 2.1 shows the percentage of children in the low-, middle-, and high-income classes in each country. The dark bar, representing the size of the middle-income group, is very large—more than three-quarters—in the Nordic countries and the Netherlands. The middle-income children in Germany, Switzerland, and Belgium number at least 70 percent. France follows, with two-thirds of its children in the middle-income group. Spain, Canada, and Australia are clustered, with around 60 percent of their children in the middle-income group. Only about half of all children are middle-income in the United Kingdom, Italy, and the United States.

There is a positive correlation between the proportion of children in the high- and marginal-income groups (.81). In the United States there are almost twice as many prosperous and rich children (17 percent) as there are poor children. The same is true in the United Kingdom and Italy. The countries with very low poverty rates also have low proportions of children living in prosperous and rich families—around 10 percent or less.

Table 2.1 shows the distribution of children in the seven income classes. Focusing more sharply on the marginal-income group, we observe that it ranges in size from 7 percent in Sweden to 34 percent in the United States, the United Kingdom, and Italy. The distribution of extremely poor children in the United States is even more distinctive. Over 9 percent of American children and nearly 11 percent of Italian children are extremely poor, while in all other countries the extreme poverty rate is 5 percent or less, and in seven it is less than 3 percent. The contrast with the United Kingdom is also striking—fewer than one-third of English poor children are extremely poor, while about half are extremely poor in Italy and the United States.

Considering the marginal-income group as a whole, we note that in most countries the great majority of those with marginal incomes are in the near-poor rather than the poor group. The exceptions are Italy and the United States, where only a minority are near-poor. In the Nordic countries, Belgium, and Switzerland, two-thirds or more of the marginal-income children are near-poor rather than poor. In the remaining countries around half of the marginal-income children are near-poor.

THE PROBABILITY OF A
LOW-INCOME CHILD BEING POOR

Every income distribution can be divided into equal-size groups ranging from low- to high-income. Typically researchers look at how

TABLE 2.1 Marginal-, Middle-, and High-Income Children in Fifteen Countries in the 1990s

	Extremely Poor	Poor	Near-Poor	Average	Prosperous	Rich	Very Rich
Sweden	0.7%	1.7%	4.6%	85.2%	6.4%	1.2%	0.3%
Finland	0.6	2.6	7.5	78.6	8.4	1.8	0.4
Norway	1.4	2.4	8.5	79.2	6.5	1.5	0.6
Denmark	1.3	2.7	9.4	78.4	6.4	1.5	0.3
Belgium	1.5	3.6	9.6	70.6	10.8	3.1	0.8
Switzerland	2.7	3.7	12.0	70.6	6.8	3.0	1.1
Netherlands	3.8	3.2	7.8	76.8	6.6	1.7	0.1
France	1.3	5.9	9.6	67.3	9.3	5.0	1.6
Germany	3.6	6.0	9.1	69.9	7.8	3.2	0.5
Spain	4.7	7.2	13.7	58.0	9.7	5.4	1.4
Australia	4.1	9.4	12.6	60.9	9.1	3.2	0.8
Canada	4.8	9.1	13.7	58.7	9.4	3.7	0.7
United Kingdom	4.8	11.5	17.0	49.0	10.1	5.6	1.9
Italy	10.6	8.9	14.9	49.5	10.2	4.6	1.3
United States	9.4	10.9	13.4	49.2	9.9	4.9	2.4

Source: Authors' calculations, using data from the Luxembourg Income Study.

much income goes to the highest decile versus the lowest, or they consider the mean income of the lowest quartile compared with the highest. We find that no country numbers more than one-third of all persons in these categories of poverty and near-poverty (although the United States and Russia come close). One way of taking a more detailed look at child poverty as an aspect of income distribution is to consider the distribution of income among children in the low-income third of the distribution. Every distribution has a lower third, but how incomes in that lower third stand in comparison with the median income is another question. Most may stand fairly close to the median, or they may be distributed from close to very far below. If their equivalent incomes are below half of the median, we are counting them as poor.

We can derive two relevant dimensions for establishing child poverty rates by focusing on the lower third of the income distribution of all persons. First, what proportion of children are in the lower third? If children in general are better off than others in society, the proportion will be less than one-third. If children live in families that are generally worse off, then the proportion in the lower third will be greater.

Among those children in the lower income third, we are also interested in the probability of a child being poor as opposed to near-poor or even middle-income. (According to the earlier definition of middle-income as an income at least 70 percent of the median, some middle-income people could fall in the lower income third.) The child poverty rate is the product of (1) the percentage of children in the lower income third of the total population and (2) the probability of being poor conditional on being in the lower third.

Figure 2.2 indicates that there is a wide variation among nations in the proportion of children who fall in the lower third of their nation's equivalent income distribution. The vertical line is drawn at one-third; countries to the left of the line are ones where children are relatively better off than all persons, and those to the right of the line are ones where children fare less well than all persons. The proportions of children in the lower third range from 22 percent in Sweden and Denmark to 40 percent or more in the United States and the United Kingdom and even higher in Italy. In nine of these fourteen nations, more than one-third of children are in the lower-third group, indicating that children tend to be relatively disadvantaged com-

FIGURE 2.2 **Children in Lower Third of Equivalent Income
Distribution in Fifteen Countries, by Child
Poverty Rates in the 1990s**

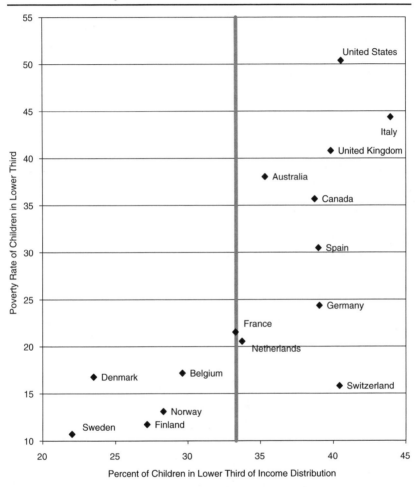

Source : Authors' calculations, using data from the Luxembourg Income Study.
Note: The survey year for each country can be found in figure 1.1 and table 1.2.

pared with older age groups. In contrast, in the Nordic countries and
Belgium we see that children are better off than other age groups.

For those who do fall in the lower third, the probability of
being poor rather than middle-income or near-poor also varies
widely—from 10 to 17 percent in Belgium, Finland, Norway,

Denmark, Sweden, and Switzerland to 35 percent or more in Canada, Australia, the United Kingdom, Italy, and the United States.

The United States has a very high overall child poverty rate because 40 percent of children are in the lower income third and there is a 50 percent probability that the children in the lower third live in families whose income is below half of the median. This snapshot of U.S. child poverty is in sharp contrast to the dominant picture in northern Europe, where no more than one-third of children are in the lower income group and only between 10 and 20 percent of them are also below the poverty line.

Note the wide range in poverty rates of low-income children in those countries where one-third or more of children are in the lower income third—from 15 percent in Switzerland to 20 to 25 percent for the Netherlands, France, and Germany, to 30 percent for Spain, to 35 to 40 percent for Canada, Australia, and the United Kingdom, to 50 percent for the United States.

As will be apparent in later chapters, the social protection transfers provided by the government for lower-income children in the United States are inadequate to protect them from poverty, whereas such protections are dramatically more effective in Europe. One task of chapters 5, 6, and 7 will be to explore the relative role of market versus government income in providing the high level of protection afforded lower-income families in almost all European countries but not in the United States.

INEQUALITY AND LEVELS OF REAL
ECONOMIC WELL-BEING

Up to this point in considering our findings on poverty and inequality across countries, we have kept to our conceptual framework, which emphasizes poverty as marginal relative income so low as to preclude participation in societal activities. But what about the consumption that these low income levels allow in different countries? In this regard it is often argued that although the United States has a more unequal income distribution than other countries, its level of income compared with those of other countries is sufficiently high that even the worst-off American has a higher income than many or all persons in other countries. The rising tide of the American economy is assumed to have lifted even the lowliest American well above the station of comparable persons in other societies. Purchasing power parity (PPP) measures (see next section) are designed to allow comparison of levels of income in different countries by replacing exchange rates with indices that take into account differences in the costs of living in different countries. These measures are derived from a large project of pricing goods and services coordinated by international organizations like the Organization for Economic Cooperation and Development (OECD). The PPP allows us to convert income amounts in our fifteen comparison countries to the U.S. dollar equivalent in purchasing power in the year of the LIS survey.

We are all aware that the American economy has grown enormously since the middle of the twentieth century. Purchasing power parity measures show that per capita income has more than doubled in real terms since 1950. (See appendix C for a discussion of the methodology for comparing real incomes.) Of course, other countries' economies have also grown. In 1950 the average real GDP per capita of our fourteen comparison countries stood at about 50 percent of American GDP per capita. By 1990 the average stood at about 75 percent. Thus, other countries have approached but still stand behind the United States in real economic production. For example, two relatively poor countries—Ireland and Spain—had GDPs equal to less than one-third of the U.S. GDP in the 1950s but had increased their ratio to about 50 percent by 1990. Among the richer countries—for example, Canada, Sweden, and Australia—the comparable shift was from somewhere in the 70 percent range to above 80 percent, a much smaller percentage increase than for the poorer countries. Interestingly, however, the rank order of our fourteen comparison countries is relatively unchanged over this period. (The correlation between their real GDP in 1955 and in 1990 is 0.89.)

Another way of thinking about the real gaps between these countries' production and that of the United States is to say that in the countries with the lowest GDPs (Spain, the United Kingdom) real income is about where American real income was in the early 1970s. For countries in the middle of the range (France, Norway, Denmark) real income stands about where it was in the United States in the 1980s, and for the richer countries it stands at a little later than that.

THE TEXTURE OF REAL CONSUMPTION

The task set by the PPP project is a daunting one. It requires estimating the cost of all of the components of a society's production and then calculating PPPs, which can be used as a cost index to convert the consumption of such items as "motorless kitchen and domestic utensils" or "travel goods and baggage items" into what they amount to in U.S. dollars. Yet we know that each country has its own culture and its own pattern of preferred consumption, given its economic constraints. Therefore, we cannot assume that if a given country has a median consumption level of 80 percent of the U.S. level, this means that in each category its consumption will be 80 percent. In some nations people may consume more of a given good than people do in the United States. The OECD provides detailed consumption amounts using this methodology (OECD, n.d.).

To put some flesh on the bones of real GDP comparisons, we take some examples of relative consumption of particular goods using the OECD tables. We can choose from such categories as food, housing, household expenditures, clothing, transportation, recreation, and medical care.[1] We can estimate expenditures for the average person and consider areas where consumption in a given country exceeds that of the United States. What we find is in some ways rather surprising.

In some categories the consumption of the average American is greater than in our comparison countries, but interestingly, there is no evidence of great deprivation in any of these categories. For example, Americans consume far more in the clothing category than people in any of the other countries, yet one would be hard put to say that the clothing of the average person in any of these countries represents great deprivation compared with how Americans dress. Similarly, the United States consumes far more in transportation goods and services, but much of this difference must be laid to the greater efficiency and use of public transportation in other countries. In the category "other goods and services," we find that American consumption is highest in such categories as hairdressers and beauty parlors, toiletries, jewelry, travel goods, restaurants, cafés, hotels, and financial services—all areas in which subsistence is hardly a concern.

The average person in Australia, Italy, Spain, Norway, the Netherlands, France, Denmark, and Belgium consumes as much food as the average American. In Canada, Denmark, Italy, Belgium, Norway, and Sweden, the average person's spending on housing and household expenditures is as great as it is in the United States. Real consumption of medical goods and services is actually higher for the average person in Belgium, France, Germany, Canada, Italy, the Netherlands, and Norway than in the United States.

We can conclude from this quick examination of aggregate levels of real consumption that even though the United States has a higher real per capita GDP than other countries and this difference has persisted for a long time, it does not follow that the consumption of an American in an average family is dramatically higher than that of comparable persons in these other societies. It appears that the average person in all but two of the fourteen countries consumes at the level of at least 85 percent of American consumption. And when it comes to "necessary" commodities, the average person in quite a few countries consumes as much as or more than his or her American counterpart.

INEQUALITY IN CHILDREN'S REAL INCOMES

Using the ratios to median U.S. equivalent income calculated as described in chapter 1, we can analyze the real incomes of average, advantaged, and disadvantaged children in each country compared with the incomes of similarly situated children in the United States. We compare American children with children in each country in the top quintile, the middle quintile, and the lowest quintile of the equivalent income distribution of children. (The average child in each group is at the tenth, fiftieth, or ninetieth percentile point.)

Table 2.2 gives the median real GDP per equivalent person of each country as a percentage of the U.S. median as derived by the method described in chapter 1. We convert the equivalent income at the tenth and ninetieth percentile points (expressed in percentages of the national median) in each of the other fourteen countries to real income amounts using these ratios to the U.S. median. Now the percentages are percentages of the U.S. median. For example, suppose we find that the median real GDP per capita in country X is 80 percent of the median real income in the United States. If the child at the ninetieth percentile point of the country X distribution of children's income has an income two and a half times greater than the overall national median, then this average advantaged child

TABLE 2.2 **Percentage of Real U.S. GDP in Fourteen Countries, per Median Equivalent Person in the 1990s**

Australia	79.00%
Belgium	89.37
Canada	88.71
Denmark	80.89
Finland	70.71
France	79.22
Germany	79.25
Italy	84.21
Netherlands	79.60
Norway	92.35
Spain	69.87
Sweden	67.79
Switzerland	98.49
United Kingdom	69.16

Source: Authors' calculations, using data from the Luxembourg Income Study.

in country X would have a real income equal to 80 percent of 2.5, or 200 percent of the U.S. median real equivalent income. If the U.S. child at the ninetieth percentile has an income three times the U.S. median, then the real income of this average advantaged child in the United States would amount to 300 percent of the U.S. real median. Therefore, the country X high-income child would have a real income equal to 67 percent (200 divided by 300) of the real income of the U.S. high-income child.

Starting with children in rich families, we find that rich American children are much better off compared with advantaged children in other countries (figure 2.3). Only Switzerland and Canada come close; in those countries the advantaged child has a real income equal to 92 and 87 percent, respectively, of the advantaged American child's real income. The other countries range down to lows of 50 to 60 percent in the Netherlands, Italy, Finland, Sweden, and Spain. Note the mix at the lower amounts of less affluent countries like Spain and Italy with moderately affluent countries of very equal income distribution like the Netherlands, Sweden, and Finland. This, then, is a picture very much in line with many Americans' conceptions of how U.S. children fare compared with those in other countries. Rich American children have much more than rich children in all our comparison countries.

FIGURE 2.3 Real Income Comparisons of the Advantaged Child Across Fifteen Countries in the 1990s

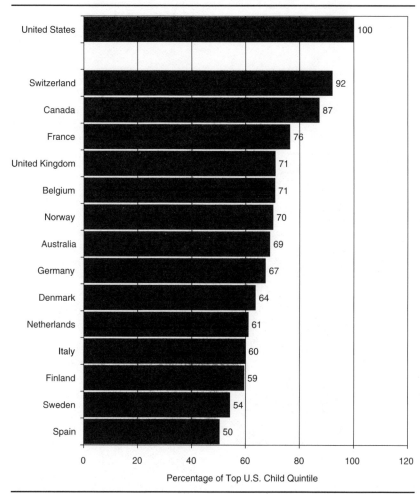

Source: Authors' calculations, using data from the Luxembourg Income Study.

But the picture changes dramatically when we focus not on high-income children but on the average child. Figure 2.4 shows the relation of the real income of the average American child to that of the average child in other countries. Here we find two countries—Switzerland and Canada—in which the average child has as much or slightly more as in the United States, and four others—France, Belgium, Denmark, and Norway—in which real income

FIGURE 2.4 **Real Income Comparisons of the Average Child Across Fifteen Countries in the 1990s**

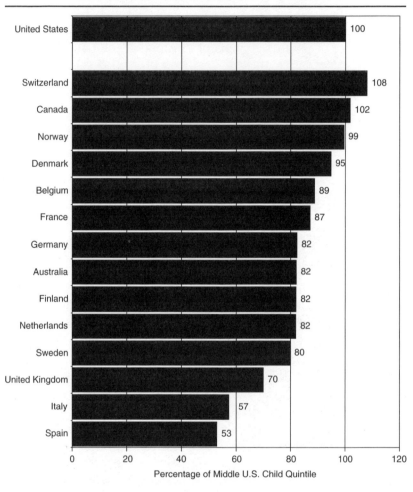

Source: Authors' calculations, using data from the Luxembourg Income Study.

approaches or tops 90 percent of the U.S. level. Thus, there is no warrant for saying that the average child in these countries is not about as well off as the average American child.

In five additional countries the average child's real income reaches or exceeds 80 percent of the American child's—Finland, Sweden, Australia, the Netherlands, and Germany. There are only two countries, Spain and Italy, in which the average child has less than 60 percent as much income as the average American child. The notion that American children are vastly better off than children in all other advanced industrial countries, insofar as that statement is based on some notion of the average child's situation, is clearly false.

We have noted that 20 percent of American children are poor. Therefore, comparing the real incomes of the lowest quintile of children in the United States with children in that quintile in other countries allows us to compare directly the level of economic well-being of American poor children with a group of the same size and relative income in other countries.

As noted, much American commentary on the poverty of children (and others) in the United States asserts that, even though poor by American standards, our poor are better off in real terms than their counterparts in other industrial countries. We see in figure 2.5 that the facts are just the opposite. In only three of our fourteen comparison countries (the United Kingdom, Spain, and Italy) is the average child in the bottom quintile (at the tenth percentile point) as worse off as the comparable poor American child. Indeed, in five countries the average disadvantaged child has one-third or more real income as the average poor American child. In Norway and Switzerland the relatively disadvantaged child has more than half again the real income of the poor American child.

If we compare one of the most equal countries, Sweden, with the United States across the whole distribution, we get a more precise picture of what lies behind the figures in these three graphs (see figure 2.6). Here we compare Swedish and American children at the same percentile points in their distributions of real income. We see that at the fifth percentile point, children in Sweden have real income roughly 40 percent of median U.S. real income, whereas in the United States such children live in families with incomes about one-quarter of median real income. We note that at each point up to about the thirtieth percentile point the Swedish child's real income is greater than that of the comparable American child. Above that point the increasingly well off American children have more income than their Swedish peers, so that by the ninety-fifth percentile point the Swedish child has a real income about 10 percent higher than the U.S. median while the very rich American child has an income slightly less than 225 percent of the median.

FIGURE 2.5 **Real Income Comparisons of the Disadvantaged
Child Across Fifteen Countries in the 1990s**

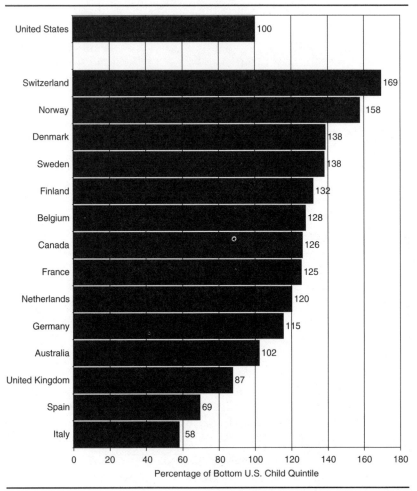

Source: Authors' calculations, using data from the Luxembourg Income Study.

Generalizing this approach, we can summarize curves like the
ones in figure 2.6 by estimating the percentile point at which each
nation's children no longer have higher incomes than the comparable American child. We see in figure 2.7 that up to the sixty-first
percentile, Swiss children's real incomes exceed those of their
American peers. In Canada and Norway this is true of about half
of children. For Denmark the crossover point is just below the

FIGURE 2.6 **Percentile Points of Child's Real Income: Sweden and the United States**

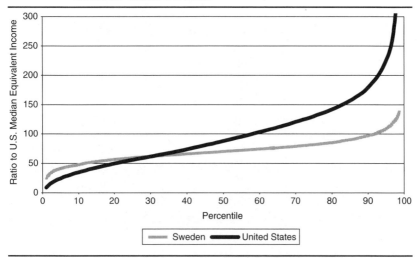

Source: Authors' calculations, using data from the Luxembourg Income Study.

FIGURE 2.7 **Percentile Point at Which Fourteen Nations' Children No Longer Have Higher Income Than Comparable U.S. Children**

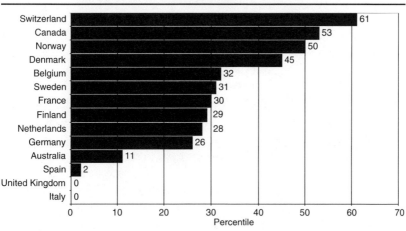

Source: Authors' calculations, using data from the Luxembourg Income Study.

median. Then there is a cluster of countries where between one-third and one-quarter of children are better off than comparable American children—Belgium, Sweden, France, Finland, the Netherlands, and Germany. Only in the United Kingdom, Spain, and Italy are almost all children worse off in real terms than American children of the same rank.

Thus, we can say that, with the exception of Australia, Spain, Italy, and the United Kingdom, *all* American poor children are worse off in material goods than the children of other nations who stand at the same point in their income distribution. That is to say, American poor children are worse off in real terms than the lowest-income 20 percent of children in ten of our fourteen comparison countries.

If we expand a bit to include the 34 percent of American children in the near-poor as well as the poor category, we find that even here, in ten of these countries, between 75 and 100 percent of marginal-income American children have lower real incomes than their opposite numbers.

CONCLUSION

This chapter has gone behind the simple rates of poverty described in chapter 1 to examine the income inequality context of those rates. By ranking the children of these nations by the size of their middle class, we arrive at the same picture as that of the pattern of poverty rates. There are the large-middle-class, small-poverty-class nations of northern Europe at one pole of inequality, and the United States along with Italy and the United Kingdom at the other. The United States and Italy are distinctive in that around 10 percent of their children are not just poor but extremely poor.

A comforting belief in the United States is that while we may have more inequality than European countries, decades of economic growth have lifted even the worst-off Americans to a higher standard of living than the marginal economic classes of Europe. Rather surprisingly, this turns out not to be the case. In half of our comparison countries roughly the lowest income third of children are better off in real terms than their American peers. And in the others (except for Australia, Spain, the United Kingdom, and Italy) the children in the same rank as the poor American children who make up the bottom income child quintile are as well or better off.

---- Chapter 3 ----

Child Poverty
and Population:
Is Demography Destiny?

W HEN AMERICANS LEARN of the large differences in poverty rates among countries, many of them ask: To what extent are differences in poverty rates a reflection of differences in population characteristics? Perhaps different parental age structures across countries, for instance, affect children's poverty rates. And surely different proportions of large and small families, differences in the number of adults in families, or differences in the number of employed family members would affect poverty figures. Most important, Americans tend to assume that differences in the proportion of families headed by a single woman would account for a significant share of the difference in poverty rates between the United States and other countries. A related variable is the extent to which countries differ in the distribution of wage earners.

Together such demographic factors make up a complex matrix of population characteristics. The implicit methodological issue is whether that matrix is very different from one country to another, and if it is, whether those differences affect the overall poverty rate. In other words, how can we meaningfully compare poverty rates across countries unless we distinguish the effects of demographic factors, including labor force characteristics, from those of the institutional factors commonly associated with the welfare state? If Germany had the demography of the United States, for instance, what would its poverty rate be? If the United States had the same kind of economic and social protection institutions that France has, how would the American poverty rate change?

To answer these questions, we have simulated the demography of each comparison country on the U.S. data and similarly simulated the U.S. demography on the data for every other country. We set up two counterfactual poverty rates to contrast with the actual poverty rates of each country:

Simulated U.S. demography: If the demographic matrix of another country were the same as that of the United States without changes in its institutions, what would the poverty rate be?

Simulated demography of other countries on the United States: If the U.S. demographic matrix were the same as that of every other country without changes in U.S. institutions, what would the poverty rate be?

A straightforward way of simulating the demography is to reweight a nation's survey in such a way that the distribution of demographic characteristics is the same as that of another nation. Using reweighting, we can examine three kinds of poverty rates—the actual rate of each nation; the simulated poverty rate of the United States when the U.S. survey is reweighted to reflect the demography of another country; and the simulated poverty rates of the other countries when they are reweighted to reflect the demography of the United States. (The methodology is described in appendix D.)

To do this, we constructed a demographic matrix for each country that cross-tabulates the following aspects of a nation's demography: the age distribution of the household head; by the number of elderly persons; by the number of children; by whether the head was a man or woman; by whether there were adults other than the head and spouse in the house; and by the earning status of the head, spouse, and any other adults. Using these cross-tabulations, we calculated weights to make each nation's distribution of population characteristics the same as that of the comparison country.

These simulations helped us up to a point in separating the effects on the overall poverty rate of demographic versus institutional factors. But this separation is not perfect considering that the number of earners in a household is certainly affected by economic and social protection institutions, and even the number of adults in a household or the number of elders is affected by wel-

fare state measures. We leave as part of "income packaging institutions" all stratification forces such as education, race, occupation, and so on, since they relate to income distribution. Income
packaging institutions are a residual referring to all of the political
economic institutions of society that produce, distribute, constrain,
or recoup the stream of income in the exchanges between society
and the family unit (Peattie and Rein 1983).

The U.S. child poverty rate in 1997 of 20.3 percent can be
thought of as the combined product of U.S. demography and U.S.
income packaging institutions. By simulating the American demography on each of the other countries, and the demography of the
other countries on the United States, we produce three poverty
rates—the nation's actual rate, the as-if rate with U.S. demography,
and the as-if rate with U.S. institutions (that is, the U.S. data
reweighted by every other country's demography). For example, we
have found that the U.K. child poverty rate in 1995 was 16.3 percent.
Our simulations suggest that if the United Kingdom had U.S. income
packaging institutions, its poverty rate would be much higher, some
30 percent (figure 3.1). On the other hand, if the United Kingdom
had retained its own institutions but had U.S. demography, its
poverty rate would have been quite a bit lower, around 12 percent.

In terms of direction, those who believe U.S. demography tends
to increase child poverty compared to that of other countries are
correct more than half of the time. But the increases are very small
except in the case of Spain. In a few countries the difference is in
the opposite direction. Overall, the changes are not very great.

We see, on the other hand, the powerful effect of institutions
when we impose other countries' demography on American
income packaging. In every case except for Italy, the combination
of the country's own demographic patterns and American institutions results in a massive increase in the simulated poverty rate
compared to the nation's actual rate. On average, the rates simulated with U.S. institutions—between 15 and 30 percent—are three
times the actual rates. This result is particularly striking in the countries with very low poverty rates. Imposing the demography of the
countries with actual poverty rates of 5 percent or less on the U.S.
sample results in poverty rates between 15 and 19 percent. Clearly
it is income packaging that drives the results we see.

Of course, none of this is to say that there are no important differences in the poverty rates of demographic groups. What this

FIGURE 3.1 **Observed and Simulated Child Poverty Rates in Fifteen Countries in the 1990s**

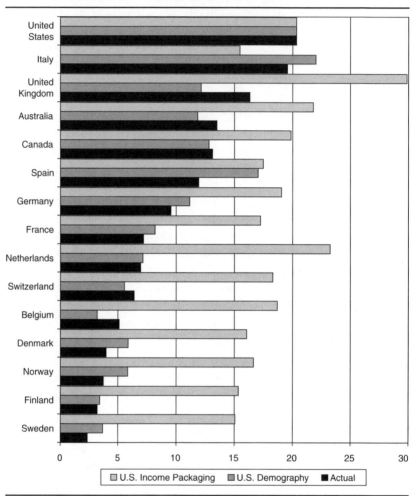

Source: Authors' calculations, using data from the Luxembourg Income Study.

exercise demonstrates is that the demographic matrices of these countries are not sufficiently different to produce large differences in poverty rates due solely to different population characteristics. Compared with institutional factors, demographic differences play only a minor role in the differences among countries. It is primarily the exceptional U.S. income packaging that produces high child poverty rates, not an exceptional U.S. demography.

CHILD POVERTY IN FAMILIES
WITH AND WITHOUT EARNERS

It will be useful to focus in detail on one aspect of the demographic matrix used in this simulation. Countries vary considerably in the distribution of the number of earners in families with children. Table 3.1 presents this distribution. We consider a person an earner if he or she received any income from work during the year. We note that the United Kingdom has the highest proportion of children living in families with no earners—25 percent. The other countries range downward from Australia, Belgium, and Switzerland at 10 or 11 percent to Finland, Italy, Norway, and Sweden with fewer then 5 percent of children living in families with no earners. In the four Nordic countries, about 75 percent of children live in families with two or more earners, followed by 67 percent in Canada and 62 percent in the United States. In most of the other countries, about half of children have two or more workers in their families. Slightly fewer than half of Italian and Dutch children live in such families. The lowest proportions of multi-earner families are found in Spain, Switzerland, and the United Kingdom. Thus, in all but one of these

TABLE 3.1 Number of Adults with Annual Earnings, by Country

	No Earner	One Earner	Two or More Earners
Australia	11.4%	34.5%	54.1%
Belgium	10.6	35.4	53.9
Canada	7.4	25.8	66.8
Denmark	6.0	17.7	76.2
Finland	4.3	21.2	74.6
France	6.4	38.3	55.3
Germany	6.1	42.4	51.5
Italy	3.8	49.9	46.3
Netherlands	8.8	46.2	44.9
Norway	4.7	20.5	74.9
Spain	5.8	58.0	36.2
Sweden	3.3	22.6	74.1
Switzerland	10.1	49.5	40.4
United Kingdom	24.8	34.3	40.9
United States	5.7	32.2	62.0

Source: Authors' calculations, using data from the Luxembourg Income Study.

countries the so-called traditional one-earner family is in the minority. In ten of these, the traditional family ranges down from slightly over one-third to a low of around one-fifth. In the United States some 32 percent of children live in one-earner families.

We would expect that children in families with no earners have high poverty rates. But, as is apparent in figure 3.2, there is a wide range in poverty rates in such families across these coun-

FIGURE 3.2 Child Poverty in Fifteen Countries, by Number of Earners in the 1990s

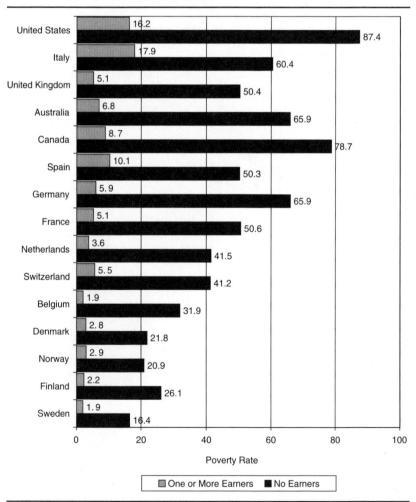

Source: Authors' calculations, using data from the Luxembourg Income Study.

tries. Fully 87 percent of no-earner children in the United States are poor. Two-thirds or more of children in families with no earners in Germany, Australia, and Canada are poor compared with around one-quarter or fewer in Finland, Denmark, Sweden, and Norway. We see that social protection systems vary dramatically in their treatment of children in no-earner families. Even so, in more than half of these countries child poverty rates in no-earner families are over 50 percent. The highly developed welfare states of France and Germany still do not fund no-earner families at a level that would keep the majority of them out of poverty.

The poverty rate for children in families with one or more earners is 3 percent or less in five countries, and an additional five countries have rates of less than 6 percent for such families. Spain and Canada have rather high rates, at 10 and 9 percent, respectively. Italy and the United States stand apart with poverty rates of 18 and 16 percent, respectively, for families with one or more earners.

The poverty rates for children in families with just one earner cover a wide range (not shown). In the United States the poverty rate of children in one-earner families is 35 percent, and in Italy it is 28 percent. The rate is 19 percent in Canada, 14 percent in Australia, and 13 percent in Spain. In the other countries fewer than 10 percent of children in one-earner families are poor. On the other hand, child poverty rates in families with two or more earners are uniformly quite low—Italy and the United States are highest with 7 percent. Twelve countries have poverty rates of 2 percent or less for multi-earner families.

We see here, in a very small way, one of the reasons demography is not destiny. Whatever the differences between the United States and other countries in the proportion of children who live in families with no earners, one earner, or two earners, we observe that American child poverty rates are considerably higher for each earner type.

The composition of the poor in terms of earning status varies a great deal from country to country, as is apparent in table 3.2. Italy and the United Kingdom stand at polar extremes—almost all of poor Italian children live in families with at least one earner, while fewer than one-quarter of British poor children live in families with an earner. In Belgium, the Netherlands, and Australia a majority of poor children live in families with no earners, and this is almost the case in Switzerland. On the other hand, three-quarters or more of poor children in Spain, Sweden, the United States, and Norway live in fam-

TABLE 3.2 **Earning Status of Poor Children's Families in Fifteen Countries in the 1990s**

	No Earner	One Earner	Two or More Earners
Australia	55.5%	36.3%	8.2%
Belgium	66.7	25.8	7.5
Canada	41.8	37.5	20.7
Denmark	33.2	29.3	37.5
Finland	34.8	40.2	25.0
France	39.3	54.6	6.1
Germany	42.4	46.9	10.7
Italy	11.8	70.9	17.3
Netherlands	58.5	38.2	3.4
Norway	26.2	63.1	10.7
Spain	21.9	62.8	15.3
Sweden	22.5	54.6	22.9
Switzerland	48.7	47.2	4.0
United Kingdom	76.5	22.4	1.1
United States	24.7	55.1	20.3

Source: Authors' calculations, using data from the Luxembourg Income Study.

ilies with at least one earner. In the other countries, the proportion of earners is in the 60 percent range.

One would expect the dominant policy issues in the countries with primarily working poor families to revolve around some combination of increasing work hours and wages or increasing family supplements to earnings. For countries where the proportion of the poor in families without earnings is high, we would expect the policy discussion to focus on increasing job opportunities for non-earners, providing job-related services like child care, and defining standards for a guaranteed income through social insurance or other mechanisms.

Our 1997 results for the United States reflect poverty rates among non-earner and earner families before welfare reform was in full swing, so the size of the working poor group was not inflated by the reform's efforts to increase single mothers' work effort. More recent data would undoubtedly reinforce the question that naturally arises even from pre-reform data: Why does so much of the discussion of poverty policy in the United States revolve around income maintenance for non-earner families, despite the fact that three-quarters of American poor children live in families with workers?

Chapter 4

Periods of Poverty: How Long Are Children Poor?

CROSS-SECTIONAL POVERTY rates give us a snapshot of how many people are poor in a given year, but they do not tell us how long people have been poor or will remain so. Faced with a 20 percent child poverty rate in one country, we therefore cannot assume (although unconsciously we often do) that 20 percent of that country's children have always been poor, or that 80 percent have always escaped poverty. We would have a much more complete understanding of cross-national inequality if we could supplement cross-national data with longitudinal data on the length of the periods of poverty experienced by children.

Although longitudinal data for cross-national research are only just now becoming available, longitudinal studies have already begun to appear. For example, Bruce Bradbury, Stephen Jenkins, and John Micklewright (2001) analyzed panel study data for several countries, including the United States and Germany. Our findings are consistent with their broader study, although they use a different definition of poverty and a different time period and therefore results are not exactly comparable.

For this analysis, we can compare only two countries: Germany and the United States. Panel surveys are available on the experience of children in Germany and the United States for fourteen years, from 1983 through 1997. The American data from the Panel Study of Income Dynamics (PSID) cover the period 1983 through 1996, and the German data from the German Socio-Economic Panel (GSOEP) cover 1984 through 1997 (see Cornell University, n.d.).

We start by examining the cohort of children who were younger than eighteen in the last year of the series and continuously present from the first survey (when they were younger than five years old). The number of children in these two samples who fit this definition is not very large: there are only 458 German children and 1,071 American children in the respective panels. For the most part, the definitions of income are the same in the LIS data and in the GSOEP/PSID dataset.[1]

On a cross-sectional basis, we find that on average a little over 5 percent of German children were poor each year compared with 20 percent of American children. (Remember that this is a cohort, so each year the children were a year older than the year before; results do not match those from a cross-section of all children.) But our question here is: How much of the time over the fourteen-year period were children poor as they matured toward the age of seventeen?

We see in table 4.1 that 76 percent of German children were never poor, compared with 49 percent of American children. Very few in either country were poor almost all the time—only 0.5 percent in Germany and 5 percent in the United States were poor for thirteen or fourteen years.

TABLE 4.1 **Number of Years Children Were Poor, 1983 to 1997: Germany and the United States**

Years Poor	U.S. Children	German Children
0	49.4%	76.4%
1	10.4	9.2
2	6.4	5.1
3	5.4	3.7
4	5.0	1.6
5	3.2	0.4
6	2.6	0.8
7	1.8	0.2
8	1.4	0.0
9	1.8	0.6
10	4.3	0.5
11	1.5	0.6
12	1.7	0.3
13	1.6	0.3
14	3.3	0.2

Source: Authors' calculations, using data from the Luxembourg Income Study.
Note: Children were continuously present in the panels and under eighteen in 1997. For the American sample the period is 1983 to 1996; the German period begins and ends one year later.

But a significant proportion of American children were poor at least half of the time. Over seventeen percent (17.4 percent) were poor for seven or more years, compared with fewer than 3 percent of German children. Thus, we find not only higher child poverty rates in the United States than in Germany in the LIS data but also comparably higher persistence of poverty in the panel data.

As we have noted several times, the poverty line is an artificial divider between those who are significantly marginal economically and those who are less so. We can expand our focus by taking into account incomes just above the poverty line. We consider patterns of poverty and near-poverty to define a broader group of economically marginal families. In this analysis, "near-poverty" is defined as an income of less than two-thirds of median equivalent income, and "economically marginal" is defined as being poor at least five of the fourteen years and at least near-poor for an additional five years, making a total of ten years of the fourteen. We find that in the United States 20 percent of children were sometimes poor and also economically marginal more than three-quarters of the time. In contrast, only 3 percent of German children were economically marginal for this long.

We obtain a more precise picture of these transitions in and out of poverty and economic marginality by examining the relationship between economic well-being in the first three years and in the subsequent eleven years. We define four groups of children in terms of their families' income experience in the first three years: those who were never near-poor; those who were near-poor at least once but never poor; those who were poor just one year; and those who were poor two or three years.

Table 4.2 presents the percentages of children in each of these categories. While there is a very large difference in the proportion of children in the two countries who were never poor, there is not much difference in the proportion of children who were never near-poor. But those who were not so fortunate are distributed rather differently. Over two-thirds of the economically marginal German children were never poor, while over two-thirds of the marginal American children have been poor one year or more.

What happens to the children in each of these groups later in life? Figure 4.1 depicts the experience of the four groups. First we plot the proportion of children who were ever poor in the subsequent eleven

TABLE 4.2 **Early Patterns of Economic Marginality Among U.S. and German Children**

	German Children	U.S. Children
Never near-poor or poor	60.7%	54.1%
Near-poor but never poor	27.4	15.1
Poor one year	6.8	9.0
Poor two or three years	5.1	21.8

Source: Authors' calculations, using data from the Luxembourg Income Study.
Note: Children were younger than five in 1984 or 1983. For the American sample the period is 1983 to 1985; the German period begins and ends one year later.

years. We also show in the bars of the chart the average number of years of poverty for those who were ever poor. We see that 23 percent of the roughly half of American children who had no experience of poverty or near-poverty in the early period were nevertheless

FIGURE 4.1 **Children's Experience of Poverty in the Later Period, by Poverty Status in the Early Period: Germany and the United States**

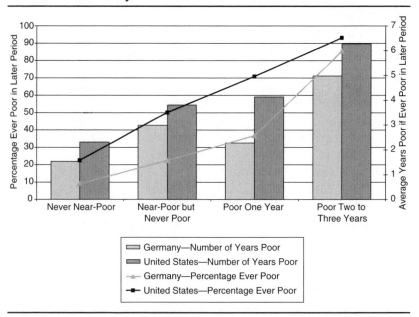

Source: Authors' calculations, using data from the Luxembourg Income Study.
Note: For the American sample the early period is 1983 through 1985, and the later period is 1986 through 1996; the German periods begin and end one year later.

poor in at least one later year compared with only 9 percent of German children. But in both countries those who experienced some poverty averaged only about two years or less.

The later poverty rates increase markedly if in the early years the family had even one year of near-poverty. In this case, half of American children and almost one-quarter of German children later experienced some years of poverty, averaging four and three years, respectively. One year of poverty in early childhood produced some years of poverty later for over 70 percent of American children, in contrast to slightly over one-third of German children. In this group, American children experienced poverty for an average of four years, whereas the average figure is a little over two years for the German children.

Almost all of the American and German children who were poor two or three years were poor at some time in the subsequent eleven years. When they were poor, they averaged six and five years, respectively.

To summarize the complex patterns of poverty, near-poverty, and better economic circumstances over these fourteen years, we divided the fourteen years into three periods: the first four years followed by two periods of five years each. We are interested in knowing how many children in each country are persistently economically marginal. For the first period we defined economic marginality as being poor for two years of the four, or poor one year and near-poor two years. For the second and third periods we defined economic marginality as being poor for three years, or poor for two years and near-poor for two additional years. These definitions treat a single year of poverty without near-poverty in a nearby year as transitional poverty. We think of families as persistently economically marginal only if their low incomes persisted.

We find in table 4.3 that, according to these definitions, almost nine out of ten German children were never persistently economically marginal, compared with 62 percent of American children. At the other extreme, 13 percent of American children were persistently economically marginal in all three periods, compared with only 2 percent of German children. In other words, American children were more than six times as likely to be marginal in all three periods as German children, and they were five times more likely to be marginal in two of the three periods. Fewer than one in eight

TABLE 4.3 **Persistence of Economic Marginality Among U.S. and German Children**

	German Children	U.S. Children
Marginal in three periods	2.0%	12.9%
Marginal in two periods	2.0	9.9
Marginal in one period	7.8	15.2
Never marginal	88.2	62.0

Source: Authors' calculations, using data from the Luxembourg Income Study.
Note: Children were younger than eighteen in 1997. For the American sample, the periods are 1983 through 1986, 1987 through 1991, and 1992 through 1996; the German periods begin and end one year later.

German children ever experienced a period of persistent marginality, compared with well over one-third of American children.

TRANSITION PROBABILITIES
OF ECONOMIC MARGINALITY

As noted, restricting the sample to only those children who were present in all fourteen years results in quite small sample sizes. To gain a more fine-grained idea of the dynamics of moves into and out of poverty, we need more cases. For that reason, we shortened the time period to the six years between 1992 and 1997 for the German sample and 1991 to 1996 for the American sample, thus gaining a much larger sample: 2,292 German children and 3,337 American children in the two panel surveys were present during those six years and under the age of eighteen in the last year.

Now we can examine the transitions in and out of poverty or near-poverty in a given year as a function of the poverty status of the child's family in the previous two years. We examine four overlapping three-year periods from the first through the third year, the second through the fourth year, and so on. We are interested in the probability of poverty or near-poverty in year 0 as a function of the economic marginality status of a child's family in year −1 (the previous year) and year −2 (two years before). We present in table 4.4 the average probabilities over the four periods of moving in and out of poverty as a function of poverty status in the previous two years.

Note that when the child's family has been poor in the previous one or two years, the transition probabilities in Germany and

TABLE 4.4 **Subsequent Poverty Status of U.S. and German Children as a Function of Poverty Status in the Previous Two Years**

	Poor		Not Poor	
Poverty Status in Previous Two Years	German Children	U.S. Children	German Children	U.S. Children
Poor in both previous two years	77.8%	76.9%	22.2%	23.1%
Poor only in previous year	50.5	52.4	49.5	47.6
Poor only two years before	18.0	27.6	82.0	72.4
Not poor either year	2.7	5.6	97.3	94.4

Source: Authors' calculations, using data from the Luxembourg Income Study.
Note: Children were younger than eighteen in 1997. For the American sample the periods are 1991 through 1994, 1993 through 1995, and 1994 through 1996; the German periods begin and end one year later.

the United States are quite similar. Three-quarters of children in both countries in families that were poor for the previous two years were poor in the third year. In both countries, if the family was poor in the previous year but not in the year before that, about half of the children were poor.

We find differences, however, for the other two patterns. German children are much less likely to become poor than are American children. We find that, when the family was poor two years earlier but escaped poverty in the previous year, a little over one-quarter of the American children were poor again in the third year, compared with slightly fewer than one-fifth of the German children. And there is a similar small difference among children whose family had not been poor in the previous two years. Here we find 6 percent of American children becoming poor, compared with 3 percent of German children. These results suggest that the dynamics of entering poverty are different in the two countries, but that the dynamics of staying in poverty are pretty much the same.

TO WHAT DEGREE IS ECONOMIC MARGINALITY INHERITED?

The fourteen years of data we have for Germany and the United States also allow us to offer suggestive findings concerning the intergenerational inheritance of poverty. That is, we can compare the economic well-being of children when they were in their teens to their economic well-being in their late twenties. To provide a definitive answer, we would have liked to be able to look at data from a longer time period—to gain more evidence for these children's experience as adults—but the results we do have are suggestive.

We selected people who were twenty-five to twenty-eight years of age in the last year; they had been twelve to fifteen years of age in the first year. We compared their pattern of economic marginality in the early three-year period with their pattern when they were in their mid- to late twenties in the last period. The sample is much smaller than we would wish: 349 Germans and 321 Americans. Table 4.5 cross-tabulates adolescent economic status in three categories—never near-poor, near-poor but never poor, and poor one or more years—with adult status in the same three categories. We find important differences in the economic fates of boys and girls, so the results are presented separately for the two sexes.

The chance of being poor at least once in one's late twenties varies from 9 percent for German men who were not near-poor as adolescents to 60 percent for American women whose families were poor at least once when they were adolescents. Among women whose families had no experience of economic marginality in adolescence, there is no hint of a difference between the two countries. But among the men, adult Americans are more likely to become poor.

For German men the effect of adolescent economic marginality, either near-poverty or poverty, does not seem very strong. But among American men there is a sharp increase in marginality as a function of family circumstances in adolescence, with poverty experience increasing from 25 percent to 40 percent. The experience of near-poverty increases these figures even more, from 35 percent to 75 percent.

Overall, economic marginality in adolescence seems to have a much greater effect on women than on men in both Germany and the United States, although in the end German women are much less likely to be poor in their late twenties than are American women.

Combining the poor and near-poor categories in both adolescence and the twenties should give us more stable findings. When we do this (see table 4.6), we find that among those who were

TABLE 4.5 Economic Marginality of U.S. and German Adults, by Economic Status in Adolescence and Gender, Comparing Poor, Near-Poor, and Never Poor Categories

	Adolescent Status					
	Never Near-Poor		Near-Poor But Never Poor		Poor One or More Years	
Adult Status	Germany	United States	Germany	United States	Germany	United States
Men						
Never near-poor	81.7%	65.1%	79.5%	49.3%	71.4%	24.8%
Near-poor but never poor	9.2	10.0	10.3	19.7	9.5	35.0
Poor one or more years	9.2	24.9	10.3	30.9	19.0	40.2
Women						
Never near-poor	68.4	68.4	56.5	17.9	47.8	20.7
Near-poor but never poor	14.0	14.1	23.9	26.0	30.4	19.3
Poor one or more years	17.5	17.5	19.6	56.2	21.7	60.0
Number of males	130	85	35	21	20	32
Number of females	102	95	42	26	20	62

Source: Authors' calculations, using data from the Luxembourg Income Study.
Note: For the American sample the periods are 1983 through 1985 and 1994 through 1996; the German periods begin and end one year later.

TABLE 4.6 Economic Marginality of U.S. and German Adults, by Economic Status in Adolescence and Gender, Comparing Poor Combined with Near-Poor Versus Never Poor Categories

			Adolescent Status					
	Never Near-Poor		Near-Poor or Poor		Total	
Adult Status	Germany	United States	Germany	United States	Germany	United States
Men						
Never near-poor or poor	81.7%	65.1%	76.7%	34.8%	80.2%	55.6%
Near-poor or poor one or more years	18.3	34.9	23.3	65.2	19.8	44.4
Women						
Never near-poor or poor	68.4	68.4	53.6	19.7	62.8	51.5
Near-poor or poor one or more years	31.6	31.6	46.4	80.3	37.2	48.5
Number of males	130	85	55	53	185	138
Number of females	102	95	62	88	164	183

Source: Authors' calculations, using data from the Luxembourg Income Study.
Note: For the American sample the periods are 1983 through 1985 and 1994 through 1996; the German periods begin and end one year later.

never economically marginal, there is no difference between men and women in the United States. About one-third are economically marginal as adults. But in Germany almost twice as many women are economically marginal as men, even though during their adolescence their families were not marginal. The German women are as likely to become marginal as American men and women.

Where there is a family experience of marginality in adolescence, women are much more likely than men, and Americans more than Germans, to be marginal in their late twenties. Thus some 80 percent of American women who come from economically marginal families are themselves economically marginal in their late twenties, along with almost two-thirds of American men. In contrast, only 46 percent of German women have an experience of economic marginality in their late twenties, and among German men the rate is only 23 percent.

CONCLUSION

Taking a longer time perspective on economic marginality through this brief exploration of longitudinal data only deepens the impression that German children experience much less economic stress than American children. Not only are more children poor for a longer time in the United States than in Germany, but American children are much more likely than German children, if they have been economically marginal as adolescents, to also experience poverty when they grow up.

—— Chapter 5 ——

Income Packaging:
Market Income and the State

U P TO THIS point we have been discussing poverty and income distribution based on a single measure of income—total money (and near-cash) income minus taxes, adjusted for family size. Because we subtract taxes, we are also taking into account the effect of tax rates and tax expenditures on disposable income. In this and the next two chapters, we want to move on to a discussion of income packaging and child poverty. The term income packaging recognizes the fact that in most countries a family's income is usually an aggregate from several different sources. An extremely detailed accounting of families' incomes in a particular country might require giving attention to as many as fifty different sources of income—different members' taxes, earnings, rent, interest, dividends, child support, and a vast array of social benefits, such as pensions, child allowances, public assistance, housing allowances, and benefits of many other transfer programs. Each source of income involves a claim and entitlement based on some activity or characteristic of family members—employment, capital, a social insurance contribution history, low income, and so forth. In the analysis of income packaging in this part, we look first at the three main aggregates of income—market income, taxes, and transfers. Then we move on to a more detailed examination of the role in the family income package of different kinds of transfers, some of which are specifically tied to the presence of children in a family and others to some other characteristics of family members. (For background on the concept of income packaging, see Peattie and Rein 1983; Rainwater, Rein, and Schwartz 1986.)

What are the roles of various sources of income—particularly earnings and the range of social protection transfers provided by governments—in enabling families with children to avoid poverty? This chapter considers the role of market income and social transfers for all children. Because labor market participation and social transfers affect children differently in single-parent versus two-parent families, our more fine-grained analysis examines their situation separately (children in two-parent families in chapter 6 and those in single-mother families in chapter 7).

POLITICS, WELFARE STATE REGIMES, AND POVERTY

The income packaging one finds in a particular society is strongly influenced by the political complexion of the nation as it has evolved over time. Taxes, social protection programs, and governmental influence on the economy and labor market are all subjects central to the programs of the political parties in the fifteen democracies we are studying. The literature on welfare state regimes developed over the past quarter-century seeks to account for the differences in the welfare states of industrial democracies (Korpi 1983; Esping-Andersen 1990, 1999; Hicks and Kenworthy 2003; Wilensky 2002; Bradley et al. 2001). Research in this tradition focuses on the role of political actors and structures (for example, parties, unions, consultation of social partners, constitutional structure), on the one hand, and the characteristics of social protection programs (for example, eligibility for benefits, equality of benefits, private as opposed to public benefits, means testing), on the other. Obviously, the regimes defined by the characteristics of social protection programs—welfare regimes proper—result from a history of political dynamics. So we start with politics.

Promoting a more equal income distribution and reducing poverty is a central goal of some political parties and a matter of indifference or hostility to others. These goals are promoted directly by tax and transfer programs but also indirectly by institutional mechanisms such as active labor market policy, government employment, support of unionization, public child care, and antidiscrimination and affirmative action policies. So, before considering the details of income packaging, we consider the impact of our nations' left-right political histories on the poverty rates we have observed. The comparative welfare states dataset assembled by Evelyne Huber, Charles Ragin, and John D. Stephens (1997) provides a measure of left cabinet share from 1946 to the 1990s with which we can test the impact of government control on the observed poverty rates. Left cabinet share is scored 1 for each year the left is in government alone, and a fraction for years of coalition.

We find that there is a very strong correlation in fourteen of these countries between child poverty and left cabinet share. (Spain is omitted since it was not a democracy in all of the postwar years.) The correlation with the child poverty rates is −0.72. If instead we define the odds ratio of escaping from poverty (100 minus the poverty rate divided by the poverty rate), the correlation with left cabinet is even higher—0.84 (see figure 5.1).

The four Nordic countries have left cabinet scores of 20 or above, and the odds of a child escaping poverty range from over forty to one in Sweden and Norway to thirty to one in Finland. At the other extreme, two countries have never had left cabinet presence, the United States and Canada, and Italy has a very low score of 5. They are also the countries with the lowest poverty escape odds of four or six to one.

A large group of countries have left cabinet scores of 10 to 15. Their odds range quite a bit—from only five to one in the United Kingdom to almost twenty to one in Belgium. Thus, despite the high correlation, variations in left cabinet share would not take us very far in understanding child poverty rate differences for this middle group of countries. Adding other variables such as Christian Democratic cabinet share or union density does not improve the fit in the middle range.[1]

A more fine-grained approach to political analysis would be required to understand the impact of politics on income packaging institutions that produces the child poverty effects we observe. The road to that understanding would require careful consideration of the role of different income sources as they contribute to total after-tax income. We begin this task in this and the following two chapters.

INCOME PACKAGING
AND THE ESCAPE FROM POVERTY

As an introduction to the analysis of income packaging, we begin by examining two general types of income. *Pretransfer income* includes

FIGURE 5.1 Odds in Fourteen Countries of Escaping Child Poverty, by Left Cabinet Share

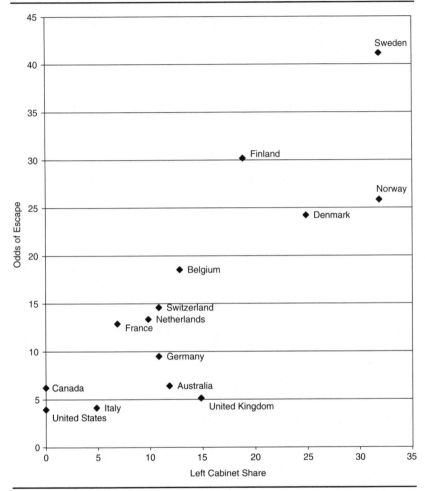

Source: Authors' calculations, using data from the Luxembourg Income Study.
Note: Spain is omitted since it was not a democracy in all of the postwar years.

salaries, self-employment income, and asset income before taxes are paid. *Post-transfer income* (disposable income) refers to the amount left after certain interventions by government, which collects income taxes and social insurance contributions and makes social protection transfers. Post-transfer income, in other words, is the net of pretransfer income minus taxes plus social and private transfers.

Government redistributes income by taxing pregovernment income and paying part of the taxes it collects to citizens in the form of social transfers. (Think of taxes and social insurance contributions as a negative transfer.) It also mandates various private transfers by law or through the courts. (We deviate from common definitions here by not including private transfers—primarily child support—in pretransfer income. We do so because private transfers often are mandated by and payment enforced by the legal system, so we categorize them as post-government.)

We compare in figure 5.2 the poverty rates of children based on their families' pretransfer income with the rates we have been examining in earlier chapters, which are based on post-transfer income. The figure graphs three elements of the redistributive process. The horizontal axis shows what the child poverty rates would be if families had only their pretransfer incomes. The vertical axis shows the poverty rates we are already familiar with, which are based on post-transfer income. The rays emanating from zero show the percentage reduction in the pretransfer poverty rate accomplished by the net of families' taxes paid and transfers received.

We note that government reduces child poverty by only a small amount (around 25 percent) in the United States and Italy. The Italian result is somewhat misleading, since the child allowances paid by employers as part of earnings are included in pretransfer income. However, child allowances are not particularly generous in Italy. The reduction is a bit greater in Switzerland, Germany, Spain, Australia, and Canada—between 37 and 46 percent. In sharp contrast, in six countries—Sweden, Finland, Belgium, Denmark, Norway, and France—the net effect of government intervention is to reduce child poverty by 75 percent or more. The United Kingdom and the Netherlands stand in the middle with a little over 50 percent reduction.

A careful look at the seven countries with pretransfer poverty rates just below and above the 25 percent range shows that, after government intervention, child poverty rates range from a high of 20 percent in the United States and Italy to 12 to 14 percent for Australia, Canada, and Spain, to 10 percent for Germany, to 7 percent in France and 5 percent and less in Belgium and Sweden. Note that the United Kingdom's pretransfer poverty rate is much higher than that of the United States, but because its government programs reduce child poverty by over 50 percent compared with 20 percent

FIGURE 5.2 **Pre- and Post-Transfer Poverty Rates in Fifteen Countries**

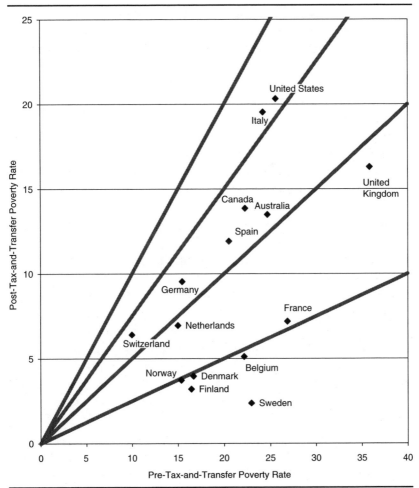

Source: Authors' calculations, using data from the Luxembourg Income Study.
Note: From top to bottom the rays indicate that 0, 25, 50, and 75 percent of children are moved out of poverty by post-tax-and-transfer sources.

in the United States, its post-tax-and-transfers poverty rate is lower. Germany has a low pretransfer child poverty rate, but it nevertheless reduces it further by almost 40 percent.

The calculation of pre- and post-transfer poverty rates is a heuristic device. After all, the redistribution process for the most part takes place simultaneously with the generation of the "primary" market income. Most Europeans in particular are not even sure what their pretax salaries are, since income tax and contributions are withheld at the source and the year-end tax return is much simpler than the American one. Many European surveys do not even attempt to ask about pretax income.

This heuristic is most useful in thinking about the effect of taxes and transfers on the situation of families with earners. For families without earners, there is very little if any pretransfer income—mostly the very small source of asset income. But since 90 percent or more of children live in families with earners (with the exception of the United Kingdom), the pattern of the government effect on poverty is not too different for children in earner families from that for all children depicted in figure 5.2.

A somewhat different perspective on the role of market and transfer income can be gained from figure 5.3. Here we plot mean equivalent income for the lowest quintile of children by the average proportion of their income that comes from net transfers (transfers minus taxes). The chart omits Switzerland, where net transfers are negative, since on average the lowest quintile children's families pay more in taxes than they receive in transfers (other than the child allowances included in paychecks).

The countries are ranged from left to right in about the same order as their poverty rates. At the extremes, the average equivalent income for the Italian bottom-quintile children is about one-third of the median, while that of comparable Swedish children is about two-thirds of the median. Of interest here, however, is the varying role of net transfers for countries at about the same level of total equivalent income. Focusing on the countries with the lowest equivalent incomes, we note that very low net transfers flow to the poorest quintiles in Spain and Italy—less than one-third of their income is from such sources—while in Australia and the United Kingdom fully 70 percent of the poorest quintile's income is from transfers.

At a higher level of average income, we find that Belgian children are the most heavily dependent on transfers, followed by French and Dutch children. In the Nordic countries, 40 percent or slightly less of income comes from net transfers; compared with

FIGURE 5.3 **Percentage Net Transfers in Fourteen Countries,
by Mean Equivalent Income for Children
in Lowest Quintile**

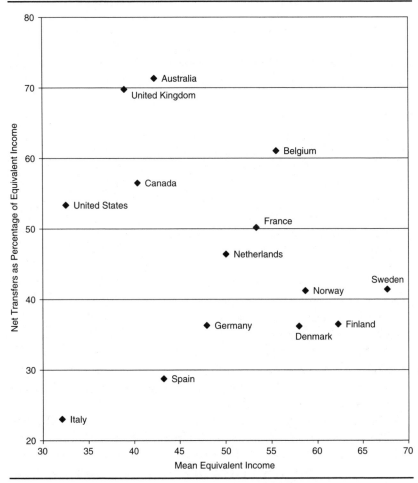

Source: Authors' calculations, using data from the Luxembourg Income Study.
Note: This figure omits Switzerland, where net transfers are negative.

most European countries, market income plays a smaller role. In
the Nordic countries, the income of the bottom quintile is higher
because both transfers and market incomes are higher than is
generally the case elsewhere.

THE IMPACT OF FAMILY TYPE
ON POVERTY AND INCOME PACKAGING

In chapters 6 and 7, we examine in detail the role of various income sources in the economic well-being of children. Although the situations of children in single-mother families and in two-parent families differ a great deal in all countries, it should nevertheless be said at the beginning that, as is implicit in the demographic simulation, there is little correlation (only–0.10) between the proportion of children in a country in two-parent as opposed to single-parent families and the overall child poverty rate.

Countries vary considerably in the distribution of family types among the poor, so it behooves us to focus on specific family types as we delve more deeply into the impact of income packaging on the distribution of families' incomes. (A reminder: cohabiting couples are included in two-parent families; single parents do not have a cohabiting partner.)

In figure 5.4, we see that the proportion of poor children in two-parent versus single-parent families varies from 91 percent of poor children in two-parent families in Italy to 57 percent in single-mother families in Norway. (Very few children in any country live in single-father families—the highest proportion is 7.4 percent in Sweden.)

We note high and low child poverty rates at all points in the range of parent types. The countries with child poverty rates above 10 percent vary from the highest proportions of children in two-parent families (Italy and Spain) to those among the lowest (the United Kingdom and the United States), with Australia and Canada in between. Similarly, there is great variance among those with child poverty rates below 10 percent, from those with relatively high proportions in two-parent families, like Switzerland and the Netherlands, to the countries with middling to high rates of single-parent families, such as the Nordic countries, particularly Sweden.

THE RATIONALE FOR COMPARING
ONE- AND TWO-PARENT FAMILIES

In all of the fifteen countries under study in this book, the great majority of children live in families headed by a couple who are

FIGURE 5.4 **Family Types of Poor Children in Fifteen Countries**

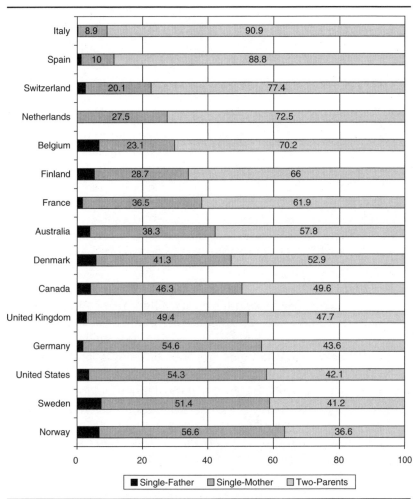

Source: Authors' calculations, using data from the Luxembourg Income Study.

either married or living together as married. Table 5.1 presents the range in the percentage of children in two-parent families. As can be seen, there is a considerable range in the proportion of children who do not live in such families, from a low of 6 percent in Spain and Italy to a high of 25 percent in the United States.

TABLE 5.1 Children Living in Two-Parent Families in Fifteen Countries

Italy	94.0%
Spain	93.9
Netherlands	91.7
France	89.9
Belgium	89.3
Switzerland	89.2
Germany	88.2
Australia	87.1
Finland	85.7
Denmark	83.3
Norway	83.0
Canada	82.3
Sweden	78.7
United Kingdom	77.4
United States	74.9

Source: Authors' calculations, using data from the Luxembourg Income Study.

Although we saw in chapter 3 that differences in family characteristics do not go very far to explain differences in poverty rates across countries, it is certainly the case that the economic lives of children in two-parent families are very different from the lives of those in families headed by a single mother. For our purposes here, however, we can only begin to understand variations in child poverty rates across nations by acknowledging the central fact that most of the children growing up in all of these countries—with the exception of a significant minority of American, British, and Swedish children—live with two parents for all or most of their childhood. To understand child poverty rate variations across countries, we need first and foremost to understand two-parent child poverty.

It is with this goal in mind that we turn in the next chapter to a detailed examination of the levels of living of children in two-parent families and consider the patterns of income packaging that directly account for these differences. Thus illuminated, these income packaging differences across countries will be even more salient for the discussion in chapter 7 of the situation of children in single-mother families.

—— Chapter 6 ——

Child Poverty
and Income Packaging
in Two-Parent Families

IN THIS CHAPTER, we look at the relation between various kinds of income packaging and child poverty rates in two-parent families in all of the fifteen countries. After a discussion of some demographic differences in poverty rates, we look in greater detail at different kinds of market and transfer income. We are then able to conclude the chapter with a country-by-country review of how income packaging affects the lives of that large majority of children who live in two-parent households.

LEVELS OF ECONOMIC WELL-BEING

Table 6.1 shows the distribution of children in two-parent families by well-being categories. The differences among countries are not as substantial as for all children but are nevertheless quite large.

Focusing first on the middle-income group, we see a range from 87 percent in Sweden to 50 percent in Italy. We can identify four clusters of countries. The most middle-class countries, all with over 80 percent in the middle-income group, are the Netherlands and the Nordic countries—Denmark, Finland, Norway, and Sweden. They are followed by four countries with middle-class incomes in the 70 percent range—Belgium, Germany, France, and Switzerland—then two other countries in the 65 percent range—Canada and Australia. Finally, we have the four countries—Spain, the United Kingdom, the United States, and Italy—at the low end of the scale with the most unequal distribution of two-parent children's income.

TABLE 6.1 Economic Well-Being Levels of Children in Two-Parent Families in Fifteen Countries

	Extremely Poor	Poor	Near-Poor	Average	Prosperous	Rich	Very Rich
Sweden	0.4%	0.8%	2.5%	86.6%	7.9%	1.5%	0.3%
Norway	0.5	1.2	4.5	83.8	7.7	1.7	0.6
Finland	0.5	2.0	5.8	80.2	9.1	1.8	0.5
Denmark	1.1	1.5	4.0	83.8	7.5	1.7	0.4
Belgium	1.6	2.5	8.4	71.3	11.9	3.5	0.9
Germany	1.7	3.1	8.5	74.6	8.1	3.5	0.5
France	1.1	3.9	8.4	69.3	10.2	5.4	1.8
Netherlands	3.6	2.0	4.3	81.0	7.2	1.8	0.1
Switzerland	2.2	3.4	10.1	73.0	6.9	3.3	1.2
Canada	2.3	5.5	10.3	66.6	10.6	4.0	0.7
Australia	2.9	6.0	10.7	65.4	10.4	3.7	0.9
United Kingdom	4.5	5.5	13.1	54.6	12.8	6.9	2.5
Spain	4.3	7.0	13.4	58.6	9.8	5.6	1.4
United States	3.6	7.8	12.2	55.2	12.2	6.1	3.0
Italy	10.0	8.9	14.2	50.1	10.8	4.7	1.4

Source: Authors' calculations, using data from the Luxembourg Income Study.

For all of the northern continental European countries, we find close to three-quarters or more of children living with two parents to be in the middle-income group. These are countries with not only relatively low proportions of children who live in poverty or near-poverty but relatively few children whose families qualify as prosperous or rich.

Figure 6.1 charts the three levels of low income for children in two-parent families. We see that very few children in any country are extremely poor. Italy has the highest rate, with 10 percent. The United States has the next highest level, though only 4 percent of American children in two-parent families have incomes less than one-third of the median. In five countries—the Nordic countries and France—the proportion of very poor children is 1 percent or less. Combining both levels of poverty, we find that only 1 to 2 percent of children in the Nordic countries are poor; they are joined by the Netherlands, Switzerland, Belgium, France, and Germany at the very low level of less than 6 percent. In the 7 to 12 percent range we find two-parent poor children in Canada, Australia, the United Kingdom, the United States, and Spain.

There are interesting variations in the proportion of children in the near-poor category (between half and two-thirds of median equivalent income). Italy has a very high proportion of children who are near-poor—fully 14 percent—followed closely by Spain and the United Kingdom at 13 percent and the United States at 12 percent. We find a group of European countries—Switzerland, France, Germany, and Belgium—as well as Australia and Canada in the 8 to 11 percent range, while in the Nordic countries and the Netherlands fewer than 6 percent of children are in the near-poor group.

Another way to look at low-income patterns is to examine the levels of living of children in the lowest third of the distribution of equivalent income of all persons. Every country has a lowest third, but no country seems to have poverty rates anywhere approaching one out of three. Focusing on the children in this low-income group can sharpen our understanding of differences in child poverty and economic marginality among countries.

The higher the incomes of two-parent families relative to the incomes of other families, the more likely they are to fall above the lowest third. In fact, we find three countries in which the pro-

FIGURE 6.1 **Children in Two-Parent Families
with Low Income in Fifteen Countries**

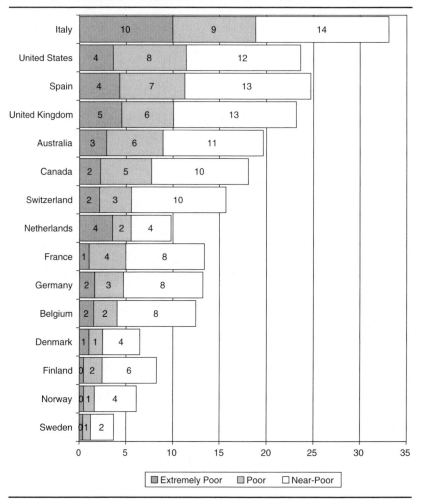

Source: Authors' calculations, using data from the Luxembourg Income Study.

portion of children in two-parent families in the lowest third is greater than one-third—Italy, Switzerland, and Spain (figure 6.2). In these nations, two-parent children's families seem to be relatively disadvantaged compared with childless families. But there is a wide spread in the percentage of lower-third children who are poor—from around 15 percent in Switzerland to around 30 percent

FIGURE 6.2 **Poverty Rate of Low-Income Children
in Two-Parent Families in Fifteen Countries**

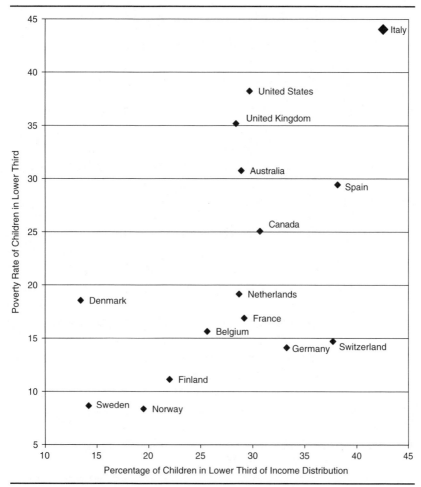

Source: Authors' calculations, using data from the Luxembourg Income Study.

in Spain and 45 percent in Italy. Germany is right at one-third, and six countries are just under that mark, in the 29 to 31 percent range—France, the Netherlands, Canada, Australia, the United Kingdom, and the United States.[1] We note that the great majority of two-parent children in Sweden and Denmark, over 85 percent, are in the middle or upper third of the income distribution, as are over three-quarters of such children in Norway and Finland.

Focusing on the majority of countries that are in the range of 26 to 33 percent of two-parent children in the lower third, we find a very wide range in the probability of these children being poor—from almost 40 percent in the United States and 35 percent in the United Kingdom to around 15 percent in Belgium, France, and Germany.

In the case of three of the Nordic countries, we see that it is the combination of a low probability of being in the lower third and a low probability of being poor that produces the overall extremely low poverty rates of two-parent children. Later in this chapter, we discuss the role that different income sources play in protecting children in these northern European countries from poverty and near-poverty. (And for the countries with high poverty rates, we consider the role of different income sources in increasing children's risk of being poor.)

It is clear, then, that American children who live with both parents have a higher poverty rate—about one in nine—than two-parent children in most other countries. This is a reflection of the fact that low- to modest-income two-parent children in the United States tend to be relatively disadvantaged compared with children at the same point in the income distribution in other countries (see figure 6.3). We find that between 50 and 62 percent of two-parent children in the four Nordic countries, France, and Belgium have as high or higher relative incomes than American children at the same point in the respective income distributions, as is the case for 94 percent of the British children. Fewer than 20 percent of children in Spain, and no children in Italy, have higher relative incomes than their American counterparts. In Switzerland, Australia, Germany, Canada, and the Netherlands, between 35 and 45 percent are as well off as or better off than their American peers.

Using the method outlined in chapter 11 to impute real equivalent income to our samples, we also compare in figure 6.3 the situation of two-parent children with respect to real income. We find that in four countries no two-parent children are better off than their American peers—Australia, the United Kingdom, Spain, and Italy. That is, the lowest-income child in each of these countries has an income lower in real terms than the lowest-income two-parent child in the United States.

Almost half of Swiss children, however, are better off than comparable American children. In Norway, Canada, and Denmark,

FIGURE 6.3 **Two-Parent Children in Fourteen Countries Who Are Equally Well or Better Off in Relative and Real Terms Than Comparable U.S. Children**

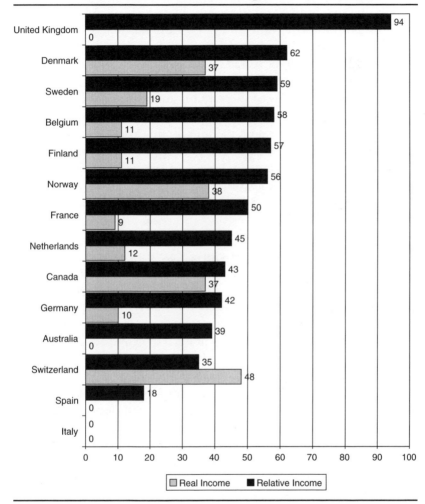

Source: Authors' calculations, using data from the Luxembourg Income Study.

a slightly fewer than 40 percent of two-parent children have higher real incomes than their American peers. This is the case for just under 20 percent of the lowest-income quintile of two-parent children in Sweden. For the remaining countries, about 10 percent have higher real incomes than comparable American two-parent children.

To compare the real income of the poor in the United States with comparable low-income children in other countries, we need to compare the lowest 11 percent of the distributions of two-parent children, since we find some 11 percent of American two-parent children to be poor. In eight of our comparison countries, all of the children who are in the lowest 11 percent of their income distributions have higher real incomes than poor American children at the same point in the distribution. This is the case with nearly all of these children in two of the other countries (not shown).

In four countries—Sweden, Denmark, Switzerland, and Norway—the average equivalent income of the lowest-income 11 percent of two-parent children is greater in real terms than the income of poor American children by one-quarter to almost one-half. In five other countries, real incomes of this lower 11 percent of children are between 5 and 14 percent higher than for American poor children (not shown).

Age of Head and Age of Child

Is the likelihood of being poor affected by the age of the parents? We find that two groups of parents are much more likely to have poor children. The effect is most apparent for children whose father is under twenty-five years of age. In only four countries—Denmark, Sweden, the Netherlands, and Switzerland—are fathers of this age not more likely to have poor children. In the United States, for example, the poverty rate for children whose father is under twenty-five is 30 percent, compared with less than 10 percent when the father is between twenty-five and fifty-four. Similar large differences are found in Canada, Belgium, Germany, Spain, and the United Kingdom. However, very few children in two-parent families have parents this young—2 percent in the United States and around 1 percent or fewer in the other countries. There is no pattern of greater or lesser poverty by father's age in the range from twenty-five through fifty-four. This range includes 95 percent or more of children, except in the United States, where 93 percent of children in a two-parent family have a father who is twenty-five to fifty-four.

Fewer than 5 percent of children live in families whose head is fifty-five or over, except in Spain, where 8 percent of children live in such families. In summary, we can say that in two-parent families the father's age is not an important factor when we try to account for which children are poor and which are not. In about half of our countries, young couples are much more likely to be poor, but there are few under-age-twenty-five couples with children.

We might expect poverty rates to vary by the age of the child for a number of reasons. Even if the age of the parents is only a minor factor, it could be that other family differences related to the age of child might be important—for example, whether the mother is employed or not. In fact, we find very little difference in the poverty rates of children of different ages. In the United States 14 percent of children under age six are poor, compared with 9 percent of children twelve years of age and older. The same pattern is found in the United Kingdom, where 11 percent of children under age six are poor, compared with 7 percent of those over age eleven. But for the other countries poverty does not seem to vary in any significant way by age of child.

THE EFFECTS OF DEMOGRAPHY
AND INCOME PACKAGING
ON CHILDREN IN TWO-PARENT FAMILIES

Just as we can examine the effects of demography and income packaging on overall child poverty, we can also use reweighting to consider their impacts on children in two-parent families. Figure 6.4 charts the results of the simulation method described in appendix D. The picture is quite similar to that for all children described in chapter 3 (see figure 3.1).

In most cases, imposing American demography on the other countries results in rather small shifts in the poverty rates for two-parent children. Only in Australia and the United Kingdom do we find a marked effect. In those countries the simulation of U.S. demography on their own income packaging would decrease poverty by three or four percentage points from their levels of 9 and 10 percent. This result probably reflects the greater proportion of multiple earners in the United States combined with the inadequacy of transfer programs targeted on families with no or low earnings.

FIGURE 6.4 **Actual and Simulated Two-Parent Child
Poverty Rates in Fifteen Countries**

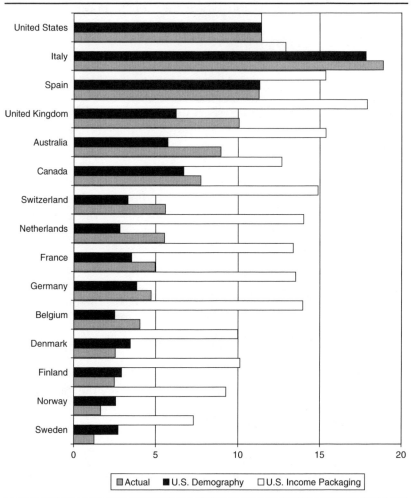

Source: Authors' calculations, using data from the Luxembourg Income Study.

Imposing American income packaging on the other countries
results in much higher two-parent child poverty rates in all countries except Italy. In fact, the simulated poverty rates are higher
than the actual rate in the United States in nine of the countries.
Only in the Nordic countries, which have very low actual rates, do

the increases not reach the U.S. level, although the proportionate increases are larger.

In short, what this exercise tells us is that for the most part other countries' lower two-parent child poverty rates are a product of their income packaging, not of a more "favorable" demographic profile than that of the United States. And more important, given its family demographics and labor force supply, the United States would have a far lower two-parent child poverty rate (less than one-third as high on average) if it had the income packaging of any of the nine northern European countries.

THE EFFECT OF MARKET AND TRANSFER
INCOME ON TWO-PARENT POVERTY RATES

To get a broad view of the role of different income sources in producing higher or lower levels of poverty, we can compare poverty rates before taking into account taxes and transfer income with those rates derived after taking them into account. In other words, we examine first the poverty rates that would result if families had only their pretransfer income—their earnings, whether from employers or from self-employment, and their asset income—and then we add their post-transfer income—the various sources of transfer income they receive. Post-transfer income includes both the positive effects on disposable income of public social protection transfers and the negative effects of taxes collected by the government.

We have not counted in pretransfer income several sources that are traditionally considered part of market income—alimony, child support, and other interhousehold transfers. Laws and government regulation have a great impact on these income sources in some countries. More to the point here, however, is the fact that these private transfers are quite small among two-parent families in all of our countries, and we include them in the discussion of transfer income more for conceptual reasons than otherwise.

Figure 6.5 charts pre- and post-transfer poverty rates of children in two-parent families. We note that France, along with the United Kingdom and Italy, has the highest pretransfer poverty rate at slightly less than one-quarter, and that Spain, Belgium, and Australia are close runners-up at slightly less than one-fifth. Five

FIGURE 6.5 **Pre- and Post-Transfer Child Poverty Rates in Two-Parent Families in Fifteen Countries**

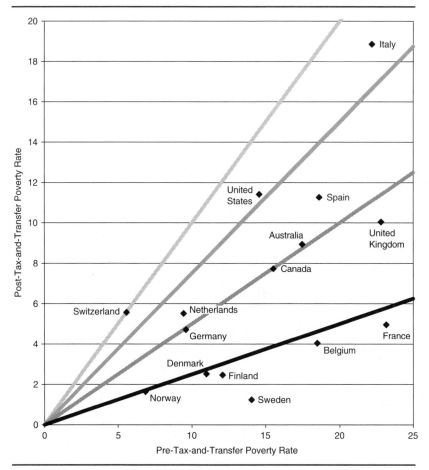

Source: Authors' calculations, using data from the Luxembourg Income Study.
Note: From top to bottom the rays indicate that 0, 25, 50, and 75 percent of children are moved out of poverty by post-tax-and-transfer sources.

of our countries are in the 11 to 16 percent range: Finland, Sweden, Denmark—all three of which have quite low post-transfer poverty rates—Canada, and the United States. Germany, Switzerland, Norway, and the Netherlands have the lowest pre-transfer poverty rates—in the 6 to 10 percent range.

We see great variation in the proportion of children who are moved from pretransfer poverty by transfers. In six countries—

France, Belgium, Sweden, Finland, Norway, and Denmark—we find that three-quarters or more of the children who are poor on the basis of pretransfer income are moved out by transfer income. In Germany, the Netherlands, Canada, Australia, and the United Kingdom, about half of the pretransfer poor children are moved from poverty by transfers. At the low end of transfer effectiveness, we find fewer than one-quarter of children are moved out of poverty by transfers in the United States and Italy. Switzerland seems to move almost no children from its low rate of pretransfer poverty.[2]

The overall pattern suggests that pretransfer income (in particular earnings, since asset income is quite small in all of these countries) is the first line of defense against poverty. In general, the countries with high pretransfer poverty levels do not moderate rates a great deal by the addition of transfers. Only two of the five countries with the highest pretransfer levels of poverty lower their poverty rates dramatically (France and Belgium). The countries with the lowest pretransfer poverty rates also have the lowest post-transfer poverty rates. It is the particular combination of pre- and post-transfer income that produces the post-transfer poverty rates that we observe.

INCOME PACKAGING IN
LOW-INCOME FAMILIES

We have seen that in no country does the poverty rate of all children exceed 25 percent, and in only two countries does the combined poverty and near-poverty rate exceed one-third. This suggests that, in seeking to understand the role of differences in income packaging, we should concentrate our attention on the low-income group. In the following section, we consider income packaging in two-parent families with incomes that place them in the lower third of the income distribution of children.

It is apparent that there are large differences in the distribution of income among children in the lower third of the distribution. We note, for example, that in Sweden, Norway, the Netherlands, and Finland, well over 60 percent of these lower-third children in fact live in middle-income families, as do about half or more in Germany, Switzerland, France, and Denmark (not shown). At the other extreme, we note that only about one-fifth of two-parent children in the low-income third in the United States, the United Kingdom, and Italy are middle-income. What is the role of different income sources in accounting for these distributional differences among countries? To answer this question, we consider the role of earnings by the family head, the spouse, and others, as well as the role of different kinds of transfers in the income packaging of the two-parent families in the lower third of the child distribution.

The Relative Importance of Factor and Transfer Income to Low-Income Families

A very general understanding of the relative roles of different income sources for the economic well-being of children in the lower third can be gained by reconceptualizing the two general categories of income—*factor income,* which is the same as pre-transfer income, as previously defined, and *transfer income,* which includes all other sources of income—whether from private transfers such as child support payments or from public transfers—but does not include taxes.

It is obvious that poverty rates will be lower the higher the average income from either factor income or transfer income.[3] It is also the case that poverty rates will be higher the greater the variance of either of these two sources. For example, if two countries have the same relatively high average income, but in one many families have very low income and many have very high income, this greater variance of income will tend to produce a higher proportion of families with incomes below the poverty line. The same applies to transfers unless transfers are heavily targeted at families with low factor income.

Much of what has been written about cross-national poverty rates tends to emphasize the role of transfers in accounting for differences across countries. For these fifteen countries, however, we find that the level and variance of factor income are as important as the level and variance of transfer income. The average factor income received by the families of children in the lowest income third is slightly less strongly related to poverty rates than transfer income in our fifteen countries, but both play a role.

THE ROLE OF EARNINGS

When we speak of factor income, we are speaking mostly of earnings (salaries and self-employment income), since asset income is very low for children in lower-third families. The highest average asset incomes are found in Switzerland and Sweden, where they amount to 2 and 3 percent of the median, respectively; in the other countries asset income averages 1 percent of the median or less (not shown).

In nine of these countries, 90 percent or more of children live in families that have persons with earnings. In the Netherlands, Sweden, and Denmark, 81 to 86 percent have earnings, while Australia and Belgium are in the 70 percent range, and the United Kingdom brings up the rear, with fewer than 60 percent having at least one earner. Thus, the reason some countries have high two-parent child poverty rates and others have low rates has more to do with the mix of earnings and transfers and the level of earnings than with whether families include an earner per se.

The LIS data do not allow us to make a clean distinction between earnings produced by the father, the mother, or others because the category of self-employment income applies to the household as a whole. Using labor force variables, we can allocate self-employment income, with some error, to the head, spouse, or others, but this allocation is rougher than we would like. We now compare the role of mothers' and fathers' earnings, but not the earnings of other members of the household. The earnings of such others are very small—the highest average (in the United States) is less than 2 percent of the median.

Mothers' Earnings

In the Nordic countries, mothers' earnings are very important, even for families of children in the lowest income third. Mothers' equivalized earnings average 20 percent of median equivalent income in Denmark, around 15 percent in Sweden and Finland, and 12 percent in Norway. Canada, the United States, and Germany are close at around 10 percent. The other countries range downward to Belgium and Spain at less than 4 percent.

How large these low-income mothers' contributions are is a product of the proportion who have earnings and their mean earnings. Mean earnings of those who work do not vary a great deal—all of the countries except Denmark and Italy are in the 17 to 26 percent range. In Denmark working mothers earn 36 percent of the median, and in Italy they earn 28 percent. There is an enormous range, however, in the proportion of mothers who have earnings. In the four Nordic countries, 56 to 60 percent of these low-income children's mothers have earnings, as do 53 percent in Canada and the United States. France, the Netherlands, Germany, and Switzerland are in the 30 to 39 percent range. In Italy, the United Kingdom, and Australia, from 22 to 28 percent of these children have working mothers, as do around 15 percent of the children in Spain and Belgium.

Thus, we can conclude that, for low-income families, variations in mothers' contributions to family income and to the escape from poverty are more a function of the proportion of mothers who have earnings than of how much they earn. Swedish, Finnish, and Norwegian low-income working mothers have about the same average earnings as do those in Australia, the United Kingdom, and Italy, yet the poverty rates of the former are very low and those of the latter very high, in part because more mothers work in Sweden, Finland, and Norway.

Fathers' Earnings

In three countries—the Netherlands, Germany, and Switzerland—fathers' average salaries are over 55 percent of the median. At 62 percent, Swiss fathers average more than double the earnings of fathers in the United Kingdom, Denmark, Belgium, and France. As with mothers' earnings, how many fathers have earnings seems somewhat more important than how much working fathers earn in accounting for differences among countries. That is, the variance in the amounts earned by low-income working fathers is smaller than the variance in how many of them have earnings. In all but three countries, working fathers earn on average about 40 to 60 percent of median income. (Working fathers in Switzerland, the Netherlands, and Germany earn considerably more.) The poverty rates of the countries in this 40 to 60 range vary from the highest to the lowest.

Overall, earnings are clearly the central line of defense against poverty for children in two-parent families. In all but four countries, the earnings of the parents of children in the low-income third average at least 44 percent of the median (that is, almost 90 percent of the poverty line). Thus, it is not difficult in most cases for social protection transfers to fulfill their designated purpose of lifting people out of poverty. Indeed, in half of the countries average earnings by these low-income parents are well over the poverty line.

THE ROLE OF SOCIAL PROTECTION
TRANSFERS IN THE INCOME PACKAGING
OF LOW-INCOME FAMILIES

The variety of social protection transfer programs in our fifteen countries is daunting. In this section, we consider the contributions of different transfers to the incomes of the families of children in the lowest third of equivalent income. There are many different transfer programs in most countries, and the benefit amounts generally range from very small to a significant contribution to the income packages of the families concerned. In one sense, every little bit helps; even small amounts from a given program will help fill the poverty gap for some families. On the other hand, understanding what produces the differences we see from country to country requires that we highlight for each country those programs that make the greatest difference in whether that country has a high or low poverty rate.

To focus on the role of social protection programs in reducing poverty, we begin by refining our analysis of pre- and post-transfer income. We consider two kinds of programs: those designed to protect workers against common risks and deprivations, which we refer to as *social wage programs,* and *social assistance programs,* which are designed to ameliorate the hardships that come from having an income below a government-established minimum. Not included in either type of program is a residual category, principally pension benefits (which are rather small for two-parent families with children) and the negative transfers of income and payroll taxes.

The social wage programs include: sickness payments; maternity and/or paternity payments; child allowances and other child support; and labor market programs and unemployment payments. These programs are designed to help families whose main source of support is earnings.

The social assistance programs provide either cash assistance or subsidized consumption of various kinds (for example, food stamps, housing allowances, and heating allowances). These benefits go to families who become eligible because, even after taking into account the benefits from social wage programs, their benefits are still regarded as too low.

Most of these programs exist in most of our countries, with the exception of the United States, which has a much narrower set of social protection programs. Sickness benefits of some kind are guaranteed to workers in all of these countries except the United States. Child allowances also exist in all of these nations except the United States. Child support payments by an absent parent exist in all countries, as do labor market and unemployment programs.

To what extent do the social wage programs move pretransfer poor children out of poverty? We find a wide range of from 3 to 60 percent of pretransfer poor children moved from poverty by these programs (not shown). In four countries—Finland, Sweden, France, and Belgium—these programs enable close to 60 percent to escape poverty. For Norway and Denmark the percentage reduction in poverty is around 40 percent, and it is around one-third in Germany, Australia, and Canada. These programs reduce poverty by 20 percent in the Netherlands and by around 15 percent in Spain and Switzerland. In Italy 9 percent of children are moved from pretransfer poverty by social wage programs, and in the United Kingdom and the United States it is a mere 3 or 4 percent.

In absolute terms these programs move many children from poverty. Child allowances alone reduce the rate in Belgium and France by seven and ten percentage points. And these plus the other social wage transfers reduce the pretransfer poverty rate by seven to fourteen percentage points in France, Belgium, Sweden, and Finland and by six points in Australia. For these countries, half or more of the reduction in poverty by transfers is due to social wage programs, as is also the case in Canada, Denmark, Germany, Norway, and the Netherlands.

Social assistance programs further reduce poverty for two-parent children by only very small amounts (three percentage points or less), except in three countries. The United Kingdom makes heavy use of means-tested programs, and we find that social assistance programs there reduce the poverty rate from 21 to 13 percent. For Sweden and Denmark the reduction is four percentage points. We will see later that the programs in the United Kingdom are quite different from those in these two Nordic countries.

In the sections that follow, we examine more closely the particular social protection transfers we have grouped together in the categories of social wage, means-tested, and social insurance.

Child Allowances

On average, in the eleven countries for which we have information, child allowances amount to about 3.5 percent of median equivalent income per child. This would be equivalent to about $100 a month per child in the United States. Almost all children are in families that receive some child allowances, the principal exception being France, where allowances are usually not paid to two-parent families with only one child. In France 12 percent of children live in families that do not receive child allowances. The countries with the most generous child allowance and other child benefit programs are clearly Belgium and France. In those nations low-income children in families that receive allowances average 14 and 13 percent of median income, respectively. Another group of countries stands out as also rather generous, averaging between 9 and 12 percent of median income—Finland at 12 percent and Norway, Sweden, the Netherlands, and Australia at 9 or 10 percent. Canada, Denmark, Germany, and the United Kingdom are in the 6 or 7 percent range. We do not know what role child allowances play in the income packages of families in Italy, Switzerland, and Spain because the allowances are for the most part paid by the employer and included in the paycheck. But aggregate statistics on social protection spending suggest that child allowances are not nearly as large as in the other countries.

It is relatively simple to simulate the effect of child allowances on the distribution of income. For example, if we impute $100 per child per month in the U.S. dataset, we can estimate how much child allowances would reduce the poverty rate of American children in two-parent families. We assume that families with average and above-average income pay for the taxes required. With such a transfer, two-parent child poverty would be cut by about one-third, from 11.4 to 7.1 percent. This is a poverty rate slightly lower than that of Canada. Thus, although these are programs that do not move many people very far from where they would be without the program, they can have a very significant impact on the poverty rate. The effect for the United States is found mainly in families with more than one child; the rate for the 20 percent of children in one-child families declines only from 9.1 to 7.5 percent.

Sickness Benefits

From one perspective, sickness benefits are not a very major source of income. Thus, we find that the highest average level of these benefits for children in lower-income families, found in Denmark and Sweden, amounts to only around 2 percent of the median income. In other countries, sickness insurance averages less than 1 percent of the median. In some countries, however, the role of sickness benefits is obscured by the nature of the programs. For example, in Germany and the Netherlands the employer covers sick leave in the first six weeks. The social security fund pays only for longer periods of invalidity. In Spain the employer must pay for the first two weeks. Thus, we have already accounted for the contribution of sickness benefits in these countries when we examined the role of earnings. For these countries our estimate of the role of earnings is somewhat exaggerated by the fact that sickness benefits are counted as earnings, whereas in other countries these benefits are counted as social insurance transfers.

Maternity benefits are also extended in all of our countries except the United States. In the Nordic countries in particular these benefits take the form of parental insurance that provides salary continuation when either parent stays home to care for a child. We find these transfers specified separately in only four countries. Again, Sweden stands out—parental insurance accounts for an average of fully 5.6 percent of median income. Finland is the only other country that averages more than 1 percent; there we find an average of 2.7 percent, which amounts to an average of 10 percent of the median for the one-quarter of Finnish low-income children in families that receive some paternal leave payments. Combining sickness insurance and parental insurance, we find that in Sweden these benefits amount to almost 8 percent of median income—in other words, 16 percent of the poverty line. And the benefits are very widely dispersed: almost 60 percent of children live in families that avail themselves of parental insurance during the year, and one-quarter live in families that took some sick leave during the year.

Labor Market and Unemployment Programs

Unemployment insurance generally goes to families that include earners. Except for the very long-term unemployed, most families that receive unemployment insurance also have earnings—either the insured earner worked part of the year or there are other earners in the family. Although the Nordic countries have rather similar labor market programs providing unemployment insurance benefits, stipends for training, resettlement, and so forth, there are significant differences between Norway and the other three in how important these programs are in the income packages of two-parent families. In Denmark, Sweden, and Finland, the average benefit for children in the low-income third is 8 or 9 percent of median income, and about one-third of these low-income children are in families that receive this benefit. For them, the average amounts are equal to about one-quarter of median income—halfway toward the poverty line. In Norway, in contrast, the average benefits amount to only 3 percent of the median, and only one-quarter of children are in recipient families.

In Belgium, unemployment and labor market assistance is the next most important social protection program after child allowances. The families of children in the lower third of the distribution receive on average 8 percent of the median income in unemployment and labor market assistance. For the 36 percent of families that receive this assistance, it amounts to a substantial 23 percent of median income. Unemployment insurance is less important in the Netherlands and the United Kingdom. Only 3 or 4 percent of families receive unemployment insurance benefits, in sharp contrast to next-door Belgium, but when they do, they receive a substantial amount—16 percent of median income.

Unemployment programs of various kinds are also important in Australia and France. Some 30 percent of two-parent low-income children live in families that receive such benefits. In those families the benefits amount to 20 percent of median income in Australia but only 14 percent in France. In Spain fewer children are in families that receive unemployment benefits (18 percent), but for those who do receive the benefits, they amount to 19 percent of the median. In Canada some 23 percent receive benefits, but the amount they receive is smaller—12 percent. In the United States only 10 percent of low-income children are in families that receive these benefits, and the average received is very small (6 percent of the median). In the United Kingdom and Switzerland fewer than 5 percent of two-parent children are in recipient families.

Social Assistance and Means-Tested
In-Kind Programs

Despite the size of their social wage programs, the low-poverty countries still rely on income-tested programs to top up the income of some of their lower-third two-parent families. These programs typically include cash assistance, housing allowances (rental assistance), unemployment assistance, food stamps (in the United States), and some other quite small categorical programs.

In Denmark such programs average 12 percent of the median. Over 40 percent of Danish low-income children live in families that receive these benefits, and those who do receive on average almost 30 percent of median income. Thus, any holes left in the Danish safety net after payment of sickness and maternity benefits, child allowances, and unemployment insurance are likely to be filled by assistance payments in the form of cash social assistance and housing allowances.

Social assistance is also important in Sweden and Finland, which have income-tested cash support and housing allowances as well as assorted smaller programs adding up to just over 10 percent of median income to the low-income family's pocket. Slightly over 60 percent of these children receive such benefits, and those who do receive about 18 percent of median income. In Sweden the cash support is general social assistance, while in Finland it is cash assistance to the unemployed not covered by unemployment insurance.

In Norway social assistance income is less important than in the other Nordic countries, amounting to around 4 percent of median income on average. But for the 32 percent of children in families that receive this support, it amounts to an important 12 percent of median income. The pattern in Germany is about the same.

The other two very low-poverty countries are the Netherlands and Belgium. In the former, cash assistance and housing allowances are important for a small group of low-income children. Some 16 percent of them are in families that receive means-tested income, for whom it amounts to 22 percent of the median. In Belgium, on the other hand, assistance programs play hardly any role, averaging 3 percent of the median for the one-quarter of children in families that receive such benefits.

Means-tested benefits are more widely received in France than in most of the countries discussed so far. The principal program is housing allowances. These benefits go to two-thirds of two-parent children in the lower income third. When received, they amount to 8 percent of median income. All told, one or another of several income-tested programs are received by 80 percent of these children, whose families receive on average 8 percent of median income from them.

In Spain means-tested benefits go to a very small 5 percent of low-income children; for them it is an important source of income, amounting to 11 percent of the median.

In Canada means-tested benefits have roughly the same importance for two-parent children as we have seen in Norway or the Netherlands. Some 18 percent of low-income children are in families that receive these benefits, which, at 20 percent of the median, are fairly high. In Australia all benefits (with the exception of child allowances) are means-tested but also categorical, so social assistance per se does not exist.

The United Kingdom and the United States are the countries that rely most heavily on means-tested transfers—over half of transfer income going to low-income two-parent children is in the form of cash social assistance and means-tested, in-kind benefits (principally rent and rate rebates in the United Kingdom and food stamps in the United States). In the United Kingdom just over half of all low-income two-parent children are in families that receive such benefits, while in the United States almost 90 percent are.

Most of these American families receive the Earned Income Tax Credit and food stamps, while a small number, 13 percent, receive cash public assistance.

The two countries are very different in how much is transferred to recipients—on average 29 percent of the median in the United Kingdom but only 7 percent in the United States. But despite this British "generosity," about the same proportion of two-parent children in the two countries are extremely poor or poor because earnings are much lower in the United Kingdom than in the United States.

We conclude that income-tested benefits can be an important part of a poverty-reducing income package when accompanied by a generous social wage package, as they are, for example, in the Nordic countries and the Netherlands. But when income-tested benefits are the principal antipoverty tool, they are far less likely to be effective.

SUMMARY BY COUNTRY OF THE IMPACT OF SOCIAL PROTECTION PROGRAMS ON TWO-PARENT FAMILIES

We now highlight the main transfer characteristics involved in producing high or low two-parent child poverty rates in each country.

The Nordic Countries

The four Nordic countries, despite the similarity of their social programs, achieve their very low poverty rates in somewhat different ways. Denmark, Finland, and Sweden combine high earnings with very high levels of transfers. All three offer a broad range of social protection programs, making heavy commitments to sickness and parental insurance, child allowances, and unemployment insurance. But we also find strong reliance on income-tested programs for those people who still slip through the social wage safety net. Norway shows a rather different pattern, with higher earnings and transfers quite a bit lower. Nevertheless, the combination of family benefits and social insurance directed to workers (sickness and unemployment) effectively moves most of the very small number of pretransfer poor out of poverty. Pension income plays a relatively small role in the income packaging of these countries. But for the few two-parent low-income families that do receive pensions, they can of course be an important source of income.

The Five Countries of Northern Europe

The Netherlands, Germany, Switzerland, Belgium, and France have two-parent child poverty rates ranging from 4 to 6 percent. These countries have more distinctive patterns of social protection than the Nordic countries. The first three have earnings that average close to two-thirds or more of median income, while the latter two average under 40 percent. Transfers are therefore much more important antipoverty weapons in Belgium and France.

We have observed that child allowances are quite generous in Belgium and France, somewhat less so in the Netherlands, and least so in Germany and Switzerland. Belgium relies primarily on child allowances and unemployment insurance to move most of the few pretransfer poor out of poverty. These two types of programs average more than 20 percent of the median. France adds income-tested programs—principally housing allowances—to this pattern to reach over 20 percent and achieve its low level of two-parent child poverty. Housing allowances are received by two-thirds of these children.

In the Netherlands means-tested assistance programs are an important source for some families. As is well known, the Netherlands has a high proportion of individuals on disability insurance. However, the proportion of two-parent children who live in families with disability insurance is rather small—only 10 percent of these low-income children are in families that receive disability insurance. When they do, however, the benefits are quite substantial, amounting to 36 percent of median income. Unemployment insurance and assistance combined are received by 16 percent of these children's families, yielding an average of one-quarter of median income. We conclude, therefore, that the extremely low poverty rate of two-parent Dutch children is based not only on the solid earnings of low-income families but on the generosity of a range of means-tested and non-means-tested social insurance programs that each benefit small numbers of low-income families, as well as child allowances, which add a modest 8 percent of median income.

Germany has a very low pretransfer child poverty rate, and unlike the other countries we have been considering, transfer income there is quite low—less than half of the average amount in the eight countries already discussed. However, this amount is sufficient to remove almost half of the pretransfer poor from poverty. The benefits from child allowances are much smaller in Germany than in the other countries. The 37 percent of children who receive social assistance average a small 4 percent of the median. Unemployment insurance and labor market stipends are received by 20 percent of children, with benefits amounting to 12 percent of the median.

Spain

Spain is the only southern European country for which we have detailed information on transfers. Spain has a high poverty rate for children in two-parent families; besides a relatively low average amount of earnings, relatively low spending on transfers is an important cause.

Not quite 20 percent of children in the lower third live in families that receive unemployment benefits, and these families receive, on average, 18 percent of median income. A smaller group, a little over 10 percent, receive some pension income, and when they do, they average a little over 30 percent of median income. Child allowances are income-tested in Spain, and the amounts received for these and other family benefits go to relatively few families.

The United Kingdom, Canada, and Australia

In the United Kingdom average transfers to low-income two-parent children are quite high. Yet the United Kingdom has a very high two-parent child poverty rate. The prime reason is that over 40 percent of these children live in families that have no earnings, and those with earnings average around half of median income, far lower than in most countries with low poverty rates. So there is a large poverty gap for transfers to fill.

Child benefits in the United Kingdom average only 7 percent of median income, quite a bit lower than in most of the other

European countries. The United Kingdom is distinctive for its heavy reliance on means-tested benefits. Slightly over half of children in this lower income third live in families that receive means-tested benefits. When these families do receive such benefits, they average 29 percent of the median. The combination of income support and rent rebates certainly improves the well-being of a large proportion of low-income children but still leaves many in poverty.

Overall, we conclude that the problem of British child poverty in two-parent families is primarily one of low earnings and only secondarily one of inadequate transfer spending.

On the one hand, Canada's total spending on transfers is not as high as in many countries, but on the other hand, it is higher than for countries like Germany or Switzerland, both of which have much lower poverty rates. The proportion of families with earners is about average, as is the mean amount earned. Canada has universal child allowances, but the amount received by children in the lower third averages only 7 percent of median income, quite a bit lower than in countries with lower poverty rates. In addition, Canada has other family programs that provide income to almost all families in this low-income group, as well as income-tested benefits that go to about one-quarter of the group. The combined income from family benefits and social assistance benefits amounts to about 10 percent of median income. Not quite one-quarter of these children are in families that receive unemployment insurance benefits; the benefits average 13 percent of median income. The range of transfer programs in Canada moves some out of poverty but, because of the low market income many start off with, also leaves half of the pretransfer poor still in poverty.

In Australia the earnings of the families of low-income two-parent children average much lower than in most of the other countries—only half of the median for the three-quarters of children in families with any earnings. All social benefits are means-tested (although in the case of child allowances the income test is at a high level). We might expect that, since means testing is supposedly highly efficient, the proportion of the poor moved out of poverty by transfers would be quite high. However, we find that transfers in Australia do not do a particularly good job of moving children in two-parent families out of poverty. Apparently the means-tested benefits are small enough that they do not have the desired effect.

Family benefits amount to 9 percent of median income. Means-tested supplements to child allowances are received by 6 percent of children, adding on average 14 percent of the median to their income. Thus, the special means-tested benefits do not go very far in topping up the income of low-income children compared with the effect, for example, of housing allowances in many European countries.

The 31 percent of children who live in families that receive unemployment benefits do somewhat better, averaging 18 percent of median income. The same is true of the 10 percent of children who live in families that receive disability pension income, where the average benefit is 26 percent of the median. In the end, Australia's transfers, like Canada's, move half of the pretransfer poor children out of poverty but leave half in that situation because of the low average earnings of their families.

The United States

Although 94 percent of low-income two-parent children in the countries under study live in families that have earnings (with the exception of Australia, Belgium, and France), average earnings are the lowest of all of our countries in the United States, where they amount to a little over half of median income.

In the United States almost three-quarters of transfer income to children in this group is means-tested. Relatively few children live in families that receive pension income (about 4 percent). Some 10 percent are in families that receive unemployment insurance payments. The benefits from pension income amount to 16 percent of median income. The average benefits received from unemployment insurance are small, amounting to only 6 percent of the median.

The three largest American social protection programs for this group of families are the Earned Income Tax Credit, food stamps, and AFDC or other welfare benefits. Some 63 percent of low-income children are in families that receive the Earned Income Tax Credit. However, they receive on average a very small amount—4 percent of the median. While for a few families the Earned Income Tax Credit may be sufficient to move above the poverty line, most find their lives only slightly improved.

Food stamps are received by over two-thirds of children in low-income families, but here also, the average received is rather small, amounting to only 3 percent of median income. Income from welfare goes to a much smaller group, 13 percent, but the benefits are somewhat larger, amounting also to 13 percent of the median.

Overall, almost 90 percent of children in this low-income group receive at least one of these three benefits. For those who do, the combined income averages 7 percent of median income.

Aside from the absence of child allowance and sickness and parental insurance, the issue concerning the adequacy of social programs in the United States is not so much whether a given program exists as whether the benefits are sufficiently great to make a serious dent in poverty. And this is the question for social insurance programs, like pensions and unemployment insurance, as much as it is for charitable programs like food stamps, compared with means-tested programs, such as housing allowances, in other countries.

In the end, all transfers together move fewer than one-quarter of two-parent poor children out of poverty. We have seen that poverty rates are very low when we simulate other countries' income packaging on the U.S. demography. Both higher earnings in other countries and more generous social benefits contribute to this result.

The northern European income package has two main aspects— a higher level of family earnings among the families of low-income children and universal transfers, particularly child allowances. As noted in the discussion of child allowances, the addition of a child allowance of around $100 per child per month alone would accomplish a significant reduction in American two-parent child poverty— from 11 percent to just 7 percent.

But higher earnings would have an even larger impact on child poverty. We can illustrate the potential effect by a simple experiment. Suppose each American family in the lower third of the child distribution had earnings as high (in ratio to median income) as the average of the eight northern European countries. For example, those European families at the fifth child percentile would have earnings two and a half times those of American families of that rank, those at the tenth percentile two times as much, and those at the twentieth percentile one and two-thirds times as much. Simulating the European family earnings distribution on the American data (without changing the distribution of transfers) produces a simulated poverty rate for American children in two-parent families of 4 percent.

CONCLUSION

In the end, it is labor market institutions that have the largest impact on a country's poverty rate. Some countries have high legislated minimum wages, and others have implicit minimum wages established in tripartite negotiations between management, unions, and the government. The higher earnings of European two-parent families are a result of a variety of influences—steadier work, higher wages for both men and women in the lower ranks of the distribution, incentives for two-career families in the form of day care, and sickness insurance. In the United States, in contrast, minimum wage legislation lags far behind overall wage growth, unions are weaker and weaker and, in any case, seldom have had solidaristic wage goals, and workers' rights to sick pay, parental leave, day care, and other supports for employment are much less developed (Gornick and Meyers 2003).

We emphasize labor market factors in the generation of poverty because they are so often ignored in American policy discussions. But, as we have seen in the countries that have low poverty rates, it is the combination of labor market supports for good earnings and the existence of a range of social wage programs that does the trick. Both these kinds of resources are weakly or not at all developed in the United States.

Chapter 7

Child Poverty and Income Packaging in Single-Mother Families

I N RECENT YEARS all countries have given special policy attention to the economic vulnerability of children in single-mother families. Most single mothers are caught between their responsibilities as mothers and heads of families, on the one hand, and the need to earn money, on the other. In quite a number of countries there is additional concern that the proportion of children who live in single-mother families may be steadily rising. Such concern has been widespread in the United States, where the increase in single-mother families is perhaps most prominent, but it has also emerged in the United Kingdom and Sweden and among various international agencies such as the OECD.

Our fifteen countries show a very wide variation in the proportion of children who live in single-mother families. We find that in the LIS surveys only 5 percent of children in Spain and Italy live in such families, while in the United States and the United Kingdom the figure is around 21 percent and it is 19 percent in Sweden. At 9 percent, Belgium, France, and Switzerland have relatively low proportions of children in single-mother families, and the rate in the Netherlands is lower still, at 7 percent. The number of these children is slightly higher in Germany, Finland, and Australia, at 11 percent, and single-mother families in Denmark, Norway, and Canada number in the 14 to 15 percent range.

The composition of single-mother families can vary significantly across countries, and so it is important to define the term from the outset. Our definition of single-mother family is a family with minor children in which a woman is the head. When other adults are present, as they sometimes are, they are likely to make contributions to the family's income. We find that not only do Spain and Italy have the lowest proportion of single-mother families, but that in over half of such families another adult is present. In the United States there is an even larger proportion of children in families that have both a single mother and another adult present; some 7 percent of all American children live in such families, or almost one-third of children in single-mother families. In the other countries a very small minority of children in single-mother families also have another adult present. Thus, with the exception of Spain, Italy, and the United States, over three-quarters of children in single-mother families in our study live in families in which the only adult present is their mother.

Given the tenuous economic situation of single-mother families, we would expect to find that children in such families are disproportionately concentrated in low-income groups. This is indeed the case. With the exception of Sweden (52 percent), Spain (56 percent), Belgium and Finland (64 percent), and Italy (65 percent), some 70 percent or more of children in single-mother families have incomes that place them in the lower third of the distribution of all persons' income. Indeed, 80 percent or more of such children in the United Kingdom, Australia, Germany, and the Netherlands are in the lower third of the total distribution.

But as we have seen in the previous chapter, being in the lower third of the distribution does not necessarily mean that one is poor or even near-poor. Figure 7.1 charts the proportion of children of single mothers in the lower third by their poverty rates. Comparing the countries with the highest levels of children in the lower income third, we see that in the United States almost 70 percent of lower-third children are poor, followed by Canada, Australia, and Germany in the mid 50 percent range. In the United Kingdom this is true of fewer than half of the lower-third children. In the Netherlands almost three-quarters of the lower-third children are not poor.

In the Nordic countries, Belgium, and Switzerland, between 12 and 20 percent of the lower-third children in single-mother families are poor, but there is a fairly wide range in the overall poverty rate: from around one-half to over three-quarters of children of single mothers are in the lower third.

FIGURE 7.1 **Poverty Rates in Fifteen Countries
of Low-Income Single-Mother Children,
by Percentage in the Lower Third**

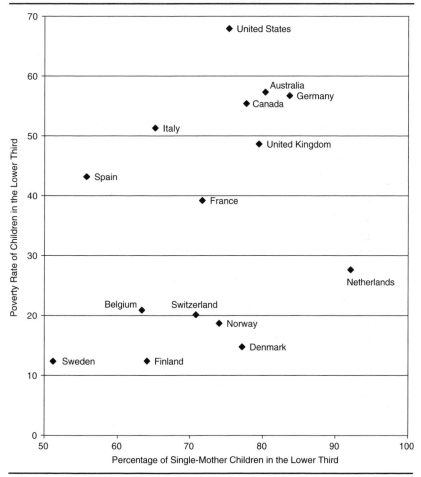

Source: Authors' calculations, using data from the Luxembourg Income Study.

Overall, we see in figure 7.2 poverty rates among single-mother children of around 50 percent in the United States and slightly lower rates in Germany and Australia. In Canada and the United Kingdom the poverty rate is around 40 percent. Single-mother children's poverty rates are higher than two-parent rates in every country, of course, but the absolute differences are much larger in these

FIGURE 7.2 **Children in Single-Mother Families with Low Income in Fifteen Countries**

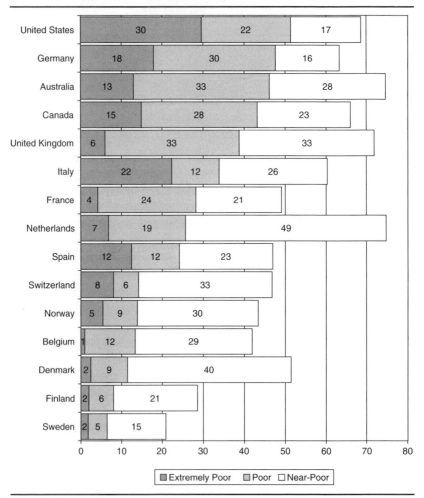

Source: Authors' calculations, using data from the Luxembourg Income Study.

five countries than in the others. We find a range of from around one-quarter to one-third in Spain, the Netherlands, France, and Italy. In the Nordic countries, Belgium, and Switzerland, single-mother child poverty ranges from 6 to 14 percent.

In the United States we find an extreme poverty rate among single-mother families that is higher than the total poverty rate for such families in nine other countries. We note that Italy and Germany also have elevated rates of extreme poverty among single-mother families, around 20 percent.

If there is another adult present in the single-mother family, the child poverty rate is generally much lower. On average, the poverty rate with more than one adult present is less than half that when there is just the mother. But the United States is an exception. Even with additional adults, the poverty rate of children in single-mother families is close to 50 percent.

We noted in the previous chapter that the poverty rate of children in two-parent families in the United States is 11 percent. We find now that in two countries the poverty rate of children in single-mother families with no other adults is in fact lower—in Finland it is 8 percent and in Sweden 5 percent. In Belgium it is the same as the American two-parent rate. If one considers that two-parent families have two adults who may work, the comparison of the U.S. two-parent rate with that of single-mother families with two or more adults finds lower poverty rates in four additional countries—Denmark, Finland, the Netherlands, and Norway. Thus, we need to ask what it is about the income packaging in these countries that allows single mothers to escape poverty so much more frequently than even two-parent families do in the United States.

We noted in chapter 3 that controls for a number of factors, including the number of children in a family, do not seem to affect dramatically the differences in poverty rates we have observed among countries. Nevertheless, the question arises: To what extent is the number of children in single-mother families related to the poverty rate?

In the United States we find a very clear pattern. The poverty rate in one-child single-mother families is 38 percent, in two-child families 47 percent, in three-child families 59 percent, and in families with four or more children 67 percent. But we do not find this neat progression in other countries. In Italy the poverty rate is actually much lower in two- and three-child single-mother families than in one-child families. We suspect that, in most countries, social transfers related to the number of children or earnings by older children temper considerably any tendency of larger families to be less well off.

These differences in poverty rates are one aspect of differences in children's relative incomes across the distribution of single-

FIGURE 7.3 **Single-Mother Children in Fourteen Countries with Higher Relative and Real Incomes Than U.S. Children**

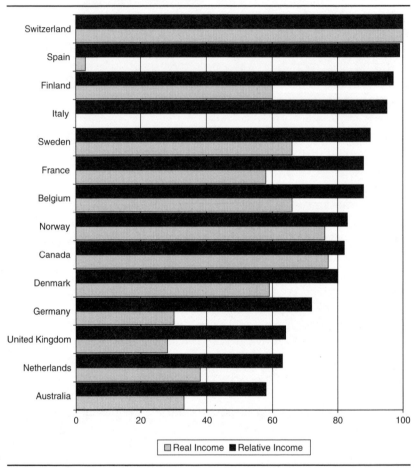

Source: Authors' calculations, using data from the Luxembourg Income Study.

mother families. We see in figure 7.3 that well over 90 percent or more of single mothers' children in five countries—Switzerland, Spain, Finland, Italy, and Sweden—have higher relative incomes than their counterparts in the United States. And this is true of over 80 percent of these children in the other countries except for Germany (72 percent), the United Kingdom (64 percent), the Netherlands (63 percent), and Australia (58 percent).

Even in real income, American single mothers' children fare worse than the majority of their counterparts in eight countries. The proportions of the latter who are better off in real terms than comparable American children range upward from close to 60 percent in Finland, France, and Denmark to two-thirds in Belgium and Sweden and three-quarters in Canada and Norway. A substantial minority (from 28 to 38 percent) of single-mother children are better off in real terms in the Netherlands, Australia, Germany, and the United Kingdom, while in Spain and Italy almost no single mothers' children are better off in real terms.

If we focus on the real incomes of the half of American children in single-mother families who are poor compared with their counterparts in other countries, we find that the American children have higher real incomes compared with only six countries. Children among the least well off half of single-mother children in the eight other countries have higher real incomes than the poor American children. In short, the poverty gap of the children of American single mothers is so great that even in countries with much lower average real incomes, single-mother children fare better.

DEMOGRAPHY VERSUS INCOME PACKAGING
OF SINGLE-MOTHER FAMILIES

The demographic and labor supply variations in single-mother families in these fifteen countries do not have a great deal of effect on child poverty rates. Using the method described in appendix D, the simulation results in figure 7.4 show that, for more than half of the countries, simulating U.S. demography produces only small differences between the simulated rate and the actual rate. The few larger differences suggest some interesting effects of labor force differences. In Italy and Spain the simulated U.S. demography rates are quite a bit higher, perhaps the effect of there being fewer multiple earners in the United States than in those countries. And the simulated rates are quite a bit lower in the Netherlands, Australia, Canada, and Belgium, perhaps a result of the fact that the United States has more employed single mothers and other family members than those countries.

FIGURE 7.4 **Actual and Simulated Single-Mother Child Poverty Rates in Fifteen Countries**

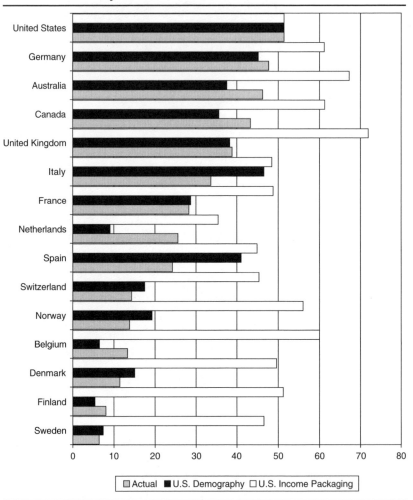

Source: Authors' calculations, using data from the Luxembourg Income Study.

Imposing the American income package on other countries' single-mother children results in a simulated poverty rate as high as or higher than the actual American rate in half of the countries. The simulated rate is almost as high in six other countries. The shifts from actual to simulated in the Nordic countries, Switzerland, and Belgium are particularly dramatic. The actual rates average around 11 percent. The U.S. packaging simulated rates are just over 50 percent, while the simulated U.S. demography rates average the same 11 percent as the actual rates. It is the very great differences in income packages between the northern European countries and the United States that produce the differences in the poverty rates of children in single-mother families. We turn now to an examination of those income packaging differences.

THE ROLE OF GOVERNMENT
AND MARKET INCOME

In most of these countries a solid majority of children in single-mother families would be poor if their families received only income from the market. The proportion of pretransfer poor ranges from just under 50 percent in Denmark and Finland to over 80 percent in the Netherlands and the United Kingdom (figure 7.5). Switzerland, Spain, Belgium, and Sweden are in the 55 to 60 percent range of child poverty if we consider market income alone. Canada, Germany, Italy, France, Norway, and the United States cluster in the 62 to 66 percent range. Then there is a rather large jump to Australia, the Netherlands, and the United Kingdom, where the pretransfer child poverty rate is around 80 percent.

There are very large differences in the proportion of pretransfer poor moved out of poverty by transfer income. In the Nordic countries as well as in Belgium and Switzerland, three-quarters or more of the pretransfer poor children of single mothers are moved out of poverty by transfer income, with a high in Sweden of over 90 percent. In the Netherlands almost 70 percent of these children escape poverty via transfers. In Spain, France, and the United Kingdom a little over half of the pretransfer poor children are moved out of poverty by transfers, slightly fewer than half in Italy, and some 40 percent in Australia. In Canada one-third of single mothers' children are moved out of poverty by transfers. But in the United States and Germany only about one-quarter of single-mother poor children are moved out of poverty by transfers.

A comparison of figure 7.5 with figure 6.5 shows that while in about half of the countries transfers move similar proportions of children in two-parent and in single-mother families out of poverty,

FIGURE 7.5 **Pre- and Post-Transfer Child Poverty Rates
in Single-Mother Families in Fifteen Countries**

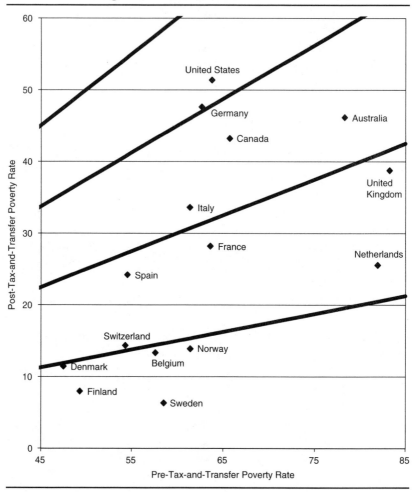

Source: Authors' calculations, using data from the Luxembourg Income Study.
Note: The diagonal lines from top to bottom denote 0, 25, 50, and 75 percent poverty
reduction by transfers.

there are marked discrepancies in a few. Switzerland, Italy, Spain, and the Netherlands are more successful in reducing pretransfer poverty among children of single mothers than among those with two parents. In contrast, Germany and France (and to a lesser extent Canada) have more success with two-parent families.

Thus, it is very clear that most single-mother families cannot depend on market income alone to rescue them from poverty or near-poverty. Social transfers are an integral part of the income packaging for single mothers. Figure 7.6 highlights the role of market and transfer income in a different way. Here we plot the average market (earnings and asset) income and transfer income received in single-

FIGURE 7.6 Mean Factor and Transfer Income of Single-Mother Children in the Bottom Child Quintile in Fifteen Countries

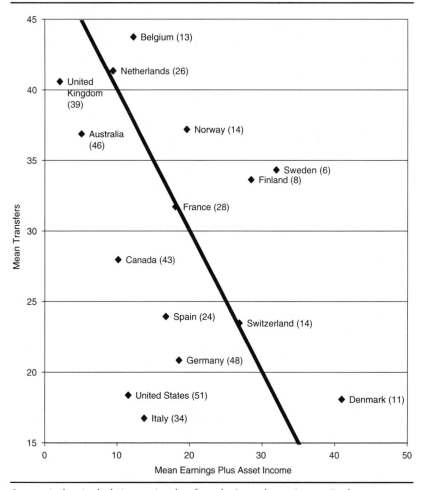

Source: Authors' calculations, using data from the Luxembourg Income Study.
Note: The diagonal line represents a total disposable income of 50 percent of median income. Figures in parentheses are poverty rates.

mother families in the lowest child income quintile. (As discussed in chapter 2, the bottom quintile of all American children is poor.) The figure charts the average income from market sources and the average income from transfer sources as a percentage of median equivalent income. The poverty rate for children of single mothers is given in parentheses after the country abbreviation.

The five countries with the lowest poverty rates vary quite a bit in the mix of income types. Denmark has a high average of market income and a relatively low average of transfers; Sweden and Finland have lower average market income and higher average transfer income, followed by Norway; and at the extreme of reliance on transfer income we find Belgium. There is the same variation in the mix of income types among the countries with middling and high child poverty rates. Switzerland and Spain show a higher reliance on market income than France and, in particular, the Netherlands, both of which rely on transfers to a much greater extent. Yet all four countries have somewhat similar poverty rates. Finally, among the countries with very high poverty rates, the United States and Germany rely most heavily on market income while the United Kingdom and Australia rely on transfers. Thus, countries may differ a great deal in the content of the income package and yet produce similar poverty rates.

We find an extremely wide range across countries in the proportion of low-income children with no market income at all. The leader here is the United Kingdom, where 85 percent of lowest-quintile single-mother children live in families that depend completely on transfer income (not shown). Belgium, Australia, and the Netherlands come next, with almost two-thirds of single-mother children in such families. In Germany and Canada we find about half of these children living without market income. Italy, the United States, Finland, France, Norway, and Spain range from 40 percent downward to one-third of single-mother children without market income. And, as noted earlier, Denmark, Sweden, and Switzerland have few children in families with no market income—ranging from 28 to 18 percent.

LOW-INCOME SINGLE MOTHERS' LABOR
FORCE PARTICIPATION AND EARNINGS

Almost all the market income for low-income single-mother families comes from earnings. In most cases, as we have seen, there is only one adult in the household, and therefore only one person who can have earnings. For the most part, then, the variations we see in the role of market income are simply variations in the earnings of the single mother who heads the household. We consider here the labor force participation of single mothers whose children are in the lower third of the equivalent income distribution of all persons.

The fact that in the four Nordic countries around three-quarters of these children's single mothers have earnings is very much a product of jobs associated with the growth of the social service sector in these countries (not shown). In Denmark and Sweden around two-thirds of single mothers with earnings in this low-income group have jobs in the government and social service sector. In Finland the proportion of single mothers with government or social service jobs is smaller but nevertheless fairly high—around half of those with earnings have jobs in the government sector. (Unfortunately, we do not have industry data for Norway.) The jobs these women hold tend to be less-skilled jobs, such as caregivers in day care centers for both children and the elderly, in schools, and in medical settings. Although these are not generally professional jobs, they do provide a certain amount of security, with full fringe benefits and standard wages.

Belgium has a somewhat similar pattern in terms of government versus private-sector jobs, although the overall proportion of mothers with earnings (40 percent) is quite a bit lower than in the Nordic countries. We do find that the majority of those with earnings in Belgium have jobs in the government sector. In France the majority of those with earnings are in the government sector also, but the proportion of low-income single mothers with earnings (about two-thirds) is a bit lower than in the Nordic countries.

A very different pattern is found in the United States, the Netherlands, and the United Kingdom. Despite the fact that two-thirds of single mothers in the United States have earnings, fewer than one-fifth of them are found working in the government sector. Instead, they are exposed to the low wages and marginal security of the least desirable jobs in the private sector. In the Netherlands and the United Kingdom, the proportion with a government job is quite small because the proportion with a job at all is small (less than 30 percent).

When the mother has earnings, we find a similar variation across countries in how much she earns. But there is only a weak positive association between the likelihood of a single mother having earnings and the average amount she earns. The working low-income mothers with the highest earnings are in Denmark, Finland, Sweden, Switzerland, Germany, and Belgium—averaging from 40 percent of median income to a high of 60 percent in Denmark. The low-earning single mothers (30 percent or less) are in Australia, the United Kingdom, and the United States.

In sum, if we think of the poverty rate for children in single-mother families as a function of mothers' earnings and social transfers, we find that across these fifteen countries market income (principally earnings) seems to play a larger role than transfers, although both are important. The correlation of the single-mother child poverty rate with low-income single mothers' mean market income is −0.70. Its correlation with mean transfers is much lower (−0.25).

THE POVERTY-CREATING EFFECT
OF TWO-EARNER FAMILIES

Of course, one reason single-mother poverty rates tend to be high is that the standard for not being poor (half of median equivalent income) is raised by two-earner families. The more such families there are, the harder it will be for single-earner families to make it above the poverty line, because the poverty line has been raised as the median family disposable income is raised by multiple earners.

To see how sensitive the poverty rates of children in single-mother families are to this factor, we can simulate a world in which at the extreme there are no second earners (mainly a situation in which no wives have earnings). This produces a lower median equivalent income amount and a lower poverty line. It increases the relative equivalent income of single-earner families and decreases the income of families that in fact have two earners. Such a simulation for the United States produces an increase in the poverty rate of children in two-parent families from 11 to 16 percent. It makes for a decrease in the poverty rate of single-mother families from 51 to 34 percent. We find a similar pattern if we take Sweden as an example of a country with a very low poverty rate. The Swedish two-parent poverty rate increases from 1.2 percent to around 8 percent, and the single-mother rate decreases from 6.4 percent to 3 percent (actually lower than that of two-parent families). In France, a country with a poverty rate in the middle of the range, we find very little effect for two-parent families but a very large effect for single-parent families—a decline from 28 to 13 percent.

Overall, we can conclude from this comparison of the role of market and transfer income that the only secure foundation for a single mother's escape from poverty is earnings. Also, the need for good earnings increases as dual labor force participation increases over time in two-parent families. Only in the Netherlands do we find the great majority of children in single-mother families escaping poverty even though they have no earnings.

Earnings and market income, however, are only a foundation. We also find that only when transfers top up the market income quite significantly does one find low child poverty rates. (Switzerland might seem an exception, but as we have noted, it is unclear what role child allowances play there because they are included in paychecks.) It takes a strong combination of earnings and social transfers to keep poverty in single-mother families below 15 percent, as in the Nordic countries and Belgium.

THE ROLE OF TRANSFERS FOR CHILDREN IN THE LOWER THIRD OF THE DISTRIBUTION

In the next sections we examine the role of the more important transfer programs for single-mother families. For the transfers considered we note the average amount received by children in the lower third of the income distribution and the percentage of children in families that receive these benefits.

Child Allowances

Child allowances are nearly universal in rich countries. Only in the United States is there no child allowance program and no guaranteed parental leave with pay. In our countries allowances are paid for almost all children except France, where there are no child benefits for the first child. In Spain, Italy, and Switzerland child allowances are paid as part of earnings, and therefore we have no separate accounting of them. From aggregate data, however, we know that child allowance spending is not as great in these countries as it is in most other European countries. Parental insurance, which allows parents to take "sick leave" with pay when their children need them, is also universal in these countries.

The average amount of child allowances and parental insurance payments received by children in low-income single-mother families is over 10 percent of median equivalent income, ranging down from Finland at 14 percent to Belgium and Norway at 12 percent, France and Australia at 11 percent, and Denmark at 10 percent. Of course, in France only families with more than one child receive benefits—thus, for the 75 percent of children who receive them, the benefits amount to 15 percent of the median. Canada, the Netherlands, the United Kingdom, and Sweden average 8 or 9 percent and Germany only 5 percent.

Child allowances are clearly important to the single-mother families in that they top up income from other sources. But they are not the major source of transfers for single-mother families in any country. Particularly for those families with no market income, other transfer sources play the major role in determining the probability that a low-income single-mother family will escape poverty.

Child Support and Other Private Transfers

Another form of family support is an important source of income for some single-mother families—transfers from absent parents or other relatives. In some countries, when the absent parent does not meet his responsibilities, the government makes the child support payment. These are the so-called advance maintenance payments. In Sweden and Norway, where government-provided advance maintenance payments are an important source of income when the absent parent does not pay, some 89 and 82 percent of children receive child support either from the absent parent or the government. Their benefits average 10 and 8 percent of median income, respectively. This means that in Sweden and Norway the combination of child allowance, parental insurance, and child support averages almost half of the poverty line.

In Belgium half of these children receive child support that amounts to 10 percent of median income. In Australia just over one-third are recipients, also averaging 10 percent of the median. In the United States one-quarter of these children receive child support, amounting on average to 8 percent of the median. Child support goes to about 15 percent of these children in the Netherlands and the United Kingdom; the former average a rather generous 21 percent of median income, and the latter 12 percent.

In Spain help from relatives for the 28 percent of children who receive such income is quite important, averaging 26 percent of median income. The pattern is similar in Germany—40 percent of recipients with benefits, averaging 15 percent of the median.

Finland, Switzerland, and France are distinctive for having single-mother families that receive fairly substantial amounts of benefits from both child support and other private transfers. In Switzerland 41 percent of these children receive child support and 45 percent receive other private transfers. The average benefits amount to 23 percent of the median in the first case and 15 percent in the second. It is these transfers that, in the main, account for the fact that three-quarters of Swiss single-mother children are moved from pretransfer poverty by transfers. We find a similar pattern of frequent receipt of these two kinds of transfers in Finland, but the benefits are quite small. The lift out of poverty by transfers in Finland comes from the more standard child allowances and labor market programs.

We find that child support is fairly important in France—25 percent of single-mother children receive child support payments that average 12 percent of the median. Only 9 percent of children receive other private transfers, however, with somewhat lower average benefits at 9 percent of the median.

Unemployment Insurance
and Labor Market Programs

Unemployment insurance plays a very important role in the income packaging of low-income single-mother families in some countries.

In Belgium 12 percent of low-income children live in single-mother families that receive unemployment insurance payments. In those families the amount received averages one-third of median equivalent income—that is, fully two-thirds of the poverty line. In Sweden and Denmark 38 percent of these children are in recipient families, and in Finland 30 percent. The benefits amount to about one-quarter of the median. In these four countries, then, the combination of child allowances and unemployment payments pulls many of these low-income families above the poverty line.

France, Germany, and Norway have a similar pattern but at a lower level. Around one-fifth of low-income single-mother families receive unemployment insurance payments. In those families the average payments amount to around 15 percent of median income in the first two, and 10 percent in the latter.

In Switzerland, Canada, and Italy 10 and 11 percent of single-mother children are in families receiving unemployment benefits that average 10 to 13 percent of the median. In the remaining countries, unemployment benefits are received by 6 percent of these children or fewer. For these few the benefits received can be fairly substantial, except in the case of the United States, where the 5 percent of children in recipient families average a benefit of only 5 percent of median income.

Social Assistance and Income-Tested
In-kind Benefits

Income-tested social protection programs are an important source of income for single-mother families. Cash social assistance may be general or linked to specific kinds of eligibility, such as being unemployed or a new single mother. So-called near-cash programs are a standard part of the welfare state in most countries—the principal ones are food stamps in the United States, housing allowances in many countries, and a range of smaller programs that provide income in connection with education.

We find that in seven countries three-quarters or more of low-income single-mother children are in families that receive benefits from cash or in-kind income-tested programs—Denmark, Australia,

France, the Netherlands, Finland, the United Kingdom, and the United States. In Sweden 67 percent are recipients. In Canada, Norway, and Germany slightly over half receive benefits, in Belgium 38 percent, and in Switzerland 30 percent. In Spain, in contrast, fewer than 10 percent receive income-tested benefits. (The LIS Italian dataset does not have information on social assistance.)

Average benefits to recipient families, however, vary a great deal. The average amount received by beneficiaries in the Netherlands is the highest (46 percent), the next highest is in the United Kingdom (35 percent), and Australia and Canada (23 percent) are third-highest in this regard. In Finland and Germany benefits to children in single-mother families average about 18 percent of the median, and in the other countries the average ranges from 10 to 14 percent.

In most countries cash social assistance programs, as opposed to in-kind programs, are the most important parts of the income-tested programs targeted at low-income families. Only in Finland, France, and Sweden does the largest share of this kind of income come from in-kind programs. In fact, in eight of the countries three-quarters or more of this income comes in the form of cash. Cash income is mostly in the form of social assistance—a general program that dispenses cash to those whose income is deemed below some subsistence standard. But in addition, in a few countries there are more specifically targeted programs. In Australia three-quarters of these children's mothers qualify for an unmarried mother's allowance with quite generous benefits amounting to almost one-quarter of the median. In Finland, Germany, and the Netherlands unemployment assistance for those who do not (or no longer) qualify for the unemployment insurance program is an important part of cash assistance.

While almost all of these countries have in-kind programs that benefit low-income single mothers' families, the size of benefits is considerable in only five. The leader is the United Kingdom, where housing benefits go to three-quarters of the children in low-income single-mother families and average 15 percent of the median. Finland and France come next with about the same proportion of housing allowance recipients and an average benefit of around 10 percent of the median. Sweden has fewer single mothers receiving housing allowances (62 percent), which average 9 percent of the median. The percentage is even higher in the United States for food stamp beneficiaries (85 percent), but the average benefit is lower at 6 percent of the median. In Germany, the Netherlands, and Norway about 40 percent of single mothers receive housing benefits; those benefits come to only 5 or 6 percent of the median, as is the case for one-third of these families in Belgium, whose average benefit amounts to 4 percent of the median. In the other countries there are either no recipients of in-kind programs or very few.

Pensions

One would not expect pension income to loom large for these families, and it does not. In general not many single mothers receive survivor's, old age, or disability social pensions or occupational pensions. Nevertheless, three countries stand out for providing substantial benefits for this group.

Italy and Spain are distinctive for their reliance on pension income, which goes to over 40 percent of low-income single-mother children. Average benefits are quite high at over one-third of median income. In Norway we find a very high 64 percent of children in low-income single-mother families receiving a survivor's pension or a temporary pension as a transitional allowance for their single parent. Their benefits amount to about one-fifth of the median.

In most of the countries with a low poverty rate, few families receive pension income—fewer than 10 percent. But benefits for those who do receive pension income tend to be high—62 percent of the median in the Netherlands and around one-third in Belgium, Switzerland, Denmark, and Sweden.

As noted in the previous chapter, much has been written about the prevalence of disability pensioners in the Netherlands. We find that some 8 percent of single mothers are recipients of disability insurance; they average benefits equal to 45 percent of the median. As observed in the case of two-parent families, disability recipiency does not seem to loom as large in the income packaging of families with children as it does in the literature.

SUMMARY BY COUNTRY OF THE IMPACT
OF SOCIAL PROTECTION PROGRAMS
ON SINGLE-MOTHER FAMILIES

To summarize the effects of income packaging for single-mother families, we discuss these findings for several clusters of countries.

The Nordic Countries

In all of these countries single mothers are likely to have fairly high market income, although between 48 and 62 percent would be poor if that were all they had. Social wage programs combined (child allowances, advanced maintenance payments, sickness and paternal insurance benefits, and unemployment insurance benefits) reduce poverty most dramatically in Sweden, Norway, and Finland. The addition of income-tested programs brings poverty to very low levels in Sweden, Finland, and Denmark. Norway is distinctive in relying on a transitional benefit for single parents that is not income-tested.

The Northern Continental Countries

Market income is central to the income packaging of Belgium, France, Germany, and Switzerland, but much less so in the Netherlands, where over 80 percent of single-mother children would be poor if their families had no transfer income. In all but Switzerland the child allowance is an additional key to a low poverty rate. There is quite a bit of diversity among these five countries, however, with respect to other kinds of transfers.

For the Netherlands, very heavy reliance on income-tested programs is key. Together all transfers make up for the relative weakness of market income to produce a moderate poverty rate for single-mother children.

In France we find a relatively high level of market income combined with moderate social wage and income-tested programs, but the end result is a poverty rate higher than those of the Nordic countries or Belgium and the Netherlands. Housing allowances are the only large transfer program besides the child allowance.

Germany has a still higher poverty rate, which is the product of lower social wage and income-tested transfers than in the other countries in this cluster and a modest level of market income. In Switzerland social wage programs are not large; instead, the main transfer programs are pensions, child support, and other private transfers. But these private benefits (family, charitable, or mixed public and/or private transfers) are quite large and do the major work in moving three-quarters of Swiss single-mother children out of poverty.

Spain and Italy

Spain has a single-mother child poverty rate about the same as France's. It does not have the rich array of social wage and income-tested programs that play an important role in France. Those Spanish single-mother children who escape from poverty do so mainly as a consequence of being in families that receive pensions or private transfers. Much the same pattern is observed for Italy; the important transfers are pensions and private transfers. Along with some other smaller transfers, these move somewhat fewer than half of these children out of poverty.

The United Kingdom, Australia, and Canada

The United Kingdom and Australia have extremely high pretransfer child poverty rates, reflecting low labor force participation among single mothers and low wages for those who do work. Canada's pretransfer poverty rate is somewhat lower but is still the fourth-highest among our fifteen countries. The task for Canadian social protection programs is thus very daunting, and Canada does not meet with the kind of success we found in the Netherlands. Social wage programs move relatively few Canadian single-mother children out of poverty. In all three countries it is income-tested programs that play the major role in reducing poverty among these children to around 40 percent. Because the United Kingdom's poverty gap is greatest, it takes more in the way of income-tested transfers (both cash social assistance and in-kind housing benefits) to reduce poverty. Australia has a similar profile but with a slightly lower level of pretransfer poverty and a higher child allowance; thus, there are fewer children who need to be moved out of poverty with cash income-tested assistance (principally an unmarried mother's allowance). Canada has a broader menu of child benefits as well as cash social assistance, as well as a smaller pretransfer gap to fill.

The United States

The United States has the fifth-highest pretransfer poverty rate for single mothers—a product of low labor force participation and low wages despite the greater prevalence of second wage earners. One-third of single-mother children are not just poor but extremely poor, with incomes below one-third of the median equivalent income. The poverty gap both before and after transfers is there-fore great. At 64 percent the U.S. pretransfer child poverty rate is close to the rate in several other countries—Canada, Germany, Italy, France, and Norway. But like Canada and Germany, the United States moves relatively few low-income children out of poverty with transfers. Unemployment insurance is the only social wage program, but it is received in the families of only 5 percent of these children, and for those the benefits are hardly generous. Because the income-tested programs provide extremely modest benefits, they too move few above the line. In the end, only 20 percent of the very large group of pretransfer poor are rescued from poverty. Together the three income-tested programs with significant bene-fits—social assistance, the Earned Income Tax Credit, and food stamps—are much smaller than the income-tested programs in the three other countries that rely very heavily on such programs. Aus-tralia, the Netherlands, and the United Kingdom have aggregate income-tested benefits to these children's families that are from half again to almost three times larger than in the United States.

Chapter 8

Is There Hope for America's Low-Income Children?

D ESPITE HIGH RATES of economic growth and improvements in the standard of living in industrialized nations throughout the twentieth century, a significant percentage of American children are still living in families so poor that normal health and growth are at risk (Duncan et al. 1998; Duncan and Brooks-Gunn 1997a, b). The previous chapters have shown that it does not have to be this way: in many other countries child poverty afflicts only one-half to one-quarter as many children as in the United States.

These numbers are startling and worrisome. For more affluent nations, child poverty is not a matter of affordability—it is a matter of priority. This country made a commitment nearly sixty years ago to deal with old-age poverty, and that effort has been fairly successful (Burtless and Smeeding 2001). When we found ourselves discussing the large federal and state budget surpluses at the beginning of the twenty-first century, that was a period when we could have made a serious commitment to reduce child poverty in the United States. This opportunity was missed. Even today, with the economy in a brief recession, making a commitment to spend the modest amount of money it would take to bring about a large reduction in child poverty is well within our grasp. Of course, such a policy would need to conform to American values (market work and self-reliance), utilize American social institutions (such as the income tax system), and continue the successful antipoverty efforts of the 1990s, such as the Earned Income Tax Credit.

Consider tax policy for a moment. There are progressive sub-
stitutes for the recent 2001–2002 regressive federal income tax
reductions that would shore up income support for the working
poor. For instance, as part of an expanded tax reduction plan, we
could make the child tax credit refundable for working families
with no federal income tax obligations; these families do pay Social
Security and Medicare taxes, of course. Similarly, we could expand
the Earned Income Tax Credit and link it to the child tax credit
(Sawicky and Cherry 2001). These modest measures would be relatively inexpensive and effective first steps in the process of further
reducing child poverty for the working poor.

While such changes are meant to be suggestive, our study
underlines the need for a comprehensive policy to reduce child
poverty rates and improve the well-being of children. Policymakers
committed to reducing child poverty must address each of the six
problem areas (employment, parental leave, child care, child-
related tax policy, child support, and education) identified in this
chapter. And they must also consider the much smaller number of
children living in families with no parent who can work.

EMPLOYMENT

The most important step in reducing poverty among children is to
ensure that at least one parent is employed. In particular, the labor
market position of mothers needs to be improved, as their earnings
are crucial for maintaining an adequate standard of living in a society where two-income families dominate. Obviously, this is doubly
true for single parents, where subsidized child care is an absolute
necessity for employment.

In low-wage, high-employment societies such as the United
States, employment is both a virtue and a challenge. Working
mothers feel better about themselves when they are employed, and
children feel better about their parents when they are employed
(Chase-Lansdale et al. 2003). However, low-skill employment is
almost always low-paying, sometimes requires working nonstan-
dard hours, can involve long commutes, and is vulnerable to lay-
offs when the economy turns down. Thus, while employment is
important, it needs to be supported by flexibility in work schedules

and other public support services (Haveman 2003). For two-parent families, some mixture of these policies will suffice. For single parents who must act as both provider and caretaker, employment must be coordinated with their children's needs. To be successfully employed, parents, especially mothers, need state support to facilitate that employment. The evidence is that low-income American single mothers work more hours than single mothers in any other nation (Osberg 2002). The evidence is also clear that American single mothers receive the least income support of any nation's low-income mothers (Smeeding 2003). American policymakers therefore must find a better mix of income support and work that makes all working single parents nonpoor (see also Gornick and Meyers 2003).

PARENTAL LEAVE, CHILD CARE SUBSIDY, AND CHILD SUPPORT

In many cases, parents—particularly mothers—need state support to enable them to work and to adequately take care of their children. The development of parental leave programs, guarantees for child support not paid by absent parents, and affordable child care are important conditions for keeping mothers in the full-time workforce and preventing poverty among their children. Child support enforcement measures are important and have become more successful over the past decade. But their potential for reducing child poverty is limited, since many of the parents who fail to pay child support are low earners themselves. The policy design issue is to find a public way to ensure child support, while not reducing the efforts that absent parents make to support their children.

The United States has lagged in these areas in all dimensions: our family leave is not universal and is, in fact, relatively short and unsubsidized; we have no child support insurance to protect single mothers from absent fathers who do not pay their obligated child support; and our child care support system helps the rich more than it helps the poor, despite many recent welfare reform–related efforts to expand child care subsidies for low-income parents (Ross 1999; Gornick and Meyers 2003).

According to the evidence presented earlier, Sweden has low child poverty rates not only because of unique cultural characteristics but because as a society it has integrated women—mothers in general and single mothers in particular—into its labor force. In its configuration of welfare state policies, Sweden has traditionally stressed the importance of women's continued attachment to the labor market and supported them as wage earners by providing child care, a good parental leave program, and a comprehensive system of child care support.

Adequate parental leave programs and child care provisions are clearly important conditions for keeping mothers in full-time employment. For instance, the increased availability in the United Kingdom of child care, maternity leave, and more family-friendly corporate policies has increased the employment continuity of British women around the time of childbirth and thus reduced the indirect cost of children to their parents (Davies and Joshi 2001). It is also reported that British women can increasingly afford to make use of child care services. However, the direct cost of child care services still proves to be too high for women with smaller earnings potential. This is one of the main reasons why British women with low earnings potential, as well as those with middle earnings potential and more than one child, are more likely to stay home (see, for example, Meyers et al. 2001).

Child Care

Clearly, the introduction of comprehensive child care provisions should be complemented by measures that would make it possible for women with lower earnings potential to make use of these services. The greater the cost of child care services relative to the mother's wage potential, the less likely it is that she will seek employment. It is therefore important to expand public support for child care services that reduces the direct cost of those services, with direct subsidies and also with indirect support through refundable child care tax credits, which would (partially) compensate low-income families' remaining expenditures for this type of service.

In 1989 the European Commission published a "Communication from the Commission on Family Policies" that underlined the importance of affordable, accessible, and high-quality child care arrangements to member states' efforts to increase the labor participation of women (European Commission 1989; Kamerman and Kahn 2001).

The British government's 1998 green paper "Meeting the Childcare Challenge" (United Kingdom 1998) contains several proposals for improving access to child care in Britain that are now being implemented. Clearly, the lack of affordable child care support is not a uniquely American problem, but it does cripple efforts by single parents in this country to find steady employment and make work economically viable.

Many governments seem to have understood the need for such measures. According to Sheila Kamerman and Alfred Kahn (2001), child care services continued to increase in supply during the 1990s in most nations, including the United States. Many governments have extended existing parental leave policies, and these policies were even introduced for the first time in a few other countries. In 1998 President Clinton pushed an initiative to improve child care for working families that would have made child care more affordable in various ways and doubled the number of children receiving child care subsidies to more than two million by the year 2003. Unfortunately, most elements of the proposal were not enacted into law. The expansion of affordable child care services was still on the political agenda in 2003, but the recession from 2001 to 2003 forced many state governments to cut back on child care services and subsidies in the face of rising state government deficits. While child care subsidies continued, even during the recession, for many single parents who were leaving welfare, support was more generally needed for parents in families who had already left welfare and become independent of the welfare system.

Parental Leave

Parental leave policy is another area where much could be done. In 2000, Canada instituted paid family leave as a national policy, and Australia did the same in 2003. In the United States, where unpaid family leave is very short and still unpaid, California has made a first step by instituting a paid family leave policy for some workers. Other states are likely to follow suit. The actions of these states may pave the way toward a more effective and expansive federal policy in the near future (Ross 1999; Gornick and Meyers 2003).

Parental leave programs and comprehensive and affordable child care services represent, of course, only some of the policy measures needed to integrate mothers into the workforce. Improving the skills of low-skilled workers (often women), job counseling, the removal of various structural obstacles (such as unemployment traps), and transportation assistance are also important initiatives that would make it easier for mothers to work full-time.

Child Support

The provision of steady, reliable child support is another important element of the semiprivate safety net in the United States and elsewhere. It is a widely held value that parents should support their children. The problem in doing so is often that absent fathers cannot or do not pay, owing to weak enforcement of child care laws or low earnings capacity. While significant progress has been made in upgrading child support enforcement for divorced mothers, much still remains to be accomplished for unmarried mothers (Ellwood and Blank 2001). Enforcement is uneven across states, paternity establishment by unwed mothers varies greatly across states, and often the fathers of the children of unwed mothers do not earn enough to support themselves, much less their children.

In Europe a different set of values prevails. The well-being of the child and the mother is usually the foremost value, and the absent father's willingness and ability to pay are of secondary concern. In these countries full child support is guaranteed by governments when absent fathers cannot or will not pay (Skevik 1998). While universal guaranteed child support on the European level would not fit American values, a more modest system might be achievable. When the custodial mother has established paternity and the absent father is deemed unable to pay (owing to imprisonment, unemployment, or low wages), a modest level of guaranteed child support—say, $2,000 per year for a first child and $1,500 for a second—could be a very important source of steady support for a single mother who is not otherwise receiving such aid. Similarly, states could increase the dollar amount of child support allowed to "pass through" to mothers receiving Temporary Assistance to Needy Families (TANF) without penalty, a measure that would increase the monthly amount received by the mother to $150 or $250, rather than only the first $50, which is the norm.

CHILD-RELATED INCOME TAX POLICY

The minimum wage is insufficient to meet the income needs of working families with children. Full-time work at the current minimum wage leaves a family of three far below the poverty line, and the Earned Income Tax Credit does not fully close the gap. If we continue to pursue this policy line, additional child-related tax benefits are necessary to ensure that working families with children are not poor. Making families headed by parents with low earnings potential more dependent on market income is not sufficient to end child poverty in a period of increased earnings inequality and slack labor markets (Haveman 2003). Earnings are often not sufficient to protect households with children from poverty, and although children living in two-parent dual-earner families are far less likely to be poor, poverty rates among children living in working single-parent families remain very high in the United States.

In recent years several countries have introduced or increased minimum wages, but these often remain insufficient to keep households with children out of poverty. Governments are reluctant to further increase the minimum-wage levels in their countries because they risk aggravating the unemployment problem faced by low-skilled workers. The "living wage" laws, which pay hourly wages of seven to nine dollars per hour to governmental contractors in some parts of the United States, are rarely applied to the private sector for this same reason—many fewer employees will be hired at this level of labor cost. Since the expansion of low-wage work might improve the job prospects of less-educated workers and make it easier for single-earner households to acquire a second income, we do not advocate significantly higher minimum wages, and certainly not "living wages" for all U.S. workers. It is clear, however, that many governments should do more to support the working poor when wages are insufficient to keep a family from becoming poor. The United States EITC is one important way to supplement earnings and help working families meet their financial responsibilities. However, it does not always guarantee that a family will avoid poverty (Moffitt 2002).

There is evidence of an increasing role for refundable tax credits in the support given to low-income working-age households in other nations as well. Many OECD countries offer social tax breaks and allowances to replace cash benefits, although they tend to be less important in countries with relatively high direct tax levies, such as Denmark, Finland, the Netherlands, and Sweden. In Germany, the value of tax allowances for the cost incurred in raising children alone amounted to almost 0.6 percent of the German GDP in 1993 (Adema and Einerhand 1998). Both the Netherlands and the United Kingdom have specific tax subsidies for single-parent families, and, as we mentioned before, many countries also use tax credits to compensate these families for expenditures such as child care costs. Yet we must emphasize that such measures have less effect on the incomes of families with earnings that are too low to fully benefit from them. It is therefore important that tax credits for child care and similar measures aimed at families with low earnings be made refundable.

In addition to the EITC, the American income tax system contains a set of tax credits that are partially refundable, but not to low-income parents who do not make enough to pay federal income tax. The several plans that have been proposed to integrate these two programs would produce a single family tax credit with more benefit adequacy and lower work disincentives than in the phase-down regime of the EITC (Cherry and Sawicky 2000; Sawicky and Cherry 2001). Adoption of these programs would give a well-targeted boost to the incomes of working poor parents.

INVESTMENT IN
A SOCIALLY ORIENTED EDUCATION POLICY

Central to the promotion of employment in a knowledge-based society is quality education for all children, regardless of their financial situation or their health. Such policies could reduce the likelihood that child poverty is passed on from generation to generation (Gregg and Machin 2001; Büchel et al. 2001). A special effort needs to be made to target education resources to the areas where they can do the most good for poor children in bad schools and to prepare low-income children for elementary school more generally.

It is the responsibility of every democracy to provide an equal opportunity from birth for every child. We sorely need to give increased attention to the quality of schooling in low-income areas and develop better and more widespread preschool programs in low-income areas if we are to increase the chances of reducing adult poverty among the next generation of children. Making schools more accountable may be a partial answer to this need, but the legislation entitled "Leave No Child Behind" is insufficient by itself to reach this goal (Smeeding 2002).

AN AMERICAN INCOME SUPPORT PACKAGE FOR FAMILIES WITH CHILDREN

The previous six policy arenas can be drawn together into a benefit or "income" package that includes a role for the state, for the family, and for work, and a package that conforms to American values. Clearly, work alone is not enough to guarantee escape from poverty for low-income working families, especially single parents (Haveman 2003). The EITC is a good step, but it is not enough by itself to reach the goal. Additional refundable tax credits, subsidized child care, guaranteed child support (for those who meet specified criteria), and paid family leave must also be woven into the policy mix. This combination of work and benefits should increase the incomes and well-being of children whose mothers work. And both low-income students and their schools need to be better prepared to advance and thrive.

Policy efforts must be redoubled to meet the needs of mothers who cannot work and of households with no workers. Perhaps the answer lies in disability policy—for example, through the Supplemental Security Income (SSI) program. We will not delve into these issues here, except to say that the remaining TANF caseload (about two million households as of early 2003) is a manageable issue that could be tackled by a reauthorization of welfare reform targeted not only at removing these last welfare recipients from the rolls but at meeting their divergent and serious human needs.

FINDING THE WILL IS FINDING THE WAY

The findings in this book underline the need for a comprehensive policy to reduce child poverty rates and improve the well-being of children. Human capital concerns in industrialized countries offer an overwhelming and very practical case for adequate investment in succeeding generations. Especially in the affluent economies of the industrialized world, there are no valid economic excuses for high child poverty rates. We can all afford low child poverty rates.

But no two countries can fight poverty in exactly the same way. Each nation's policies must fit its own national culture and values. Thus, the policy suggestions made here must be hewn together into a system of child poverty reduction that will work in the United States. Moreover, these policies cannot simply be taken off the shelf and plugged in. It takes political leadership to make such policies national priorities and to make programs mesh in a supportive fashion.

In recent years Prime Minister Tony Blair of the United Kingdom has shown that when a nation makes a commitment to reduce child poverty, much can be accomplished (see, for example, Bradshaw 2001; Walker and Wiseman 2001). Since 1997 the Blair government has spent an additional 0.9 percent of GDP (about $1,900 per family) on poor families with children (Hills 2002). An equivalent degree of effort in the United States would cost $90 billion. The high poverty rates of the late 1990s in the United Kingdom are now being gradually reduced (Bradshaw 2001; Hills 2002). Unfortunately, not all countries share this priority, particularly not the United States (Danziger 2001; Smeeding 2002).

The American social assistance system has now achieved a primary goal: increasing work and reducing welfare dependence for low-income mothers. Fewer than five million persons (two million cases) remain dependent on TANF benefits. The "welfare problem" is no longer. However, as welfare rolls have been trimmed, corresponding decreases in child poverty have not been achieved because market income alone is not enough to bring about serious reductions in child poverty. The United States needs to make this goal a top priority for its political agenda. Even a commitment of $45 billion—half the effort of the Blair government—could at least partially fund most of the policy options listed in this chapter. The integrity of our democratic values will be ensured and the cultural and economic fabric of our society enriched when we can say that many fewer children grow up poor in America.

— Part II —

Choice and Method
in Research on Poverty

Chapter 9

Establishing
a Poverty Line

IN THIS CHAPTER, we review the rationale for a social conception of
poverty rather than one that is narrowly economic, and we
explore the implications of such a view for defining an overall level
for a poverty line in terms of the kinds of measurement choices that
have to be made.

It has long been recognized (reference is usually made to Adam
Smith or Karl Marx) that a society's poverty is relative to its mainstream standard of living. Poverty is the absence of those necessities that allow citizens to participate in the mainstream. In *The
Wealth of Nations,* Adam Smith (1776, book 5, chapter 2, article 4)
defines necessities in the following relativistic manner:

> By necessaries I understand not only the commodities which are indis-
> pensably necessary for the support of life, but whatever the custom of the
> country renders it indecent for creditable people, even of the lowest order,
> to be without. A linen shirt, for example, is, strictly speaking, not a nec-
> essary of life. The Greeks and Romans lived, I suppose, very comfortably
> though they had no linen. But in the present times, through the greater
> part of Europe, a creditable day-labourer would be ashamed to appear in
> public without a linen shirt, the want of which would be supposed to
> denote that disgraceful degree of poverty which, it is presumed, nobody
> can well fall into without extreme bad conduct. Custom, in the same man-
> ner, has rendered leather shoes a necessary of life in England. The poor-
> est creditable person of either sex would be ashamed to appear in public
> without them. In Scotland, custom has rendered them a necessary of life
> to the lowest order of men; but not to the same order of women, who
> may, without any discredit, walk about barefooted. In France they are nec-
> essaries neither to men nor to women, the lowest rank of both sexes
> appearing there publicly, without any discredit, sometimes in wooden
> shoes, and sometimes barefooted. Under necessaries, therefore, I com-

145

prehend not only those things which nature, but those things which the established rules of decency have rendered necessary to the lowest rank of people. All other things I call luxuries.

The location of this definition of relative poverty in the modern sense (not having a linen shirt in "the greater part of Europe") is especially interesting. Immediately following this definition, Smith argues that we cannot understand the effect of consumption taxes without first understanding the role of necessities versus luxuries:

As the wages of labour are everywhere regulated, partly by the demand for it, and partly by the average price of the necessary articles of subsistence, whatever raises this average price must necessarily raise those wages so that the labourer may still be able to purchase that quantity of those necessary articles which the state of the demand for labour, whether increasing, stationary, or declining, requires that he should have. A tax on those articles . . . must, therefore, occasion a rise in the wages of labour proportionable to this rise of price.

A fuller social theoretical base for such a notion was quite well developed by social scientists in the 1940s and 1950s, particularly by sociologists like Talcott Parsons and David Riesman and a few economists such as James Duesenberry. The latter argued that after some quite minimum income is reached, the impulses "to increase expenditure for one individual depend on the ratio of his expenditures to the expenditures of those with whom he associates" (Duesenberry 1949, 32).

This argument implies that poverty is essentially a matter of social standing or social class. Poverty in this view is a persistent shortfall of resources that results in a person not being able to act out mainstream social roles. It leaves aside the issue of transitory poverty, which could conceivably strike people of any social class (although we would expect the working class to be most vulnerable to episodes of transitory poverty).

Sociologists have argued that social behavior is oriented to conceptions that people have of the so-called standard package of goods and services that obtains in a society at a given time (Riesman and Roseborough 1960). The standard package is the patterns of consumption characteristic of average members of the society—in social class terms, the stable working class and the lower middle class.

From this perspective, a social minimum is defined as "a certain minimum of possessions in order for the family to meet cultural definitions (as opposed to the mere legal definitions) of a family" (Parsons and Smelser 1956, 9). Thus, if a family's income is insufficient to supply the required minimum, we may well call them poor.

Nothing in this conception of poverty implies that the definition of poverty is merely subjective, or even that poverty is defined consensually. Rather, the argument is that objectively people cannot carry out the roles, participate in the activities, or maintain the social relations that are definitive of mainstream members of society if their resources (over some period of time) fall short of a "certain minimum." In such a situation, inadequacy of resources precipitates a lower-class style of life that is reactive to the inability to live the life identified with the standard package (Davis 1946; Rainwater 1974; Coleman, Rainwater, and McClelland 1978). This definition of poverty as a social phenomenon has been very well expressed by Peter Townsend (1979, 31) in his classic study of poverty in the United Kingdom:

> Poverty can be defined objectively and applied consistently only in terms of the concept of relative deprivation. . . . The term is understood objectively rather than subjectively. Individuals, families, and groups in the population can be said to be in poverty when they lack the resources to obtain the types of diet, participate in the activities and have the living conditions and the amenities which are customary, or are at least widely encouraged or approved, in the societies to which they belong. Their resources are so seriously below those commanded by the average individual or family that they are, in effect, excluded from ordinary living patterns, customs and activities.

Note that this conception of poverty makes central what is customary, encouraged, or approved for everyone. Poverty is the condition of being excluded from the life made possible by the customary level of consumption.

To say that poverty is a matter of relative deprivation is to raise the question: Relative to what? Relative deprivation is a concept in reference group theory—the deprivation is relative to the situation of a group of which the deprived person is a member. But we are all members of many different groups, some of which are merely statistical (all high school graduates) and some of which involve face-to-face relations with neighbors or coworkers. Townsend specifies the relevant reference group for poverty discussion as "the society to which they belong." In that group it is assumed that members share a conception of what is "customary, or at least widely encouraged or approved." Members cannot escape being evaluated in terms of whether they have the resources for such participation. In a highly stratified society no subgroup can openly set up and maintain standards that are different from those of the whole group. Efforts to do so bring forth repression and definitions of the alternative standards as deviant or immoral.

This objective reality of poverty standards is no secret from the members of a society. Those standards are part and parcel of its workings. Thus, members of society respond to others in terms of their perceived social standing and reinforce definitions of each other as poor or prosperous, average or just getting along. When people are asked to describe poverty, their statements fit well with the perspective outlined here. Survey respondents can give lively descriptions of different living levels—comfortable, just average, getting along, having a hard time, poor. And they see these types of socioeconomic situations as having the largest role in defining a person's social standing. Contrary to the view of many sociologists, income rather than occupation or education dominates the factors that people consider in determining their own and others' social standing, as is apparent in a summary of what survey respondents said about living in poverty:

> Poverty, people tell us, is not just not having things. It is also a social and psychological condition in which there are specific effects on how people feel about themselves (depressed, angry, miserable) and on how they behave (family problems, neighborhood conflict, crime). The difference between getting along and being poor is the difference between hard-pressed optimism and pessimism, between a good chance for things to get better and nothing ever changing. The person living in poverty is not the Middle American; he has passed over an invisible border. (Rainwater 1974, 135)

People who are not poor shy away from confronting poverty because they find the experience painful. More important, people who are poor try not to admit it to themselves, because the admission of "failure" adds to the misery they feel from their objective situation. Thus, in interviews poor, lower-class people are often able to characterize the situation of others like themselves in lively detail but often seek to distance themselves personally from that common plight (Coleman, Rainwater, and McClelland 1978).

The argument that relative poverty is objective is central. Otherwise, this approach to poverty could be seen as simply a question of "how people feel" and therefore seem somehow not real—at least to those who do not accept sociology's central tenet about social facts.

Such a definition of poverty is consistent with a large number of studies of low-income communities that find in one way or another that inability to participate in mainstream activities generates various kinds of social deprivations and disadvantages for those communities. These studies span more than half a century of the American sociological enterprise—from Allison Davis's (1946, 1948) Chicago studies of white and black slum cultures in the 1930s and 1940s to Elijah Anderson's *Code of the Street* (1999), a study of a black lower-class area in Philadelphia.

DISCOVERING THE OBJECTIVE SOCIETAL POVERTY LINE

Most governments use income standards to define those families who are objects of social concern because of inadequate consumption or, more usually, because their income is judged to be insufficient for subsistence. Such government standards can be thought of as *state poverty lines.* These poverty lines may be tacit or explicit. Explicit lines define poverty or low income as a condition—examples would be the U.S. "poverty line" or the Swedish "existence minimum." These lines are then used to determine eligibility for different social programs. Tacit poverty lines are determined by examining eligibility requirements for public assistance or other minimum-income programs—thus, we find supplementary benefits guarantees in the United Kingdom used as a poverty line.

But our interest here is in *societal poverty lines,* not state poverty lines. (For an argument on this point, see Sen 1981.) There is no necessary connection between the two. States' poverty lines are politically determined and may differ quite dramatically from the economic resources that define a person as poor in the ongoing life of a society. It is the latter objective condition that we wish to index. A more generous state will have a high state poverty line; a less generous one will have a low state poverty line. Where the explicit or tacit line is drawn will be a subject of political contention. But the experience of poverty, though affected by eligibility as defined by the state's rules, is independent of where the state draws the line.

The argument for a fully relative standard of poverty is qualitative (or at least not exclusively quantitative), based either on impressions from general observation and reading or, in modern social science, on qualitative studies of community life. The hypothesis that issues from these community studies is that what makes for poverty (or any other living standard category) changes as the economy grows or declines. We see this in the quote at the beginning of this chapter from Adam Smith in the eighteenth century, and we could cite many similar conclusions in the writing about poverty since. (See the history of poverty lines in Fisher 1993, 1995.)

To describe the poverty population, it is necessary to concretize the complex qualitative assessments of the situation of the poor with some readily measured characteristic—usually family income or family expenditures. But there is no unambiguous way to derive a poverty line from observation of the living conditions of a people. The choice would always be a simplification because in fact there is no hard and fast demarcation between adequacy and poverty. To speak of poverty is to characterize one aspect of the pattern of inequality in society. No sooner is a poverty line defined than writers find themselves needing to also deal with the condition of being not just poor but very poor, or not poor but just above the poverty level. The underlying reality we simplify for convenience is one of a continuum of misery or well-being, and to chase the real poverty line is to chase a will-o'-the-wisp.

That said, practical concerns lead us to count people who are probably poor by defining income levels that seem to characterize poverty. Based on an assessment of the qualitative writing about the poor and on general knowledge of their societies, experts have tended to focus on incomes around half of the median family income as the best choice for a single poverty line.

One way of establishing the level of the poverty line at a given time is to ask people at what income they believe poverty starts. A

Gallup Poll survey in the summer and fall of 1989 (O'Hare et al. 1990, v) asked a sample of Americans: "People who have income below a certain level can be considered poor. That level is called the 'poverty line.' What amount of weekly income would you use as a poverty line for a family of four (husband, wife, and two children) in this community?" The average response was around $15,017, which was 24 percent higher than the official 1988 poverty line of $12,092. This Gallup average was a little less than half of the median income of four-person families and a little more than half of the median equivalent income as defined in this book. If this question were asked periodically over several decades, we could discover the income elasticity of the poverty line. No such time-series study has been done, but we see in the following section that other survey questions have shed light on changing standards for economic marginality.

Sometimes researchers define the poverty line as a ratio of mean income rather than median. Which choice one makes reflects an underlying assumption about the influence of the incomes of the nonpoor on the definition of poverty. The poverty definition of the European Commission (1985) quoted in the introduction ("The poor shall be taken to mean persons, families and groups of persons whose resources [material, cultural, and societal] are so limited as to exclude them from the minimum acceptable way of life in the member state in which they live") would seem to focus on the mainstream for defining an "acceptable way of life," but the EU's operationalization of the poverty line was some ratio (40, 50, or 60 percent) of the mean consumption of families. The choice of the means tends to bias statistical results unnecessarily, we would argue, for the following reason.

Anchoring the poverty line in terms of the median is a way of focusing on mainstream incomes and taking them as a point of departure in defining poverty. The median represents the average person in the society, and we count income deficit from there. Using the mean income implies that all incomes, not just mainstream ones, must be taken equally into account, with a weight proportional to income amount. Given that income distributions are positively skewed, the choice of the mean implies that the societal poverty line is as much or more a function of the incomes of the rich as of those in the middle of the distribution. The practical consequence is that the more unequal the income distribution, the higher the poverty line and consequent poverty rate. For example, if we had used mean equivalent income to define the poverty lines of our fifteen countries, we would be finding that poverty rates in all countries are higher than the results described in previous chapters and that the differences are even greater between low-poverty countries like Sweden or Belgium and the United States at the high end. The median, in contrast, is not affected by the inequality of the distribution.

That choice serves well for defining poverty at a given time in a given country, but what about comparisons among countries or across time? Is it reasonable to assume a fully relative poverty line, or does the standard of what makes for poverty shift in relative terms over time? A common assumption of those who focus on consumption rather than social participation in defining poverty is that with economic growth the poverty line declines relative to the average person's standard of living, even though it increases in absolute terms. Our assumption is instead that the income elasticity of the poverty line is unitary. The contrary assumption is that the elasticity is something less than one—for example, around 0.8 (Citro and Michael 1995).

THE INCOME ELASTICITY
OF THE POVERTY LINE IN THE FIRST HALF
OF THE TWENTIETH CENTURY

We have emphasized the objective nature of poverty and its dependence on patterns of relationships, activities, and cultural images. But two kinds of additional evidence on how members define living levels in their societies come from the judgments of experts who have established minimum budgets based on their knowledge of consumption at a particular time and on public attitudinal measures concerned with income standards. Given the perspective developed thus far in the chapter, it should be clear that experts' judgment and attitudinal data are a shortcut to testing the ideas developed from more grounded community studies that shed light on living standards. The views of experts and survey respondents, then, are taken not as defining poverty but as indexes of the patterns of social behavior relevant to understanding the effects of low income. The views of the two groups are testimony to the cultural understandings about economic marginality that exist at a particular time.

To gain an understanding of what made for poverty before the advent of opinion surveys (to be discussed in the next section), we must rely on experts' definitions of poverty. Oscar Ornati and his colleagues (1966) published some sixty "quantity" budgets for a family of four developed by experts between 1900 and 1960. A quantity budget defines the amount of money required to provide a family with particular quantities of goods—food, clothing, housing, and so on. These budgets spelled out the incomes necessary for "health and decency," for "minimum adequacy," and for "minimum subsistence." The last two categories were designed to mark the dividing line between poverty and nonpoverty. The "minimum adequacy" budgets defined a standard somewhat greater than poverty, but not by a lot.

These budgets served as tools for social agencies in their consideration of whether supplicants actually "needed" income support (minimum subsistence) or free services (minimum adequacy). Ornati (1966, 8) notes that the governmental and charitable organizations that prepared these budgets were "interested in establishing living standards for a particular time only." Since each budget was prepared based on what poverty meant at that particular time, examining how the amounts changed over time provides a good test for locating the income elasticity of the poverty line. Ornati found that

> budget makers customarily base their budgets on (1) what people "ought" to buy and (2) what they actually *do* buy. . . . Clearly there is considerable circularity in these computations. . . . Income largely determines choice; choice determines alleged needs. . . . The criterion to a large extent is "What is a person at this income level accustomed to?" The budget is worked out in terms of what the available money will buy. Thus, standards particularize customary expenditure.

A similar conclusion concerning the inherent circularity of the quantity budget method is found in the report *New American Family*

Budget Statistics (Expert Committee on Family Budget Revisions 1980; see also Watts 1980).

It would seem that the budget makers know unconsciously the approximate location of the poverty line when they start on a budget; their budget making merely concretizes and tests that conception (see also Applebaum 1977). Through an iterative process, they arrive at an amount that seems right. If in setting their tacit target they were guided by their understanding of consumption at that particular time, we would expect a fairly high income elasticity over time. But if they believed that economic growth would reduce the relative income needed to escape poverty or near-poverty, that elasticity would be lower. On the other hand, if they assumed that growth would do nothing to reduce the relative resources needed to escape from poverty, then the elasticity would be one.

Ornati's results strongly suggest a nearly unitary elasticity of the experts' poverty lines. We can estimate the income elasticity by selecting the nine budgets for minimum subsistence and the thirteen budgets for minimum adequacy for the years in which they were first developed. (The rest of the budgets in Ornati's tables are interpolated from these.) They cover the period 1907 to 1963 (the latter date being the first year of the official U.S. poverty line). We have no data on median family income for the years before 1947, so we rely on per capita disposable income. We calculate the budget amount as a percentage of per family (that is, four times per capita) disposable income. We regress this amount on (1) the year, (2) a dummy variable that equals one for adequacy budgets and zero for subsistence budgets, and (3) a dummy variable for the war years (1917, 1918, 1942, and 1945).

Considering the vagaries of the budget-making process and the unknown degree of comparability of the national accounts income estimates over time, the 0.786 coefficient of determination for this regression is quite high. The coefficient of year should be zero if the income elasticity of the lines is exactly one—in fact it is −0.001, which indicates that we should expect the lines to decline by 0.1 percent a year in relation to per family disposable income. This translates to a decrease for the subsistence budget from 41 percent before World War I to 39 percent by 1963, and of the adequacy budget from 59 percent to 57 percent.

THE INCOME ELASTICITY
OF THE POVERTY LINE SINCE WORLD WAR II

As we have just seen, there is highly suggestive evidence to support the hypothesis that the minimum subsistence budgets increased proportionately with increases in per capita national income in the first half of the twentieth century. More recently, researchers have turned to public opinion polling questions about the amount of money that respondents associate with particular living standards.

For forty-five years (1946 to 1989, and again in 1992) the Gallup Poll asked respondents a question about how much income was necessary to "get along": "What is the smallest amount of money a family of four (husband, wife, and two children) needs each week to get along in this community?" (Citro and Michael 1995, 137). Beginning in 1978, a second question was asked about the smallest amount of money the respondent's own family needed. The answers have sometimes been used to define a poverty line (Goedhart et al. 1977), but in fact the level of living tapped by this question is somewhat higher than the established poverty line (Rainwater 1974).

Four surveys have asked questions that allow us to link the average answers concerning how much income is necessary to get along with average answers concerning how much income is necessary simply to escape poverty. These include surveys in Boston in 1971 and in Kansas City in 1972 (Rainwater 1974), a survey in Boston in 1983 (Dubnoff 1985), and the 1989 national Gallup survey referred to earlier (O'Hare et al. 1990). These surveys provide the following estimates of the ratio of the poverty line to the get-along amount: 63.9 percent (1971), 63.2 percent (1972), 55.9 percent (1983), and 71.8 percent (1989). For these four surveys, the average poverty line is 64 percent of the get-along amount.

We would be justified in concluding that over this period of almost twenty years the public carried around in its head an income map in which the incomes of the poor were somewhat less than two-thirds of the amount necessary to get along. Since we know the historical relationship of the get-along amount to mean household income (as discussed later), we can conclude that over this period of time a poverty line would have amounted to between 45 and 50 percent of median family income. Patricia Ruggles (1990) observes that in 1963 the poverty line arrived at by Orshansky was about half of median family income. The results here would suggest that the Orshansky choice was not too far off from the amount that the average member of society would have chosen at that time.

It was the logic of an absolute poverty line that caused the official poverty line to diverge further and further from society's poverty line. By the late 1980s the official poverty count was missing more than 12 million people whom the public would have called poor—the official poverty rate was 13 percent while the public's poverty line defined 18 percent of all Americans as poor (O'Hare et al. 1990). Gordon Fisher (1992) provides a rich historical analysis of failed efforts by government statisticians to increase the poverty line as median incomes rose.[1] Their efforts were to no avail against the overwhelming resistance of political executives.

Since the amount deemed necessary to get along in Gallup surveys is significantly below the average level of living in U.S. society, it would seem reasonable to conclude that the income elasticity of this get-along amount may be a good estimate of the income elasticity of the poverty line. Two early studies (Kilpatrick 1973; Levenson 1978) claimed to have established an income elasticity of the get-along amount of less than one. These analyses would imply that people's perceptions of how much income is necessary to get along increases more slowly than median incomes. These studies, however, were based on only a few years of the Gallup question. Now that it is possible to analyze the full range through 1992, we can come to a firmer conclusion.

The hypothesis we wish to test is that the get-along amount is a constant proportion of mainstream income. As mainstream income rises, the average get-along response will rise by an equal proportion. This is the meaning of unitary income elasticity. The simplest test of the hypothesis is to determine whether the get-along average is a constant percentage of median income or, as others have argued, a declining proportion.

A number of choices are available for an index of mainstream income. Denton Vaughan (1993) uses the median income of families of four. On theoretical grounds, we prefer a measure that is less influenced by changes in family types over time, so we have tested the hypothesis using the median income of all families (including single-person families) from the Consumer Income Series of the U.S. Bureau of the Census and per couple personal consumption expenditures (that is, twice per adult expenditures) from the U.S. National Accounts. For the latter two measures, we adjusted the income measure to represent the month of the Gallup survey by linear interpolation across the years, assuming the census amount represented the middle of the year.

The results from these three different ways of calculating the size of the get-along amount in relation to mainstream income turn out to be identical. We find that for the late 1940s to around 1990, the get-along average as a percentage of the median income of four-person families, as a percentage of median income of all-person families, and as a percentage of per couple consumption expenditure is the same: 72 percent.

Inspection of the time series for all three calculations shows a sharp decline in the relative get-along amount during the early 1960s and a flattening out from 1963 on. To test this perception, we regressed the get-along percentages (and the natural logarithm thereof) in Vaughan's analysis and for our median-income-of-all-families measure on three variables: YEAR (ranging from sixteen for 1947 through zero for 1963, to twenty-nine for 1992), AFTER62 (zero through 1963, then one to twenty-nine for 1964, through 1992), and LATE (a dummy variable for the period from 1963 on).

If there were absolutely no change over time in the get-along percentage, then all three of these variables would be zero and the constant would equal the average get-along percentage. If the income elasticity were less than one for the whole period, then the coefficient for YEAR would indicate the rate of decline of the get-along percentage, and the other two variables would be zero. In fact, we have a mixed case, as is shown in table 9.1.

It is apparent that the results are very similar whether we use our all-family median or Vaughan's family-of-four median to represent mainstream income. The year variable indicates a decline over the whole period in the get-along percentage, but the dummy variable for the period after 1962 produces a compensating increase in the percentage for those years. The dummy variable tells us that the percentage in the later period averages seven or

TABLE 9.1 **Regression of Get-Along Percentage by Year Among Gallup Respondents, 1947 to 1992**

	Get-Along Percentage		Ln Get-Along Percentage	
Variable	All-Family Median	Family-of-Four Median	All-Family Median	Family-of-Four Median
(Constant)	75.769%	78.284%	4.328%	4.359%
YEAR	−0.367	0.025	−0.004	0.000
AFTER 62	0.349	−0.073	0.004	−0.001
LATE	−7.102	−8.58	−0.099	−0.116
Adjusted R-squared	0.765	0.638	0.777	0.632

Source: Authors' calculations, using data from Gallup surveys for 1947 to 1986, and Vaughan (1993).

eight percentage points less than in the earlier period. The regressions with the logged percentage tell the same story.

The most plausible interpretation of these results is that the get-along percentage is constant, but that something happened in the 1961 to 1963 period in the way people thought about choosing a get-along amount or (much more likely) in the way the Gallup surveys were conducted. Since that change, the get-along amount has varied randomly around an average just under 70 percent of mainstream income. Figure 9.1 charts the get-along percentage since 1963 derived in three different ways: the two total sample percentages using our median and Vaughan's median and the percentages for persons who are themselves in a family of four. Note that respondents who are themselves in a family of four give responses very similar to those of the whole sample (more on this later).

It is interesting to compare our results with those of Peter Saunders and Bruce Bradbury (1989), the one comparable study. In their Australian study, they too found unitary elasticity of aggregate income measures (per capita disposable income and per capita consumption expenditures). However, their question was different. These researchers asked respondents what amount was needed to "keep in health and live decently." This question echoes a U.S. Gallup Poll question that has not been asked since 1963 (Rainwater 1974, 50–52). That year Gallup asked both questions; the "health and comfort" mean was about one-third greater than the get-along mean, or roughly equal to per couple consumption. Saunders and Bradbury

FIGURE 9.1 **Get-Along Income as a Percentage of Mainstream Income, 1963 to 1992**

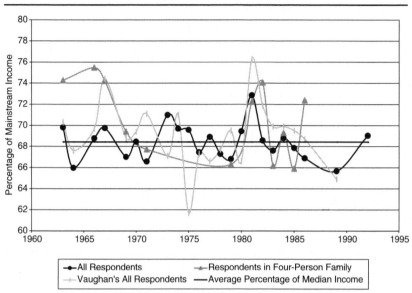

Source: Authors' calculations, using data from U.S. Census Bureau (various years), *Consumer Income Reports;* U.S. Department of Commerce, Bureau of Economic Analysis (various years), *National Economic Accounts;* Gallup Poll survey results reported in Citro and Michael (1995), O'Hare et al. (1990), and Rainwater (1997); and Vaughan (1993).

used per capita (rather than per adult) consumption expenditures and household income as their aggregate income variables, so it is hard to compare their percentage with those given here. They found that on average the health and decency amount was 1.786 times per capita consumption. This might translate into an average of around 1.2 times per couple consumption as defined here.

HOW MUCH CONSENSUS?

Because the sociological argument for a social standard of poverty requires that there be a high degree of consensus in society about relative living levels, we need to examine the extent to which people's judgments about the get-along amount vary systematically by social category. We looked at the effects of age, family size, and income on people's responses to the get-along question.

Although we might have expected that respondents in a family of four would have different views from those in other families, figure 9.1 indicates that this is not so. On average, the get-along amount is 70.6 percent of mainstream family income for the former compared with 68.4 percent for the total sample (for the twelve years beginning in 1962 in which we can identify families of four). More generally, we do not find very much variation by age or family size in conceptions of how much a family of four needs. Table 9.2 shows the average variations for the surveys between 1951 and 1986 for which we have the microdata.

In general, the pattern of differences is not stable from one survey to the next. With respect to age, we find that persons fifty-five and over seem to think that the two-parent, two-child family needs less than do younger respondents. But up to that age there are very small average differences. The variations by family size are also quite small. For both age and size, it is possible that the differences we find are a function of differences in income rather than age and size.

TABLE 9.2 **Deviation of Mean Get-Along Amounts in Selected Surveys 1951 to 1986, by Age and Family Size**

	Deviation of Mean Get-Along Amount
Age	
Younger than twenty-five	−3.9
Twenty-five to thirty-four	−1.4
Thirty-five to forty-four	0.0
Forty-five to fifty-four	−3.4
Fifty-five to sixty-four	−7.8
Sixty-five and older	−13.8
Family size	
One	−4.5
Two	−3.2
Three	−2.5
Four	0.0
Five	−1.6
Six	0.7
Seven or more	−6.2

Source: Authors' calculations, using data from Gallup surveys.

To assess the role of respondents' family income, we have data for fourteen surveys beginning in 1962. We estimate the impact of family income on response to the get-along question by regressing the (ln) get-along response on (ln) family income. Table 9.3 presents the regression results for each year. On average the family income elasticity (b) of the get-along amount is 0.157, and the average coefficient of determination is 0.073. This indicates that respondents' answers vary systematically with income but that the effect is small; income is very weakly correlated with people's answers. The regression implies a point (YMIN) at which respondents' incomes just equal their responses. That point is equal to the regression constant divided by one minus the regression coefficient. On average, YMIN is 96.3 percent of the geometric mean of respondents' get-along amounts.

We can interpret this result as suggesting a rather high degree of consensus about perceived living levels in society. Even higher-income people do not exaggerate very much the needed income of the family specified by the Gallup question. The same conclusion can be drawn from two studies that ask about a wider range of living levels from poor to rich (Rainwater 1974; Dubnoff 1985).

TABLE 9.3 Loglinear Regression of Family-of-Four Get-Along Amount on Family Income, 1962 to 1986

Year	Coefficient	Constant	Adjusted R-squared	Mean Need	Ln(YMIN)
1962	0.184	6.735	0.086	8.297	8.252
1963	0.142	7.107	0.066	8.309	8.28
1966	0.182	6.846	0.072	8.433	8.366
1967	0.177	7.011	0.088	8.565	8.523
1969	0.154	7.259	0.083	8.626	8.585
1971	0.156	7.352	0.064	8.757	8.705
1978	0.141	7.925	0.055	9.254	9.222
1979	0.171	7.711	0.072	9.339	9.305
1981	0.148	8.126	0.061	9.557	9.538
1982	0.125	8.355	0.049	9.569	9.549
1983	0.123	8.414	0.045	9.612	9.591
1984	0.171	7.981	0.097	9.669	9.629
1985	0.175	7.971	0.089	9.711	9.665
1986	0.147	8.282	0.085	9.754	9.711

Source: Authors' calculations, using data from Gallup surveys.

This result implies that, in judging their own family's well-being, people are more strongly influenced by their own incomes. But interestingly enough, we find that YMIN is about the same whether we examine the influence of respondents' own income on their judgment of how much the family of four needs or its influence on their judgment of how much their own family needs to get along.

DEGREES OF POVERTY

Our language is rich with words to capture the quality of life associated with different amounts of economic resources. We say that someone is not only "very rich" but perhaps even "stinking rich." And we qualify degrees of being poor, from "a little poor" to "dirt poor."

It can be difficult to move from these qualitative characterizations to quantitative measures of economic well-being. As discussed at the beginning of this chapter, researchers simplify by defining a poverty line and counting the people below it. Or they make more elaborate tables showing the percentage of people below 40 percent, below 50 percent, or below 60 percent of median income. We have not moved beyond this kind of measure in this book because we want our findings to be readily understood. Any more encompassing measure would be quite a bit more complicated to relate to the real world. It is worth discussing here, however, how we might move toward such a fuller index of the degree of economic deprivation in a society.

We would like to develop a measure that weights how many people are economically deprived with how deprived they are. To do that, we need to know how society evaluates different levels of income deprivation. But our methods for measuring quantitatively how people evaluate the social circumstances of people at different income levels are poorly developed, despite our considerable knowledge about how they go about using these evaluations in daily life (Coleman, Rainwater, and McClelland 1978).

One way to capture the distribution along the qualitative continuum of poor to rich is to use summary measures of income distribution. The literature on models of inequality has been particularly lively for some years now (see, for example, Atkinson

1970; Sen 1973; Cowell 1978). Those whose particular interest is in social policy have adapted inequality analysis to studying in finer detail the distribution of income below a poverty line—or more broadly, below the median (see, for example, Hagenaars 1991; Cowell 1988; Atkinson, Rainwater, and Smeeding 1995).

With respect to poverty, this literature seems to arrive at a consensus as to the kinds of measures we need to describe aggregate poverty in a society:

The proportion of the population below a poverty line: This is the so-called headcount ratio (H). It is this measure that we have adopted in parts 1 and 2 of this book.

The average poverty gap (I): This is the difference between a poor person's income and the poverty line. It can be summed to the aggregate poverty gap to describe the transfer of income to the poor required to eradicate poverty. We occasionally make use of this measure in parts 1 and 2.

The inequality among the poor: Any one of a number of measures designed to summarize the distribution of incomes of the poor (for example, gini coefficient, Atkinson index).

Some of the latter measures take into account inequality aversion—the degree to which lower incomes should be weighted more heavily in summarizing the distribution. Inequality aversion is an index of how much loss of aggregate income could be tolerated to have a more equal distribution. But inequality aversion is thought to characterize either a detached observer of social welfare or a policymaker. It does not seek to capture the social meanings associated with particular levels of income.

However, the mathematics of these measures may summarize social misery as well as an observer's inequality aversion. This can be illustrated with data from a small pilot study some years ago that sought to measure people's sense of the magnitudes of poverty associated with different incomes (Rainwater 1974, 147–58). The study sought to develop a measure to be used in a poverty index that would take into account the fact that "poverty becomes more severe at an increasing rate as successive decrements of income are considered" (Watts 1969, 326).

Respondents were asked to indicate whether they considered families described in terms of given income and family size to be poor or not. If they considered the family at least somewhat poor, they were then asked how poor they considered the family to be on a ratio scale compared with a family of five with an income of $2,400 a year. The average responses of the sample can be represented quite well as a function of the income deficit (D) of the family. D is defined as the ratio of median equivalent income minus the equivalent income of the stimulus family to median equivalent income. Poorness (P) is estimated using the following loglinear equation: $P = a + bD$. The coefficient of determination in this small pilot study was over 0.99, and the parameter b was 3, indicating that poorness increases very rapidly as income deficit rises.

Obviously, a small pilot study carried out in one city at one time cannot establish the parameter determining the relationship between income and degree of poorness as a social and psychological experience. But the results are highly suggestive. Poorness increases in proportion to at least the cube of the equivalent income deficit, implying that a person who has twice the deficit of another person is thereby eight times poorer. In short, absolute increases in poverty are larger and larger the lower the income—as envisioned in Harold Watts's formulation, which in turn fits well with common sense and popular usage. (See also the discussion of "images of Lower America" in Coleman, Rainwater, and McClelland 1978, 190–209.)

Aggregating poorness, then, could be a central measure of poverty, along with headcount and poverty gap measures. Simplifying our deficit measure, let us say that $P = 0$ for those with incomes at the median or above and for those with incomes below the median $P = [(m - y)/m]^a$, with m referring to median equivalent income and y to a given family's equivalent income. Poorness ranges from one with zero income to zero at the median. The exponent a is conservatively assumed to be 3 until empirical work modifies that assumption. (Obviously, it could differ from country to country. For example, in a country with a broader range of public services, we might find that poorness increases less sharply with income deficit than in one with fewer public services.) The advantage of this kind of measure is that it is additively decomposable both by income level and by demographic group (for an example, see Cowell 1984).

This measure can be aggregated by calculating the mean of P. This is the poverty index proposed by James Foster, Joel Greer, and Erik Thorbecke (1984), with one modification. In their formulation, m is the poverty line; here it is median equivalent income. Calculating deficit from the median obviates the necessity to define a poverty line and takes into account the public opinion that people are somewhat deprived at levels above the poverty line.

If we calculate the aggregate poorness of children in our fifteen countries and compare it with the child poverty rates of figure 1.1, we find the two highly correlated at 0.98. This suggests that although there are theoretical attractions to having a deeper measure of poverty than simply the headcount ratio, we would not in fact have a different impression of the range of poverty across these fifteen countries with any other measure.

Thus, while a poorness measure avoids the roughness and false specificity of a poverty line and emphasizes instead the salience of the degree of inequality below the median as the driving force in social exclusion in these countries, a poorness measure does not seem to add useful information. Given the accessibility of a poverty rate based on a poverty line at half of the median, it seems prudent to keep things simple. Also, analysis of the categories of extreme poverty and near-poverty can yield some of the information buried in an overall poorness measure.

CONCLUSION

We have reviewed the theoretical considerations and empirical evidence that support the following assumptions that have guided our choices concerning a poverty line. On balance, we have seen that there is strong support for these assumptions. In the next chapter, we take up the evidence for the way we have adjusted family income to take account of differences in family composition.

1. In rich countries poverty is a meaningful concept only if it is defined in terms of material deprivation that leads to inability to participate meaningfully in the social and cultural activities that constitute mainstream life in the society.

2. Poverty is relative to the mainstream life of the society, and the standard of poverty rises proportionately with the standard of living of average persons.

3. For cross-national studies, these considerations imply that the poverty standard must be defined for each country in relation to its mainstream standard of living, not by the poverty standard of some other nation.

— Chapter 10 —

Establishing Equivalent Family Income

IN THIS CHAPTER, we discuss the choices that must be made in order to adjust incomes for differences in family composition. Efforts to measure economic well-being require some adjustment of income to take account of need. How this is done can make a very great difference in whom we call poor and whom not poor, as well as in the proportion of people who are defined as poor. In the case of child poverty, different adjustments can alter the rate by as much as 50 percent for all children, and for children in larger families they can increase or decrease the poverty rate by a factor of four. It is unfortunate, therefore, that in much poverty research so little attention is given to choosing a measure of variation in need by family composition.

Equivalence scales are designed to take account of need by adjusting for those family characteristics deemed to affect need. We can choose to adjust for factors such as family size, age of adults, or age of children. Most commonly, we take account only of the size of the family. The most primitive and long-standing adjustment is simply to divide family income by the number of persons and use per capita income as the measure of economic well-being. But such an adjustment ignores economies of scale in household consumption related to size and also ignores other differences in need among household members. In this chapter, we consider evidence for establishing an equivalence scale that does take into account economies of scale as a function of size. In addition, we show that there is good reason to consider variation in need by the age of the family head. People perceive need as varying by both the number of family members and the age of the head.

167

After examining the evidence for the equivalence scale used in this study, we consider the sensitivity of the measure of poverty to the scale chosen. The specific formulas used by various social scientists and government experts to establish need are quite varied. A scale can be simple—for example, 1.0 for the first adult, 0.7 for other adults, and 0.5 for children. Or it can be quite elaborate, with different weights depending on the ages of adults and children as well as their number. Despite their complexity, the equivalence scales proposed by experts can be quite well represented by a single parameter—the family size elasticity of need.

Therefore, we can explore various approaches to defining equivalent income (Y) by defining it as equal to disposable income (D) divided by family size (S) raised by some equivalence elasticity (e):

$$Y = D/S^e \tag{10.1}$$

The equivalence elasticity can vary from zero for disposable income unadjusted for family size to one for per capita income. In between, an e of increasing size denotes diminishing economies of scale. Many equivalence scales are expressed simply as ratios to the need of one person. However complex the scale, it can be very closely approximated by equation 10.1. Doing so makes it more straightforward to compare scales since we need only to compare the e factor. It is the case that almost all known equivalence scales (even ones that depend on age of child as well as family size) have correlations close to one with a scale based on equation 10.1 (Buhmann et al. 1988).

WHAT IS EQUIVALENT WELL-BEING?

What we wish to establish in using the social definition of economic well-being outlined in the previous chapters are possibilities for equivalent social participation. From the perspective of economics, equivalence scales are designed to establish equivalent consumption. From a social perspective, however, need and equivalence are issues of the resources required for social participation. What must be established is the relation between family characteristics (size, age) and opportunities for gratifying social participation. An equivalence scale should represent the net of additional consumption required by an additional family member *and* the gain to the family's lifestyle contributed by that additional member.

Establishing socially relevant definitions of economic well-being should proceed by asking the real experts—that is, the members of society—through the use of survey questionnaires. In one approach, people are asked to report their expenditures and then an equivalence scale is derived from the analysis of how expenditures vary by family size. In the other approach, people are asked to report income levels that match some specified level of living. It is the latter approach on which we rely because it seems to take into account both the perceived cost of having a family of a given size and age and the compensating benefits. These benefits are primarily personal and social and therefore are not measured by an approach that considers only consumption expenditures.

FAMILY SIZE, AGE, AND SOCIAL EQUIVALENCE

Several studies have sought to establish levels of living as defined by the public. As noted in chapter 9, for forty-five years the Gallup Poll asked a question about how much income was necessary for a family of four to get along. A question only about a family of four will not take us very far in this effort to choose an equivalence scale, but it does provide some suggestive evidence. Fortunately, this approach has been extended in some studies with other questions that allow a more direct assessment of socially relevant standards of equivalence.

A negative finding from the analysis of the Gallup question about how a family of four gets along suggests consensus about how much the family of four needs regardless of the respondent's own situation. We might expect that respondents in families of four would have different views from those in other families. This turns out not to be the case. Over the forty-five-year period covered by the "get-along" question, the average response of those in four-person families differed from the average for the total sample by only 1 percent.

As noted earlier, a wide range of equivalence scales are used to establish well-being by adjusting income for need (Whiteford 1985; Buhmann et al. 1988; Bradbury 1989). Scales in use in various countries at various times have equivalence factors covering almost the whole range from zero to one. Our task is to select a power—an equivalence coefficient—that properly, even though very roughly, captures the extent to which socioeconomic need increases with family size.

Several efforts have been made to construct social equivalence scales from survey questions. There are two approaches. In the first approach, respondents are asked how much income they feel is necessary for families of different sizes to achieve a particular level of living—for example, getting along, being comfortable, being rich, or being poor (Rainwater 1974; Dubnoff 1985). The second approach analyzes responses to questions about respondents' own needs—in particular, how much their own family needs to get along. If we regress responses on income, family size, and age, we can determine the implicit equivalence scale that respondents are using.

Beginning in 1979, the Gallup data have allowed us to use a version of this minimum income question (MIQ), developed by Bernard van Praag, in what is sometimes called the Leyden approach to poverty measurement (Goedhart et al. 1977). Immediately after the question about how much a family of four needs to get along, the Gallup survey asks the question: "What is the smallest amount of money your family needs to get along in this community?"[1] We have analyzed seven surveys (1979 and 1981 to 1986) that include the MIQ question and have information on respondents' family income, size, and age of head.

Most of the interest in the MIQ question has centered on extracting family size equivalence from the answers. Before moving on to that matter, however, let us examine the effect of age on the answers. When age is taken into account in defining equivalence scales, it is usually with respect to either the ages of children or the differing needs of elderly and retired persons. For example, the equivalence scale implicit in the U.S. official poverty line is that to be equally well off persons sixty-five and over need 10 percent less income than those under sixty-five.[2]

AGE DESCRIBES A NEED TRIANGLE

Analysis of each of the seven surveys with all of the relevant information produces a highly consistent picture of economic need: it increases steadily with age to the early forties, then decreases steadily into old age. To demonstrate this relationship most clearly, heads of household were selected and the surveys were pooled for a multiple classification analysis to extract the coefficient for the effect of each single year of age on the get-along response controlling for income, family size, and year of survey. The get-along response, income, and size were logged; the year of survey and age were analyzed for the effects of each value.

Figure 10.1 charts the smoothed coefficients of each year of age. There is a lot of noise in the raw results, but smoothing shows the underlying relationship. The rates at which need increases to the apex in the early forties and then decreases are about the same. Controlling for family income and size, need increases about 0.8 percent a year to ages forty to forty-five, then decreases at the same rate to the late ages.

This result suggests that individuals' judgments about how much their families need to get along assume that living is cheaper for younger and older people than it is for those in midlife. Through the broad middle years the age factor in need does not make a lot of difference in the distribution of well-being, but at the extremes it has important effects.

We might wonder whether this age-of-head effect somehow masks an age-of-child effect. This is not the case. We analyzed separately the responses of heads in families with no children (and also analyzed separately heads with one, two, three, and four or more children). We found the same pattern of increasing need with age up to the forties, and then decreases, regardless of the presence or number of children in the family.

We have found one European survey (Rabier and Inglehart 2002) that asks the minimum income question and provides information on the amount needed by the respondent's family, family income, family size, and age of head. Unfortunately, responses to the minimum need question are categorized in the same broad income levels as is family income; as a consequence, the results of regression analysis are quite gross. Nevertheless, we found that the age-of-head effect was the same as in the U.S. Gallup surveys, although a little weaker. We did not distort results very much by using the U.S. results on age and need in our cross-national analysis.

FIGURE 10.1 **Effect of Age on Respondents' Own Family's Income Need in Seven Gallup Surveys, 1979, 1981 to 1986**

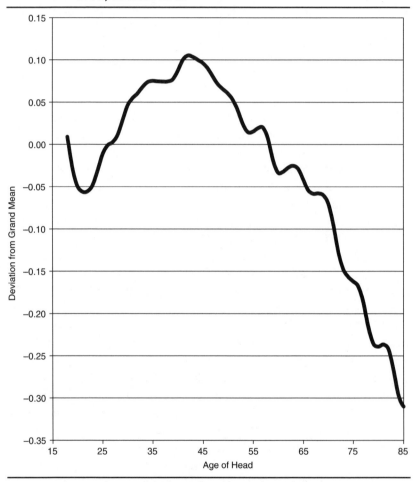

Source: Authors' calculations, using data from Gallup surveys.
Note: Single year of age coefficients (deviations from grand mean controlling for family income and size) have been smoothed by a compound data smoother.

CHILDREN ARE CHEAP

Responses to questions that tap social equivalence suggest that commonly used equivalence scales rather strongly exaggerate the amount of income needed by larger families compared with smaller ones. For example, the official U.S. poverty measure has an equivalence factor of 0.55. Several scales used in European countries are as high as 0.7. As we will see, a more socially oriented approach produces a much lower equivalence factor, suggesting much greater (social) economies of scale.

We can elaborate on the family-of-four get-along question by asking about different levels of living besides "getting along" and different family sizes. This approach yields a map of equivalence levels as perceived by the general public (Rainwater 1974; Dubnoff 1985). In Rainwater (1974), questions in the following form were asked about hypothetical families that were known as rich, prosperous, and substantial; comfortable; getting along; and poor: "Mr. and Mrs. Jones have four children and are generally considered rich. What is the lowest income they could have and still be considered rich?" Items varied the number of children from none to five children. All of the items specified two parents, so family size varied from two to seven.

To extract an equivalence scale from the responses to the matrix of six family sizes by five living levels, we regressed the responses on dummy variables for each family size and each living level. Then we tested for variation in equivalence scales at different living levels. Finally, we tested for the extent to which respondents' characteristics (income, family size, age) affect responses.

These analyses indicated that there were no important effects of respondents' characteristics on their responses—adding these variables to the regression equation increased the explained variance by only 1 percent compared with the 60 percent of variance explained by the stimulus variables of living level and size. Similarly, there seemed to be no systematic variation in equivalence scale from one living level to another—the deviations from a one-size-fits-all scale were not significant. A dummy variable analysis yielded the following equivalence scale for need as a function of family size:

Two adults, no children	1.00
Two adults, one child	1.12
Two adults, two children	1.26
Two adults, three children	1.30
Two adults, four children	1.40
Two adults, five children	1.49

We can also simplify the calculation of the implicit equivalence scale in these responses by regressing the log of the amounts that respondents gave to the question on the log of the family size and dummy variables for the living levels. This yields an equivalence factor of 0.311.

We checked the degree of stability of the implicit structure of these definitions of living levels and family size–based needs by predicting the average value of each item from a regression equation that excluded that item. Comparing these estimates with the actual averages, we found an average difference for the twenty-six items of 0.1 percent. In short, there seems to be a high degree of consensus on these matters despite a good deal of roughness in the estimates that people make.

To tease out the effect of family size on people's perception of their own family's well-being, we estimate the effect of age (A)—defined as the absolute difference between age forty-three and the respondent's age—and the logs of size (S*) and family income (Y*) on the logs of the (annualized) response to the get-along question (G*).

$$G^* = a + bY^* + cS^* + d\,|A - 43|\qquad\qquad(10.2)$$

The results of this regression for each of the seven Gallup surveys are shown in table 10.1.

TABLE 10.1 **Respondents' Own Family Get-Along Amount as a Function of Income, Family Size, and Age (Loglinear Regression)**

		Equivalence Elasticities					
Year	Adjusted R-Squared	Income	Size	|Age-43|	Constant	Size	|Age-43|
1979	0.406	0.385	0.257	−0.009	5.338	0.418	−0.015
1981	0.318	0.296	0.262	−0.007	6.353	0.372	−0.011
1982	0.271	0.282	0.226	−0.008	6.529	0.315	−0.012
1983	0.272	0.271	0.211	−0.009	6.697	0.289	−0.012
1984	0.311	0.307	0.168	−0.012	6.492	0.243	−0.017
1985	0.342	0.372	0.243	−0.001	5.628	0.387	−0.001
1986	0.335	0.286	0.186	−0.01	6.686	0.26	−0.014
Mean	0.322	0.314	0.222	−0.008	—	0.326	−0.012

Source: Authors' calculations, using data from Gallup surveys.

The regression implies a point (YMIN) at which respondents' incomes just equal their responses when family size is one and A − 43 equals zero. The loglinear specification is:

$$YMIN^* = a \mid (1 - b) \tag{10.3}$$

The adjusted coefficients of determination are much larger for the regression of the response for the respondent's own family than the responses for a family of four. The coefficient of determination is almost four times higher for judging the respondent's own situation—on average 0.322 compared with 0.084. (Size and age make little difference in judging the family of four; for the most part the coefficients are not significant.) The own-family income coefficient indicates that doubling family income increases the get-along amount by about one-quarter.

Comparing YMIN for a family of four for the two get-along questions indicates that the average difference between the two over the seven survey years was only 2 percent. In short, regressions for both a family of four and the respondent's own family yield the same estimated YMIN.

The coefficient for family size averages .222 and that for age −0.008. To calculate the implicit family size and age equivalence scale, we need to adjust each size and age coefficient for the effect of income by dividing it by (1 − b), as in equation 10.3. This tells us the effect of size and age on any particular level of needed income—for example, YMIN.

With this adjustment, the equivalence elasticity for family size averages 0.33 and that for age −0.012. The coefficients vary quite a bit, but with no particular pattern over this seven-year period. It would be difficult to invent a theory that would entail changes in equivalence from year to year with no particular trend.

To simplify, we can say that need increases in proportion to the cube root of family size. Need decreases by about 1 percent for each year's difference between a person's age and age forty-three. An individual in his or her early twenties needs about 80 percent as much as a forty-three-year-old; an individual in his or her late sixties needs about three-quarters as much.

For family size, need increases by the following ratios compared with a one-person family:

Two persons	1.26
Three persons	1.44
Four persons	1.59
Five persons	1.71
Six persons	1.82
Seven persons	1.93

The hypothesis that there is an interaction between income level and equivalence is a plausible complication of this simple equivalence scale. We might expect that at higher and higher levels of income, adjustments for family size would need to be progressively smaller to confer equal well-being. We did not find this effect in the seven Gallup surveys we analyzed, nor was it apparent in the questions about living levels from poor to rich discussed earlier. To test for the interaction, we divided the sample into three income groups: a low-income group with 28.7 percent of the cases; a middle-income group with 37.7 percent of the cases; and a high-income group with 33.7 percent of the cases. (A neat division into low, middle, and high thirds was not possible because Gallup categorizes the income variable.) The surveys were pooled after adjusting for changing mean income over the 1979 to 1986 time period. The coefficients for each group are listed in table 10.2.

It is apparent that the size coefficient of the low-income group is larger than for the other two groups. However, when the coefficients are adjusted by the income coefficient $(1 - b)$, the size elasticities are 0.30, 0.35, and 0.29, respectively, and the age elasticities are −0.011, −0.010, and −0.012, respectively.

Thus, the conceptions of need implicit in the regression relations do not seem to differ systematically by level of income of the respondents. It is, of course, always possible that more refined techniques would reveal the expected larger impact of size on need at low levels of income compared with higher levels.[3]

TABLE 10.2 Regression Coefficients by Income Level of Respondent

	Income	Size	Age
Low-income	0.171	0.248	−0.009
Middle-income	0.426	0.202	−0.006
High-income	0.330	0.196	−0.008

Source: Authors' calculations, using data from Gallup surveys.

We have reviewed the results of the two different approaches to establishing social equivalence—evaluations of others' situation and of respondents' own situation—and find that they yield essentially the same size equivalence scale, which we simplify to the cube root of family size. Figure 10.2 charts the implicit scales we have found expressed as both dummy variable coefficients and the equivalence factor as a power of family size. We can observe how very close the lines are. Both the judgment of others' situation and of one's own indicate that there is very little difference perceived between the needs of a family with two children and those of a family with three children. Overall, an equivalence factor of the cube root of size fits very well.

We do not have to rely only on these surveys for estimates of size equivalence. Numerous investigators have used this approach to determine how people perceive need as a function of size. Two basic approaches have been taken. The minimum income question (MIQ) approach exemplified by the Gallup question about what one's own family needs has been used in other surveys in a wide range of countries. A variant, the income evaluation question (IEQ), asks respondents to indicate incomes with which they would be dissatisfied, satisfied, or in between. Isolating the effect of family size on this set of answers yields an equivalence scale (Kapteyn and van Praag 1976).

Table 10.3 summarizes the range of responses to the various questions tapping conceptions of need. There is obviously considerable overlap between the United States and the European series. It will take more systematic research to determine whether there are important differences among countries in size equivalence. The only European country for which we have multiple measures (six) is the Netherlands, where the range is from 0.20 to 0.36 and the mean is 0.27. For our purposes, we have chosen 0.33 rather than a lower power as the more conservative choice, since most research using equivalence scales uses an even higher elasticity.

WHAT DIFFERENCE DO DIFFERENT
SCALES MAKE?

As noted, survey-based equivalence scales produce size elasticities much lower than the average of ones derived by other methods (Whiteford 1985; Buhmann et al. 1988; Bradbury 1989; Atkinson, Rainwater, and Smeeding 1995). We find particular

FIGURE 10.2 **Four Measures of Equivalence as Social Need**

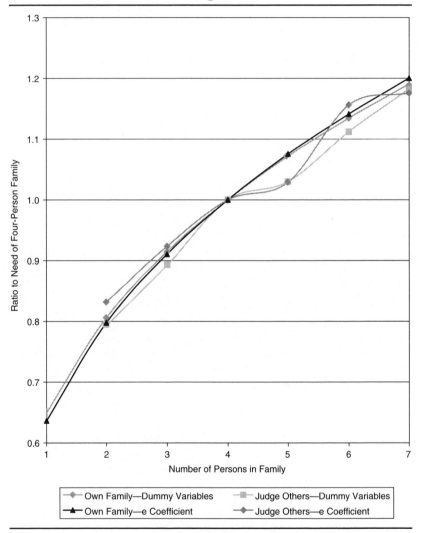

Source: Authors' calculations, using data from Gallup surveys.

scales covering almost the whole range of possible elasticities, from no adjustment for size to per capita adjustment. Scales based on minimum budget estimation and consumption theory average elasticities in the 0.45 to 0.55 range, while those based on the Engel method often run even higher, particularly if based mainly

TABLE 10.3 Size Elasticity in Thirty-Seven Surveys

Surveys	Size Elasticity	
	Range	Mean
U.S. Gallup surveys 1979 to 1986	.26 to .42	0.33
Fourteen other U.S. surveys	.19 to .43	0.33
Sixteen European surveys	.12 to .40	0.26

Source: Authors' calculations, using data from Gallup surveys and Rainwater (1994).

on food. But there is no simple way of accounting for differences among so-called objective scales—studies that seem to use the same methods on the same population often produce widely different results. (See particularly the review by Whiteford 1985.) It is possible to find objective scales within the range covered by the subjective ones. (Whiteford's list includes nine objective scales with elasticities below 0.4.) But a consensus budget-consumption theory scale in the range of 0.5 to 0.55 implies much larger increases in need with each additional family member than do the scales that tap social equivalence.

What might account for the difference? If we focus on the maintenance of particular kinds of lifestyles—as the product of combining goods, services, and the activities of family members—rather than on the maintenance of a particular level of material consumption, the lower elasticities elicited by a wide variety of different survey questions make sense. Expenditure-based scales tend to exaggerate need because an overly rigid pattern of consumption is assumed to be required to maintain economic well-being. Thus, Theo Goedhart and his colleagues (1977, 516), in discussing the fact that their results suggest much greater economies of scale than implied by consumption-based equivalence scales, argue that "our small estimates of the increase in needs reflect the fact that the preferences within the family shift in such a way that material needs do not increase very much. . . . In our opinion, substitution possibilities of this kind are not fully taken into account in current literature on the family equivalence scale."

From a more sociological point of view, it can be argued that equivalence scales should also take into account the contribution to the construction of the family's lifestyle of the participation of additional family members (Rainwater 1974; Bradbury 1989). That is, we want an equivalence scale that defines need in terms of the income necessary for the maintenance of a particular quality of lifestyle rather than the maintenance of a particular level of material consumption. For example, a young couple may prefer watching the antics of their newborn over going to a movie.

Given all of these considerations, it seems not unreasonable to take 0.33 as the ballpark estimate for size equivalence, following the sociological logic that has guided us in this analysis. Simplifying the regression results reviewed earlier, we have defined equivalent income (EI) in this study as:

$$EI = Y \mid (S^{.33*} .99^{|(A - 45)|})$$ (10.4)

That is, equivalent income is defined as disposable income (Y) divided by the product of (a) the cube root of family size and (b) .99 compounded by the number of years' difference between an individual's age and age forty-five. (To avoid too dramatic an age effect for the very young and old, we have arbitrarily limited the age multiplier to no less than 0.8.)

But what of other possible scales? How different would the results presented in part 1 have been if we had used an equivalence factor at one or another point on the scale from zero to one? The flexibility allowed us by the LIS database makes it possible to calculate inequality statistics for the fifteen nations of interest with any equivalence scale we might choose based on size and age of head. Here we present some comparisons of poverty rates based on our scale with results using family size equivalence factors incremented by 0.1 from zero to one.

It turns out that there is a characteristic shape to the relation of poverty rates to equivalence scales that applies in each of the fifteen countries, even though the level of poverty varies, as do the details of the shape, for all persons, elders, and children. Figure 10.3 presents the average rates across the fifteen countries at each point on the equivalence continuum. It is apparent that the poverty rate of the total population declines steadily from 15 percent at an equivalence factor of 0 and then flattens out at around 10 percent at an equivalence elasticity between 0.3 and 0.4. (The dip in poverty between the 0.3 and 0.4 elasticities is produced by our scale with an elasticity of .33 and an age adjustment.)

FIGURE 10.3 **Poverty Rates by Equivalence Factor, Average of Fifteen Nations**

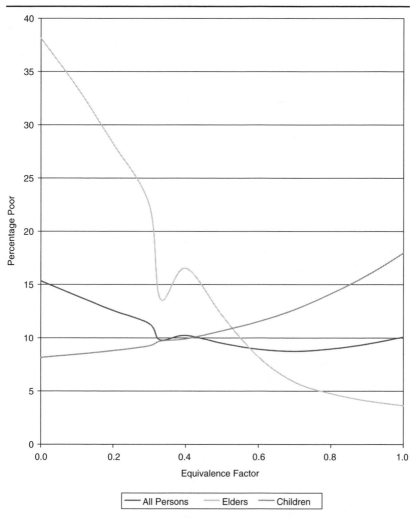

Source: Authors' calculations, using data from the Luxembourg Income Study.

The child poverty rate, on the contrary, increases with increasing elasticities. In general, the lower the poverty rate at low elasticities, the greater the increase. For example, for Sweden, Finland, and Belgium the child poverty rate triples, while for the United States, Italy, and Canada the increase is only about 75 percent.

The elderly poverty rate is much more sensitive to the equivalence factor used. It is much higher at low elasticities. It declines sharply from a high of almost 40 percent to below 10 percent in the region of e = 0.6, and it continues to decline at a lower rate to 5 percent at e = 0.8. While the age adjustment does not have much effect on the child poverty rate, it has a rather large effect on the elderly poverty rate that carries over to the total population rate.

But interestingly, the countries tend to keep their ranks across all equivalence elasticities. One finds six countries—Finland, Sweden, Norway, Belgium, Denmark, and the Netherlands—tracking each other at very low child poverty rates ranging upward from 5 percent at zero elasticity to 8 to 12 percent on a per capita basis. At the other extreme, the United States stands alone with the highest rates (19 to 33 percent), followed by the United Kingdom (15 to 31) and Italy (16 to 37) at slightly lower rates.

Of course, some children are poor under all the equivalence factors, and some are never poor or even economically marginal. Over 70 percent of children in all of the countries are either poor or have average income regardless of the equivalence scale used. Only around 20 percent of children are not always in one of three categories: average or above-average income, near-poor, or poor.

In short, we can say that with respect to ranks in child poverty across countries, different equivalence scales change things hardly at all. But different scales do affect our conception of the prevalence of poverty in any particular country. The higher the equivalence factor, particularly above 0.6, the higher the number of children who will be considered poor.

This is not the case, however, with children in single-mother families. These child poverty rates are high whatever the equivalence scale, and though the rates vary a bit as the scale changes, there is no overall tendency for the rates to increase significantly from low to high equivalence factors. Thus, it is principally the poverty rate of children in two-parent families that varies by equivalence factors.

Chapter 11

Whence the Poverty Standard—Nations or Communities?

IN PREVIOUS CHAPTERS, we have assumed that in defining mainstream and poverty standards, the relevant community is the nation as a whole. Thus, we have defined the poverty line as one-half of a nation's median equivalent income. But we have begged a question: What difference does it make for our understanding of poverty in a society if we focus not on the nation as a whole but on particular communities within the nation? In this chapter, we explore this question by considering possible variations in child poverty rates among the fifty states of the United States plus the District of Columbia. To provide a broader context for this discussion, we also use Luxembourg Income Study data to make comparisons with variations by regions in four other countries—Australia, Canada, Italy, and Spain.

DIFFERENCES IN FOCI OF POVERTY POLICIES

Studies of poverty, particularly comparative studies, almost always take the nation as their prime focus, certainly with respect to the definition of the poverty line but also often more broadly than that. This focus on the nation is very much taken for granted, and it is difficult to find thoroughgoing discussions of whether the nation is the appropriate unit for defining and then measuring the extent of poverty.

For example, while the definition of poverty adopted by the European Union in 1984 (see introduction) reflects a conception of poverty grounded in an understanding of the nature of social stratification in prosperous industrial societies, it adopts without discussion the nation as the unit for defining "limited resources," "exclusion," and "minimum acceptable way of life." Yet there could be important variations among different regions or communities within a country in how these characteristics of the standard of living are defined. Alternatively, the question of who is poor could move beyond national borders to encompass groups of nation-states on the continental level, such as the European Union broadly defined.

If the responsibility for fighting poverty lies at the national level, the nation seems to be the logical unit of poverty measurement, and antipoverty effectiveness can be judged on a national basis. However, there are important exceptions to this rule as they apply both to nations and to their subcomponents and supracomponents. Even as policy takes the nation as its focus, the reality of social exclusion may develop in different ways in different communities.

The recent devolution of the primary social assistance program in the United States, Temporary Assistance to Needy Families (TANF), to each of the fifty states marks a new era in federal-state relations. Increasingly, antipoverty policy has moved from the national level to the state level. Before 1996 a number of national programs had important interstate variations; different matching rates for federal support, different options for supplementation, and even differences in state administration have been part of the history of the U.S. safety net since 1935. Programs like Supplemental Security Income (SSI) and Medicaid have had significant interstate variations. However, the Personal Responsibility and Welfare Reform Act (PRWRA) of 1996 gave states wide latitude over the design, structure, and entitlement status of the former Aid to Families with Dependent Children (AFDC) programs (now called TANF). In fact, in turning AFDC into a capped state block grant, the act set a few overarching rules but otherwise gave the states full latitude to determine who should be entitled to what and for how long.

This devolution has produced a myriad set of state differences in efforts to move persons off welfare, to help low-income mothers and children, or to punish them (imposing sanctions, for example, for overstepping state-imposed rules). While the jury is still out regarding the successes and failures of welfare reform, there is considerable new interest in interstate differences in the poverty status of children and the antipoverty effect of policy in reducing (or increasing) child poverty. Think tanks and other groups (see, for example, Loprest 1999; Flores, Douglas, and Ellwood 1998) have begun to produce a number of studies of children's budgets and state-specific reports. Hence, there is a renewed policy interest in U.S. state estimates of child poverty.

Because states (provinces) also play a strong role in poverty alleviation in the Canadian and Australian nations, there is a similar interest in these countries. For instance, the Canadian "social union initiatives," a set of political agreements between Canada and its provinces, have taken the National Child Benefit program as its early test case for joint federal-provincial budgetary and programmatic support (Government of Canada 1999).

In contrast, as the European Union becomes a more important political entity, interest is growing in the effort to move beyond the nation-state and to develop measures of poverty for groups of nations. The European Community Household Panel (ECHP) project was begun to collect data on the lives, incomes, and conditions within the original thirteen EC member states. It has published reports on poverty and income distribution in these states using both "national" and "European" poverty lines (see, for example, Eurostat 1998). European-wide microsimulation models are being built to estimate the antipoverty effects of adopting different social programs across the EC (see, for example, Immervoll, Sutherland, and de Vos 2000).

THE IMPACT OF LOCAL VERSUS NATIONAL
FOCI ON RELATIVE AND ABSOLUTE
CONCEPTS OF POVERTY

Whether we take an absolute or relative approach to defining poverty affects how we think about this question of national versus subnational regions as the proper focus of that definition. With either approach, there are two possibilities in examining regional variations in poverty. First, there can be variations in poverty rates in different regions even when the standard for defining the poverty line is a national one. This kind of question is routinely dealt with in poverty studies in the United States but less frequently in European countries.

Second, there is also the possibility of variations in standards for defining poverty across the regions of a nation. With an absolute approach, a shift of focus from the national to the local level involves defining a market basket that is adjusted for local prices instead of the more common practice of applying the market basket and national prices across the whole country. The content of the market basket would stay the same; only the cost would vary by regions. This is the kind of recommendation made by the United States National Academy of Sciences in its recent report—that we adjust national poverty lines to account for differences in regional housing costs (Citro and Michael 1995).

With a relative standard, there is the more consequential choice of substituting a local relative standard for the national one. This is the approach that we take in this book. In previous studies using the Luxembourg Income Study, the poverty line has been defined as one-half of the national median equivalent income.[1] Shifting to an approach that takes regional standards seriously, we would define the poverty line as one-half of the median equivalent income in the local area, however that local area is defined. We believe that this approach brings the definition of a poverty line closer to the social reality of the lives of the people being studied in that it approximates much better, although not perfectly, the community standards for social activities and participation that define persons as being of "average" social standing or of "below average" or "poor" social standing (Rainwater 1991, 1992).

A conception of poverty based on an absolute standard is not as likely to make this shift to local standards as well as local prices. Conceivably, a researcher could choose to define market baskets that take into account differences in consumption in different regions, but as far as we are aware, this has not been done, nor is a rationale for it at all developed in the literature. Perhaps that is just as well.

Using a local relative standard takes into account not only the relevant variations in the cost of living but also the relevant differences in consumption *and* the relevant differences in social understanding of what consumption possibilities mean for social participation and evaluated social activities. Economic well-being refers to the material resources available to households. As explained in the introduction and chapter 9, the concern with these resources is not with consumption per se but rather with the capabilities they give household members to participate in their communities and societies (Sen 1992). These capabilities are inputs to social activities, and participation in these activities produces a given level of well-being (Rainwater 1974; Coleman, Rainwater, and McClelland 1978). The social meaning of any given package of economic resources is defined in the context of the resources of the community. With this as our theoretical stance, we now move on to operationalize the concept.

THE 1995 TO 1997 LIS U.S. DATABASE

For the focus on the states of the United States, we used a LIS database that provides enough cases to produce reasonably stable estimates of state-level poverty lines and poverty rates: a combination of the 1995, 1996, and 1997 Current Population Surveys (CPS), which yields a total sample of 150,239 households. Because the populations of some states are rather small, even this number of households does not give us a good statistical base for all states. We were able to make separate analyses for twenty-seven states; we had to combine the other twenty-four states into nine multistate regions of two to four units. In the tables that follow, these combined units are indicated by a name that compounds the standard abbreviations for the states; for example, "ME-NH-VT" combines Maine, New Hampshire, and Vermont.

We define a "state" poverty line as the average of one-half of the median equivalent incomes in that state (or multistate region) in each year.[2] The U.S. median equivalent disposable income in 1995 was $25,756, $26,801 in 1996, and $28,012 in 1997. The state poverty line is defined as half of the state median, just as the national poverty line is defined as half of the national median. In the analysis that follows, we express the state medians as a percentage of the national medians, and states' poverty lines are expressed as a percentage of the national poverty line.

For context we have chosen four other countries that have quite different political and economic dynamics—Australia, Canada, Italy, and Spain—to examine how much difference regional variations might make in other national contexts. We chose these nations either because they are geographically large and have multilevel national and state or provincial governments (Australia, Canada) or because they are nations with important regional differences in political, ethnic, or other groupings (Italy, Spain). The pattern of child poverty in each nation also differs: the high U.S. rate has plateaued at about 20 percent; Australia and Canada have stable (flat) trends at the 13 to 14 percent level; Italy has a rising rate at 19 percent; and Spain is holding steady at 12 percent. In addition, we provide national poverty rates for a group of other European nations—again, to emphasize the range in poverty rates now found across subnational regions and nations.

TO WHAT EXTENT DO STATES DIFFER
IN AVERAGE INCOMES?

The first empirical issue we must address is the degree of heterogeneity in average standards of living among regions. The second, discussed in the next section, is the difference among regions in amounts of poverty.

Table 11.1 gives state medians as a percentage of the U.S. national median, while figure 11.1 charts the deviation from the national median of each of the state medians. In figure 11.1, we see that in two states—the combined Rhode Island–Connecticut region and New Jersey—the state median is more than 20 percent greater than the national median. Interestingly, New York, which is often thought of as a very rich state, does not have a higher median. In fact, its median, which is 2 percent less than the national median, is comparable to those of North Carolina and Oregon, both 4 percent less than the national median.

The next most prosperous states appear to be Massachusetts, at 15 percent above the national level, and Washington, at 12 percent above. Just as New York does not stand out, California's median is only 2 percent above the nation's median. Of course, these two large states (with 12 and 7 percent of the national population, respectively) have a great impact on the national median, so we might not expect their medians to be very far from the nation's. The second-largest state, Texas, however, has a state median that is 8 percent below the national median.

It is also not surprising that the less prosperous states are in the South. From West Virginia to Texas, we find medians that are below average. West Virginia, Mississippi, Arkansas, and New Mexico have medians at least 20 percent below the national standard. Overall, we find a significant range among the fifty American states (and the District of Columbia), from a high in New Jersey of 25 percent above the national median to a low in Arkansas of 25 percent below. While not quite half of the states have a median in the band of minus to plus 10 percent, there is still significant variation across states.

We would therefore expect significant variations in the state poverty rates based on the national median. What is not clear is whether there would be similar variations in poverty based on the state medians. If the income inequalities, particularly the inequalities in the distributions below the median, were more or less the same in all of the states, then we might well find roughly the same poverty rates based on the state standards despite dramatic variations based on national standard. Or indeed, the relationship might go in the other direction if it turned out that the more prosperous states also were states with a greater degree of inequality in the distribution of income below the median. We might find rich states with high poverty and low-income states with low poverty.

In fact, we find a very low correlation between the median equivalent income in a state and its poverty rate based on the state standard—only 0.12. In contrast, the correlation between the median income of the state and its poverty rate based on the national standard is high, −0.77. As expected, the less affluent states have higher poverty rates by the national standard, but that is most definitely not the case with state standards. We return to these state-based poverty rates later in the chapter.

HOW DOES U.S. STATE VARIATION COMPARE
WITH VARIATION IN OTHER COUNTRIES?

We have selected four countries to investigate for variations in regional affluence so as to compare the results with those for American states. In figures 11.2 and 11.3, we show state medians in these countries as a percentage of their respective national medians. Because the samples are rather small, these results may

(*Text continues on page 195.*)

TABLE 11.1 U.S. Median Incomes and Poverty Rates According to National and State Standards

		Poverty Rates					
	State Median Income as Percentage of National Median	Children (Age Eighteen or Younger)		Working-Age Adults (Age Eighteen to Sixty-Four)		Elders (Age Sixty-Five and Over)	
State		National Standard	State Standard	National Standard	State Standard	National Standard	State Standard
ME-NH-VT	102.6%	12.7%	13.7%	10.2%	11.0%	21.2%	22.3%
Massachusetts	114.6	18.4	24.2	10.4	13.9	19.9	25.3
RI-CT	120.8	17.3	22.7	10.0	13.8	16.0	25.1
New York	98.3	26.9	26.3	16.2	15.9	23.1	22.4
New Jersey	125.3	13.6	21.8	8.3	13.9	18.6	29.3
Pennsylvania	102.7	17.6	18.4	12.7	13.3	20.8	21.9
Ohio	103.5	17.5	18.6	11.7	12.5	19.0	20.3
IN-MO	100.9	13.4	13.8	10.5	10.6	18.0	18.3
Illinois	108.1	18.8	21.7	10.7	12.5	18.4	22.3
Michigan	107.2	16.9	19.5	11.0	12.6	17.8	21.5
Wisconsin	107.9	13.1	15.1	8.9	10.4	18.5	21.6
Minnesota	110.1	12.3	15.8	12.3	11.3	19.1	17.2
ND-SD	93.0	14.9	12.3	8.7	10.7	24.8	28.9
IA-NE-KS	96.0	14.4	13.0	14.0	12.0	26.6	23.4
DE-MD-VA-DC	110.2	14.9	18.8	10.5	13.2	17.8	23.0
West Virginia	79.2	27.9	18.5	21.1	14.0	28.8	16.1

State						
North Carolina	95.7	19.8	17.2	12.9	11.2	23.9	22.9
South Carolina	90.8	22.6	18.0	14.6	12.1	30.0	22.9
Georgia	95.3	20.9	18.8	14.1	12.8	25.1	23.3
Florida	95.0	23.0	21.2	15.2	13.8	20.2	18.2
Kentucky	90.9	25.1	20.5	17.5	14.6	25.3	19.9
Tennessee	91.1	22.4	18.2	16.7	13.3	27.0	23.3
Alabama	88.2	25.0	20.3	17.8	13.3	28.0	21.7
Mississippi	77.0	30.6	18.9	21.9	12.7	30.0	18.1
Arkansas	75.2	25.7	14.1	19.2	10.4	33.8	19.8
Louisiana	87.0	28.0	22.8	19.3	15.8	27.1	20.4
Oklahoma	83.9	24.2	17.6	17.7	13.2	26.0	17.8
Texas	92.1	24.7	20.7	16.9	14.3	25.9	22.2
New Mexico	76.3	33.3	21.6	24.6	15.8	26.3	16.5
Arizona	91.3	27.1	23.6	17.2	14.3	17.4	15.3
MT-ID-WY	87.7	20.3	13.9	16.0	11.5	19.4	13.6
CO-UT-NV	105.9	10.7	13.1	9.9	11.4	15.1	16.8
Washington	111.8	15.8	19.0	11.1	13.8	15.6	19.0
Oregon	95.9	17.7	16.2	11.9	10.9	15.3	12.3
California	102.3	24.6	25.7	15.5	16.1	18.1	18.8
AK-HI	108.5	12.6	16.1	9.8	11.7	15.3	17.0
United States	100.0	20.3	20.1	13.6	13.4	20.9	20.8

Source: Authors' calculations, using data from the Luxembourg Income Study.

Note: Equivalent income is age-adjusted cube root of family size. National median income is calculated for each year (1995 to 1997) and set at 100. State medians are percentages of national median. Poverty line is one-half of relevant median.

FIGURE 11.1 U.S. State Median Equivalent Incomes

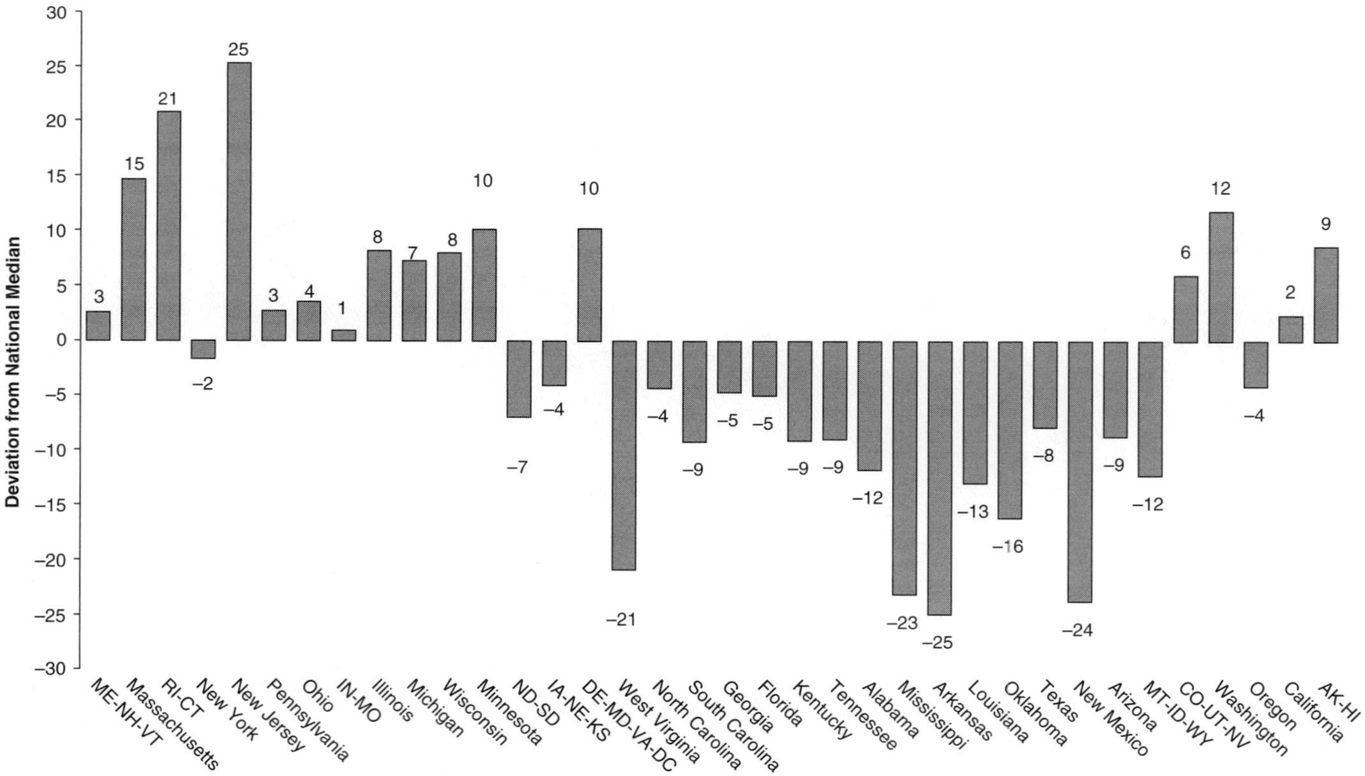

Source: Authors' calculations, using data from the Luxembourg Income Study.

FIGURE 11.2 State Median Equivalent Incomes in Canada and Australia

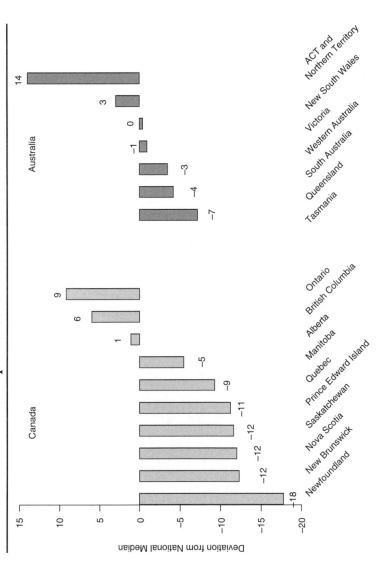

Source: Authors' calculations, using data from the Luxembourg Income Study.

FIGURE 11.3 State Medians in Italy and Spain

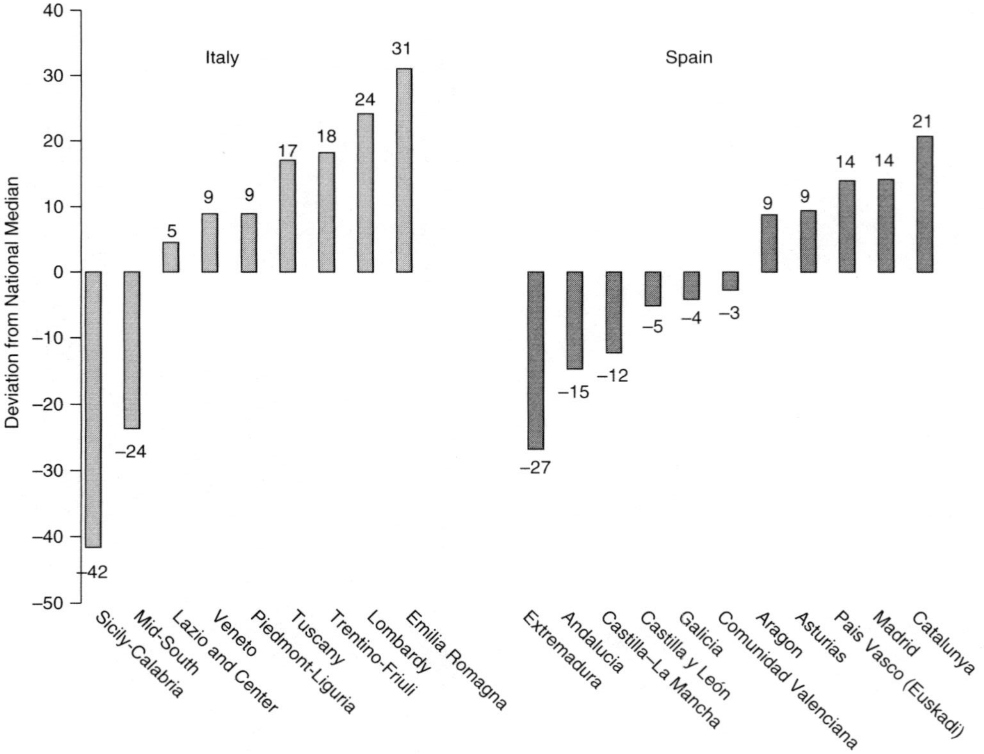

Source: Authors' calculations, using data from the Luxembourg Income Study.

be unstable.[3] In some cases we have combined regions in the LIS data to produce somewhat more reliable results.

We find that in Canada the provincial variations are not as dramatic as they are for U.S. states. The range is from 9 percent above the national median for Ontario to 18 percent below in Newfoundland and 11 or 12 percent below in New Brunswick, Nova Scotia, Saskatchewan, and Prince Edward Island. British Columbia also appears above average, but only by six percentage points. In Australia we find a similar pattern, with a range from 7 percent below the national median in Tasmania to 14 percent above in the Australian Capital Territory (ACT) and the Northern Territory. In the other five regions the deviations from the national median are quite small. These other large nations thus have less variation in income across them than the United States. Although it is arguable that breaking an aggregate into fifty pieces rather than seven (Australia) or ten (Canada) is bound to produce such a result, a breakdown by the nine census regions makes no significant change in the U.S. result: the West South Central and East South Central regions (the so-called Deep South) still have median incomes 20 percent below the U.S. national median. Moreover, the nine Italian states show even larger regional variation than do the fifty American states.

In the geographically smaller nations of Spain and Italy (but larger in population), yet another pattern emerges. In Italy we find very dramatic regional variations. As might be expected, the southern regions have medians far below the national line. In Sicily-Calabria the median is 42 percent below the national median, and in the Mid-South (four other southern provinces) it is 24 percent below. In contrast, Emilia Romagna and Lombardy are very far above average, with medians at 31 and 24 percent above, and Tuscany and Trentino-Friuli are also quite prosperous.

The Spanish range of state medians is not as dramatic, but more so than in either Canada or Australia; in fact, Spain resembles the United States, with a range from 27 percent below the national median in Extremadura and 15 percent below in Andalucia and nearby provinces, to 21 percent above in Catalunya and 14 percent above in Madrid and the Basque region. So we might expect interesting variations between provincial poverty rates and the national average in Spain.

CHILD POVERTY RATES IN THE UNITED STATES AND OTHER NATIONS BY NATIONAL AND STATE STANDARDS

When we apply national and state or local standards to these five datasets, we find a very interesting result for the countries as a whole (see figure 11.4). In four of the countries the national poverty rate differs very little whether we use the national or the state standard. In the United States the child poverty rate is 20.3 percent according to the national standard and 20.1 percent according to the state standard. The difference in the two rates is even smaller in Australia— 13.5 percent versus 13.4 percent. In Canada the difference is slightly larger but still not as large as 1 percent. In Spain the difference is yet again a bit larger, with the national standard producing a rate of 11.9 percent and the state standard a rate of 11 percent. It is only in Italy that we find a substantial difference: by the national standard 19.5 percent of Italian children are poor, but using a local standard cuts the poverty rate by almost one-quarter, to 14.7 percent.

FIGURE 11.4 Child Poverty Rates for Five Nations Based on National and Local Standards

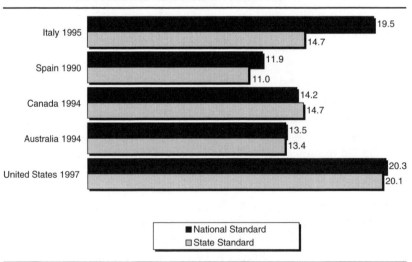

Source: Authors' calculations, using data from the Luxembourg Income Study.

We present U.S. child poverty rates according to national and local standards for twenty-seven states and nine regional combinations of small states (see table 11.1). For comparison, we have also given the poverty rates for working-age adults and for elders, though one should be careful in comparing poverty rates across these groups.

Examination of the two child poverty rates in the United States shows that there is not a very high correlation between them—only 0.534. Thus, we can expect a fair amount of reshuffling when we move from the national to the local standard. For example, the four states with the highest child poverty rate according to the national standard are New Mexico, Mississippi, Louisiana, and West Virginia. The four states with the highest poverty rate according to the local standard are New York, California, Massachusetts, and Arizona. The four states with the lowest poverty rate according to the national standard are Minnesota and the combined Colorado-Utah-Nevada, Alaska-Hawaii, and Maine–New Hampshire–Vermont areas. Even by the local standard, these states have below-average poverty, but the honors for the very lowest local standard poverty rates go to North Dakota–South Dakota, Iowa-Kansas-Nebraska, Colorado-Utah-Nevada, and Maine–New Hampshire–Vermont.

Figure 11.5 charts the relationship between state and national child poverty rates in a way that highlights the differences between them. Here we show the percentage increase or decrease represented by the state poverty rate compared with the national standard poverty rate. We see very large increases of one-quarter or more in the poverty rates for Massachusetts, Rhode Island–Connecticut, New Jersey, Minnesota, and Delaware–Maryland–District of Columbia–Virginia. On the West Coast we also find three states with a very large percentage increase in their poverty rate—Colorado-Utah-Nevada, Washington, and Alaska-Hawaii. We find very little change in New York and California child poverty rates, as might be expected given the fact that these state medians are about the same as the national median.

We note that local standard poverty rates are lower than the national rate in the southern states in general—beginning with West Virginia and moving on around the southern rim to Texas—and also in the Rocky Mountain states. We find that poverty rates in Massachusetts, Rhode Island–Connecticut, and New Jersey

FIGURE 11.5 Percentage Increase or Decrease of U.S. State Child Poverty Rate over National Child Poverty Rate

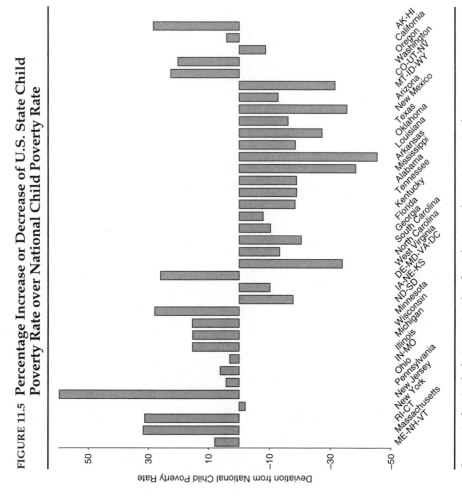

Source: Authors' calculations, using data from the Luxembourg Income Study.

increase by six to eight percentage points, while in contrast, West Virginia's rate decreases by nine percentage points and we see even greater decreases for Mississippi, Arkansas, and New Mexico of twelve percentage points.[4] There is also a decrease in the range of six percentage points in Montana-Idaho-Wyoming.

It clearly matters whether the state or national standard is used. If we use state standards, New York, California, and Massachusetts are the poorest states. These states are also relatively large in population terms (and California is large geographically). They also contain relatively large shares of recent immigrants (southern California and New York City in particular) and relatively large ethnic and racial minorities (in all three states).

New Mexico and Louisiana have above-average poverty rates by either standard, while the state-specific poverty rate in Arkansas (14.1 percent) is much closer to the lowest state median–based rate of 13 percent (Iowa, Kansas, Nebraska) than to the average state (20.1 percent). In fact, when we move to state standards, a very large variation emerges within groups of states often thought to be homogeneous. The state-specific poverty rate in Arkansas (14.1 percent) is very different from that of the contiguous states of Louisiana (22.8), Mississippi (18.9), and Tennessee (18.2), all of which are considered high-poverty southern states by most observers.

RESHUFFLING CHILD POVERTY RATES
IN OTHER COUNTRIES

How does this shifting among the regions of the United States compare with the situation in the four other countries whose regional variations we are examining? In the case of Australia (see figure 11.6), as might be expected, we find relatively little difference in the poverty rates according to the two standards. It is only in the ACT and the Northern Territory that we find a difference greater than two percentage points. In the other states the state poverty rate is about the same as the national standard poverty rate.

In Canada, shifting to a provincial rate makes a bigger difference. We find fairly large decreases, on the order of 20 percent, in Newfoundland and Nova Scotia. The decrease is about one-third in Prince Edward Island. The child poverty rate increases by about one-quarter in Ontario, the only province in which there is a

FIGURE 11.6 **Child Poverty Rates in Australia and Canada**
According to State and National Standards

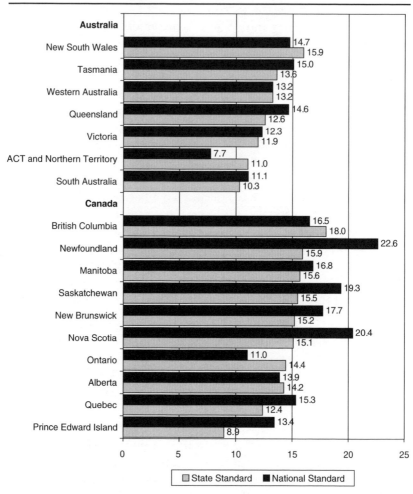

Source: Authors' calculations, using data from the Luxembourg Income Study.

notable increase. Overall, the shifting in Canada is more like that of the United States than is the case for Australia.

What is notable in Canada is that the provincial poverty rates make Canadian regions seem much more homogeneous than does the national standard. Thus, we find provincial standard child poverty rates converging from just below to just above 15 percent in Newfoundland, Manitoba, Saskatchewan, New Brunswick, Nova

Scotia, Ontario, and Alberta. Only British Columbia, with a higher rate, and Quebec and Prince Edward Island, with lower rates, stand apart. This is in contrast to Australia, where the differences among regions are about the same for both state standards and the national standard, with a range from around 10 percent to 16 percent.

Figure 11.7 presents results for Spanish and Italian child poverty rates. With the exception of southern Spain (the Andalucia region and Extremadura), there seems to be a rather high degree of similarity in the local standard child poverty rates. The rates range from about 8 percent to about 11 percent. It is in the southern regions of Spain that we find the largest discrepancy between local and national standards. Shifting from the national to the local standard, we find decreases of almost one-third in the Andalucia region, almost one-half in Extremadura, and over one-third in Castilla–La Mancha. In the other regions the changes are much smaller. The effect of using a local standard rather than the national standard tends to be to increase the poverty rate of the more prosperous regions while decreasing it slightly in the less prosperous ones (outside of the South). The end result is that the state standard produces a much greater degree of similarity across regions.

In Italy we find that both the national and state standards produce a considerable diversity in poverty rates across regions, but the state rates moderate considerably the differences found with the national standard. We note that in Sicily-Calabria the national rate produces a 45 percent child poverty rate, but that it is 19 percent according to the regional standard. The four provinces of the mid-South also show very large decreases, amounting to more than one-third—from 27 percent down to 16 percent. By both standards, Emilia-Romagna and Tuscany have the lowest child poverty rates, but the provincial standard increases the rates to nearly 10 percent. This is not too different from the rate of around 13 percent for such regions as Piedmont-Liguria, Trentino-Friuli, Veneto, and Lazio and the surrounding region. Another example of the dramatic effect of shifting to a regional standard is the comparison of the mid-South region with Lombardy. By the national standard, Lombardy has a poverty rate almost one-quarter that of the Mezzogiorno, but by its own local standard there is a difference between the two regions of only one percentage point.

(*Text continues on page 206.*)

TABLE 11.2 State Poverty Rates in the United States, Canada, and Australia and National Rates in Fourteen European Nations

Rank of Poverty Rate	United States, 1995 to 1997		Canada, 1994		Australia, 1994		Europe	
	State	Rate	Province	Rate	State	Rate	Country	Rate
Total	**United States**	**20.3**[a]	**Canada**	**14.2**[a]	**Australia**	**13.5**[a]		
Under 5 percent							**Sweden (1995)**	**2.4**
							Finland (1995)	**3.2**
							Denmark (1992)	**3.4**
							Norway (1995)	**4.0**
							Belgium (1997)	**5.1**
							Luxembourg (1994)	**4.3**
							Austria (1987)	**5.3**
Under 10 percent			Prince Edward Island	8.9			**Netherlands (1994)**	**7.0**
							France (1994)	**7.2**
							Germany (1994)	**9.5**
Under 15 percent	ND-SD	12.3	Quebec	12.4	South Australia	10.3	**Israel (1992)**	**10.6**
	IA-NE-KS	13.0			ACT and Northern Territory	11.0	**Spain (1990)**	**11.9**
	CO-UT-NV	13.1			Victoria	11.9		
	ME-NH-VT	13.7			Queensland	12.6		
	IN-MO	13.8	Alberta	14.2	Western Australia	13.2		
	MT-ID-WY	13.9	Ontario	14.4	**Australia**	**13.4**[b]		
	Arkansas	14.1	**Canada**	**14.7**[b]	Tasmania	13.6		

	US jurisdiction		Canadian province		Australian state		Country	
Under 20 percent	Wisconsin	15.1	Nova Scotia	15.1			**United Kingdom (1995)**	**16.3**
	Minnesota	15.8	New Brunswick	15.2				
	AK-HI	16.1	Saskatchewan	15.5				
	Oregon	16.2	Manitoba	15.6				
	North Carolina	17.2	Newfoundland	15.9	New South Wales	15.9		
	Oklahoma	17.6						
	South Carolina	18.0	British Columbia	18.0				
	Tennessee	18.2						
	Pennsylvania	18.4						
	West Virginia	18.5						
	Ohio	18.6						
	DE-MD-VA-DC	18.8						
	Georgia	18.8						
	Mississippi	18.9						
	Washington	19.0						
	Michigan	19.5						**Italy (1995)**	**19.5**
Over 20 percent	**United States**	**20.1**[b]						
	Alabama	20.3						
	Kentucky	20.5						
	Texas	20.7						
	Florida	21.2						
	New Mexico	21.6						
	Illinois	21.7						
	New Jersey	21.8						

(*Table continues on page 204.*)

TABLE 11.2 State Poverty Rates in the United States, Canada, and Australia and National Rates in Fourteen European Nations *(continued)*

Rank of Poverty Rate	United States, 1995 to 1997		Canada, 1994		Australia, 1994		Europe	
	State	Rate	Province	Rate	State	Rate	Country	Rate
	RI-CT	22.7						
	Louisiana	22.8						
	Arizona	23.6						
	Massachusetts	24.2						
	California	25.7						
	New York	26.3						

Source: Authors' calculations, using data from the Luxembourg Income Study.

a. National rate using one-half median national income.

b. National rate using one-half median state incomes, or weighted average of state poverty rates.

FIGURE 11.7 **Child Poverty Rates in Spain and Italy According to State and National Standards**

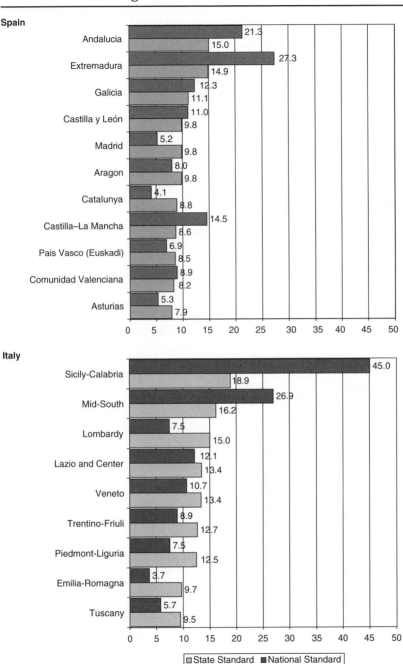

Source: Authors' calculations, using data from the Luxembourg Income Study.

We combine the national and state child poverty rates for the various regions in these five countries in figure 11.8. Here we plot the local standard child poverty rate against the national standard rate. We observe that the overlap is greatest according to the national poverty lines. There tends to be much greater compression according to the state poverty lines.

We note that there is overlap between a number of Canadian provinces (those with higher poverty rates) and some American states (those with lower poverty rates). And there is some overlap between the American states with very low poverty rates and Australian states. There is also some overlap between a few of the Italian regions and some of the low-poverty American states. But with respect to Spain, there is almost no overlap, except in the case of the two high-poverty southern regions.

These overlaps are shown more fully in table 11.2, which tabulates child poverty rates according to state standards for the United States, Canada, and Australia and national standard rates

FIGURE 11.8 Child Poverty Rates in the States of the United States, Canada, Australia, Italy, and Spain

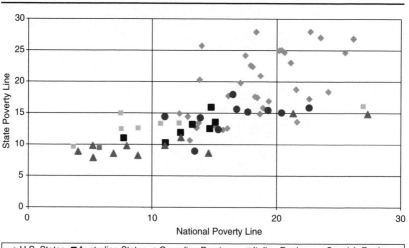

Source: Authors' calculations, using data from the Luxembourg Income Study.
Note: Sicily is excluded because it would appear off the chart with a local child poverty rate of 45 percent and a national rate of 18 percent.

in Spain, Italy, and eleven other European countries, all based on LIS data. Here we find the full range of child poverty rates, from a rate of less than 3 percent in Sweden to a high of 26 percent in New York State. We note that the two regions with the highest rates in our comparison countries still have much lower rates than some American states. Thus, Sicily and the Italian mid-South, at 19 and 16 percent, respectively, have lower rates than thirteen of the American states if we use state standards to define poverty rates.

Clearly, the range of poverty rates across the American states (12.3 to 26.3 percent) is greater than the range in Canada (8.9 to 18.0 percent) or Australia (10.3 to 15.9 percent), by a large margin. By state standards, many American states have poverty rates below those found in the United Kingdom or Italy and are comparable to those in Israel and Spain. In contrast, California, New York, Massachusetts, and Illinois have high poverty rates for any national or subnational breakdown. But even the lowest-poverty American states have rates well above those of all the northern and central European and Scandinavian states.

CONCLUSION

We would argue that local standards are more in line than national standards with societies' definitions of some people as poor, some as almost poor, some as not at all poor, and some as prosperous. That is, it is in the local community that these evaluations and self-evaluations are made. Approximating local living standards presents practical problems for statistical studies, however, and therefore in part 1 of this book we fell back on national standards. Were the requisite data available, moving from the national level to the state level would seem to be a move in the right direction. Table 11.3, for example, illustrates the difference in poverty rates among the U.S. states when national and state standards are applied. And given the problems of small sample size as we move toward the local community, the most realistic choice may be using the state or region as the unit for defining a poverty line.[5] In the United States it may also be the most policy-relevant grouping for fighting child poverty, as

TABLE 11.3 U.S. Poverty Rates and Number of Poor Children According to National and State Standards

State	State Median as Percentage of National Median	Percentage Poor		Poor Population (in Thousands)		
		National Standard	State Standard	National Standard	State Standard	Difference
ME-NH-VT	102.6%	12.7%	13.7%	1.14	1.23	0.09
Massachusetts	114.6	18.4	24.2	2.74	3.60	0.87
RI-CT	120.8	17.3	22.7	1.82	2.39	5.68
New York	98.3	26.9	26.3	12.57	12.32	−0.25
New Jersey	125.3	13.6	21.8	2.78	4.44	1.66
Pennsylvania	102.7	17.6	18.4	5.19	5.42	0.22
Ohio	103.5	17.5	18.6	5.11	5.43	0.32
IN-MO	100.9	13.4	13.8	3.99	4.12	0.12
Illinois	108.1	18.8	21.7	6.11	7.05	0.94
Michigan	107.2	16.9	19.5	4.36	5.02	0.67
Wisconsin	107.9	13.1	15.1	1.81	2.09	0.28
Minnesota	110.1	12.3	15.8	1.58	2.03	0.44
ND-SD	93.0	14.9	12.3	0.55	0.46	−0.09
IA-NE-KS	96.0	14.4	13.0	2.75	2.48	−0.28

DE-MD-VA-DC	110.2	14.9	18.8	4.88	6.15	1.27
West Virginia	79.2	27.9	18.5	1.20	0.79	-0.41
North Carolina	95.7	19.8	17.2	3.77	3.27	-0.50
South Carolina	90.8	22.6	18.0	2.21	1.76	-0.45
Georgia	95.3	20.9	18.8	4.24	3.81	-0.43
Florida	95.0	23.0	21.2	8.09	7.46	-0.63
Kentucky	90.9	25.1	20.5	2.49	2.03	-0.45
Tennessee	91.1	22.4	18.2	3.03	2.36	-0.57
Alabama	88.2	25.0	20.3	2.77	2.25	-0.52
Mississippi	77.0	30.6	18.9	2.38	1.47	-0.91
Arkansas	75.2	25.7	14.1	1.75	0.96	-0.79
Louisiana	87.0	28.0	22.8	3.47	2.83	-0.64
Oklahoma	83.9	24.2	17.6	2.18	1.59	-0.59
Texas	92.1	24.7	20.7	13.98	11.74	-2.24
New Mexico	76.3	33.3	21.6	1.71	1.11	-0.60
Arizona	91.3	27.1	23.6	3.46	3.03	-0.44
MT-ID-WY	87.7	20.3	13.9	1.49	1.02	-0.47
CO-UT-NV	105.9	10.7	13.1	2.18	2.67	0.49
Washington	111.8	15.8	19.0	2.35	2.82	0.48
Oregon	95.9	17.7	16.2	1.47	1.35	-0.13
California	102.3	24.6	25.7	22.58	23.52	0.94
AK-HI	108.5	12.6	16.1	0.64	0.82	0.18
United States	**100.0**	**20.3**	**20.1**	**144.81**	**142.95**	**-1.87**

Source: Authors' calculations, using data from the Luxembourg Income Study.

antipoverty policy continues to devolve to lower levels of government in the United States.

Whatever the level at which it is measured, accurate and comparable measures of poverty are important to identify and gauge the well-being of our most vulnerable citizens, our children. As we hope is now clear, millions of America's kids do not prosper by any sort of comparison—state, nation, or locality, measured by relative or real incomes. If we are to do better in the fight against child poverty and to raise the living standards of these kids, we need to arouse the leadership of ardent activist policymakers, those who truly do not want any child left behind, not those who pay only lip service to this slogan.

——— Appendix A ———

The Luxembourg Income Study Project

THE LUXEMBOURG INCOME Study (LIS) project is one of the oldest and best-known examples of cross-national social science infrastructure. As of this writing, some twenty-six nations and twenty sponsors are teaming together to provide Internet-accessible, privacy-protected household income microdata to over four hundred users in thirty nations. The project is financed by annual contributions from sixteen nations' National Science Foundations and/or National Statistical Offices as well as from the Luxembourg government.

The LIS research and databank project has provided harmonized, cross-national household income microdata for social science research for over fifteen years. These data provide the basis for cross-national comparative research projects by providing access to household income microdata for all research users who are connected to the Internet; these users promise to respect the privacy of survey respondents and to use the LIS microdata for research purposes only.

The LIS project has five goals:

1. To *harmonize* cross-national data by relieving researchers of this task and building an expert staff to accomplish it and to handle user questions and user services

2. To test the feasibility of *creating* a database consisting of social and economic household survey microdata from different countries

3. To provide a method of allowing researchers to gain *access* to these data under the various privacy restrictions required by the countries providing the data

211

4. To create a system capable of *quickly processing* research requests and responding to users *at remote locations*

5. To *promote comparative research* on the economic and social status of populations in different countries, through training and networking activities

Up-to-date information on the project, the countries and variables included in the database, and the several hundred working papers that have been completed using the data can be found on the LIS project website, www.lisproject.org.

Appendix B

The U.S. State Database and Regional Combinations in Other Countries in the Luxembourg Income Study

THE U.S. STATE DATABASE

To facilitate the comparisons in chapter 11 of countries in the LIS database with individual American states, a special dataset has been created and placed with other LIS datasets. This dataset was created by combining three separate March Current Population Survey (CPS) files—those for March 1996, 1997, and 1998 (income in 1995, 1996, and 1997, respectively). These three datasets were combined in order to increase sample sizes and reduce the sampling variances that would otherwise have resulted if we had used data for only a single year. Data from these files were "lissified" (converted to the standard LIS format) and then concentrated. The survey weights on each file have been divided by three so that the results from the combined file sum to the average for the three-year period. Income amounts are stated in the prices of the income reference year. (Users may price-adjust the files using the price deflator of their choice.)

The data from some states have been combined because the sample size, even after combining the three surveys, was deemed too small to provide reliable estimates at a 5 percent confidence level. The states that were combined and shown as groups were:

Maine, New Hampshire, Vermont

Montana, Idaho, Wyoming

Colorado, Utah, Nevada

Indiana, Missouri

Iowa, Nebraska, Kansas

North Dakota, South Dakota

Delaware, Maryland, Virginia, District of Columbia

Alaska, Hawaii

All other states are identified separately. The resulting dataset includes a total of 150,239 households, 301,771 adult records, and 92,089 child records. This file can also be used to undertake research at the national level for population subgroups whose sample sizes may be somewhat too small for any single year.

The survey weights provided by the U.S. Bureau of the Census on the public use data file sum to population controls by detailed age, race, and sex at the national level. These controls are based on the bureau's best estimates of the civilian non-institutional population as of the survey month and are adjusted for the estimated 1990 census undercount. Unfortunately, the bureau does not require that the sum of these survey weights correspond to its best estimates of the population at the state level. At the state level, control is maintained only for estimates of the population age sixteen and over. This lack of control at the state level for important population subgroups, such as children under age eighteen, has resulted in year-to-year fluctuations in the estimates within states that can make the data difficult to use.

The data used in this study have been adjusted ("reweighted") so that the sum of weights at the state level correspond to the census state estimates of the number of persons under age five and the number of persons age five to seventeen. A multivariate ranking procedure was employed to derive weighting adjustment factors that ensure that the sum of weights at both the national and state levels meets population controls. In this case, national level counts were controlled to the original survey estimates for the under-eighteen population by poverty status, relationship, sex, and race-ethnicity.

REGIONS COMBINED IN CANADA, AUSTRALIA, SPAIN, AND ITALY

In Australia no states were combined. In Canada no provinces were combined, but the Northwest Territories and the Yukon Territory were excluded.

In Spain the following regions were combined:

Asturias, Cantabria, and La Rioja

Andalucia, Ceuta and Melilla, Murcia, and the Canary Islands

Aragon and Navarra

Catalunya and Baleares

In Italy the following regions were combined:

Sicily and Calabria

Mid-South: Molise, Basilicata, Campania, Puglia, Sardinia

Lazio, Abruzzi, and Umbria

Piedmont and Liguria

—— Appendix C ——

From Relative Income to Real Income

Most of us have a general idea of the economic well-being of people in different nations. We think of people in developing countries as having low standards of living; we view Eastern Europeans as having much lower incomes than Westerners; and people in Western Europe, we assume, are somewhat less well off than Americans.

The task of measuring in detail the real cost of various goods and services is given to purchasing power parities (PPP), the end product of extremely elaborate projects to assess the cost of a common list of hundreds of goods and services in more than one hundred countries. The total cost of the given basket in local currencies can then be phrased in dollars, and the conversion of one to another gives a real purchasing power measure of the local currency. That measure can deviate quite a bit from the exchange rate since the latter is affected not only by the domestic cost of living but also by the relative demand for a country's products in international trade.

In considering trends in GDP growth in our fifteen countries in chapter 2, we made use of the statistical series on real gross domestic product developed by Robert Summers and Alan Heston (1991) in their Penn World Tables (PWT Mark 5.6). These tables give us the real GDP from 1950 to 1994 of most of the countries in the world. The tables provide a measure of the real GDP per capita of each of our countries as a percentage of the real GDP of the United States in the same year.

For comparisons in the previous chapters of the distribution of economic well-being at the time of the LIS surveys, we made use

216

of OECD purchasing power parities (OECD, n.d.) because the OECD PPPs are coming to be more widely used and continue where the PWT leaves off. The OECD PPPs are based on the Summers and Heston methodology but produce somewhat different numbers. However, for our countries the discrepancies are not large except in the case of Australia and Sweden, where the OECD PPPs suggest that buying power is about 10 percent less than what is predicted by the Penn World Tables.

FROM PER CAPITA TO PER EQUIVALENT DOMESTIC PRODUCT

The OECD and PWT PPP measures express an average per person level of real income. Thus, the U.S. per capita real GDP in 1997 was around $31,352. That is, for each woman, man, and child in the country, there was about $31,352 worth of real domestic product. But we have seen that in thinking about economic well-being we need to adjust income for family size. We would like to compare real income per equivalent person in different countries because we want to take into account any differences across countries in the economies of scale that arise from differences in family composition or age distribution.

To rely exclusively on a per capita measure is to underestimate real opportunities for socially meaningful consumption in a country that has a higher average number of children per family, a higher proportion of married versus single-person households, or a lower proportion of elders compared with another country. For this reason, we have made a first adjustment to the OECD's estimates of real GDPs per capita by calculating instead the GDP per equivalent person. We make this adjustment by estimating from the LIS data the ratio of mean income per equivalent person to mean income per capita. If, compared with the United States, a given country has larger families or fewer elders, then its GDP per equivalent person will be higher relative to that of the United States than it would be on a per capita basis. If, on the other hand, a country has smaller families and/or more elders, it will have a lower GDP per equivalent person relative to that of the United States than it would on a per capita basis.

For example, in our 1997 U.S. dataset, per capita gross income is $19,428 and per equivalent person gross income is $42,553—a ratio of 2.19. A higher ratio in another country means that its per capita GDP underestimates opportunities for social consumption. So we adjust each country's OECD real GDP per capita percentage by multiplying it by the ratio of the country's per equivalent person to per capita ratio to the U.S. ratio of 2.19. This adjustment for our fourteen comparison countries is given in the second column of table C.1.

It is apparent that for most countries this adjustment to bring the aggregate income measures in line with our equivalence measures does not change the relation of the country to the United States by much. In six countries the adjustment shifts the percentage of U.S. real GDP by less than 5 percent. But in a few countries the shifts are much more significant. In Spain, where families are larger and fewer elders live alone, the adjustment increases the ratio of real GDP to U.S. real GDP by 20 percent. A similar shift is observed for Italy (7 percent). Because Sweden and Denmark have many small households, the adjustment moves those countries in the opposite direction—the ratio to the United States declines by 19 and 15 percent, respectively.

We also need to take into account the impact of inequality on measures that rely on a mean (either per capita or per equivalent person). The more unequal the income distribution in a country, the less accurate is the mean as a guide to the situation of the average person. The mean is, after all, an average of money per person. Since we are interested in the economic situation of persons at different points in the distribution, we need to start with an understanding of the real (equivalent) income of the person who is in the middle (at the median) of the distribution.

To take inequality differences into account, we estimated the ratio of the median to the mean equivalent income using the LIS data. With the result, we adjusted the measure of a country's real income relative to the United States to estimate the situation of the median equivalent person in the country compared with the median equivalent person in the United States.

As is well known, the income distribution of all of the other countries is less unequal than it is in the United States. This means that the equivalent income of the average (median) person in those

TABLE C.1 Measures of Real Income and Adjustments to Estimate Median Real Income in Fourteen Countries

Nation	Percentage of Real U.S. GDP Per Capita[a]	Ratio of Per Capita to Per Equivalent Person[b]	Ratio of Median to Mean Equivalent Gross Income[b]	Total Adjustment for Equivalence and Mean/Median Difference[c]	Percent of Real U.S. GDP per Median Equivalent Person[a,d]
Australia	72.13%	0.97	1.13	1.10	79.00%
Belgium	78.56	0.98	1.17	1.14	89.37
Canada	80.22	0.98	1.13	1.11	88.71
Denmark	76.64	0.85	1.23	1.06	80.89
Finland	67.09	0.90	1.17	1.05	70.71
France	74.80	0.98	1.09	1.06	79.22
Germany	76.67	0.93	1.11	1.03	79.25
Italy	72.85	1.07	1.08	1.16	84.21
Netherlands	72.98	0.94	1.16	1.09	79.60
Norway	85.14	0.91	1.19	1.08	92.35
Spain	53.35	1.20	1.10	1.31	69.87
Sweden	70.20	0.81	1.20	0.97	67.79
Switzerland	96.52	0.95	1.08	1.02	98.49
United Kingdom	66.87	0.97	1.07	1.03	69.16

Source: Authors' calculations, using data from the Luxembourg Income Study.

a. As a percentage of U.S. GDP per capita.

b. Ratio to U.S. ratio.

c. Product of columns 2 and 3.

d. Column 5 is the product of columns 1 and 4. The results may not be exact due to rounding.

societies is higher relative to the average person in the United States than we would believe based on the per capita or even the per equivalent person measures. In our U.S. data we find that the median equivalent gross income is $33,405, compared with the mean of $42,706, a ratio of 0.782. A country with a higher ratio as a result of having a more equal distribution will have a higher median GDP per equivalent person relative to that of the United States than one would expect based on the mean. The ratio for a country to the U.S. ratio indicates how much higher than its mean is its median relative to the United States. We find the ratios for our fourteen comparison countries in the third column of table C.1.

Focusing on the average person increases our measure of real economic well-being relative to the United States in all the countries—by 15 to 20 percent in Denmark, Sweden, Finland, Norway, and the Netherlands. The increases are over 10 percent in Australia, Canada, Belgium, and Germany.

With these two adjustments, we are able to examine questions of real income in the context of the measures of relative poverty that we have examined in previous chapters. First, what was the relative economic well-being of the average person in each of our comparison countries compared with the average person in the United States that same year? Table C.1 shows the two adjustments that transform per capita GDP to median equivalent person GDP, both as a percentage of the relevant measure for the United States. Our estimate of median equivalent person GDP (expressed as a percentage of estimated U.S. median equivalent person GDP) is the product of per capita GDP, the adjustment that takes into account differences in household and age composition and the adjustment for differences in the ratio of median to mean. (That is, column 5 of the table is equal to the product of columns 1 and 4.)

Figure C.1 charts the per capita GDP and the median equivalent person GDP as a percentage of the U.S. median. One sees that the adjustments do not have much effect on the rank order of these countries, but they do increase real income relative to that of the United States in all the countries except Sweden, where small family size overwhelms the effect of greater income equality. The greatest increases are in Spain, Italy, Australia, Belgium, and Canada. Spain's equivalent person GDP is much higher than its per capita GDP because it has larger households and elders are more likely to

FIGURE C.1 **Percentage of U.S. Real GDP per Capita and per Median Equivalent Person**

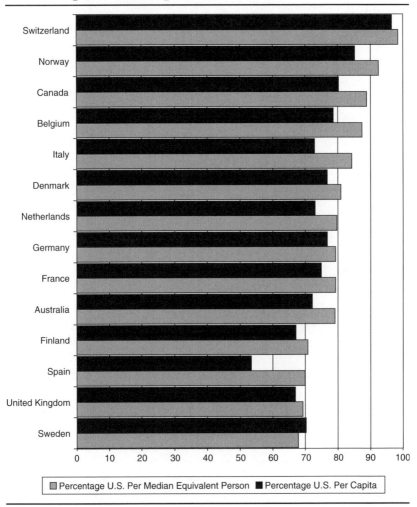

Source: Authors' calculations, using data from the Luxembourg Income Study.

live with others; thus, economies of scale in Spain are obscured by the per capita measure. The same factor has a weaker but significant effect in Italy. For the most part it is the adjustment for differences in inequality that dominates that for family equivalence differences.

We note that in four countries the average person has a real equivalent income equal to 85 percent or more of the average American's income—Norway, Belgium, Canada, and Switzerland. The average Swede has an income equal to 68 percent of the average American's. The two other countries whose citizens are least well off are the United Kingdom at 69 percent of the average American income and Spain at 70 percent.

It should be noted that the measure of real income in a country includes not only personal consumption expenditures and savings but collective consumption as well. It would require a major research project to impute in a detailed way the collective portion of national income to each household in our surveys. On the other hand, to ignore this collective portion is to ignore differences across countries in how large a role these resources may play. In comparing nations, we need to include some measure of collective consumption, because each nation "chooses" some balance between collective and personal consumption. Moreover, the economic well-being of the population is reflected in both collective and personal consumption.

As a very rough approximation of these resources, we make an assumption about how they are distributed in proportion to money income. When we make comparisons of real income at different positions in the income distribution, we are assuming that the distribution of collective consumption per equivalent person is the same as that of equivalent disposable income.

This is a conservative assumption for our comparison of the economic situation of less well-off people in the United States and other countries; a more common assumption is that the distribution of collective consumption is biased toward lower-income groups. In that sense, we may be understating the economic well-being of lower-income people in countries that have relatively high levels of collective consumption.

Our scaling up of money income per equivalent person to GDP per equivalent person also compensates for any differences across countries in the extent to which the aggregate money income in the surveys falls short of actual totals because of under-reporting. But it does that by assuming that unmeasured income is distributed in the same way as measured income—that is, proportionally to the distribution of equivalent disposable income. Other assumptions might be made, but we believe ours is a reasonably conservative one.

MOVING FROM RELATIVE TO REAL SURVEYED INCOME USING PURCHASING POWER PARITIES

An alternative approach to comparing poverty in different countries based on real incomes is much simpler. Instead of reaching for a measure of "full" income by imputing the collective portion of GDP to the households in our sample and making an assumption about underreporting of income in surveys, we could simply convert the survey income from national currencies to U.S. dollars using the OECD purchasing power parities.

Table C.2 shows the conversion of national median equivalent disposable incomes to real median incomes. The first column of the table shows the median in national currencies, the second column the OECD PPPs, and dividing the first column by the second yields the third—the median in U.S. dollars. For comparison, in the last column of the table we repeat from table C.1 our estimated median real GDP per equivalent person as a percentage of the comparable U.S. amount. Differences between the median equivalent income ratios and GDP per capita ratio are a product of differences across countries in all four of the factors we discussed earlier: equivalence versus per capita, median versus mean, underreporting, and in-kind and collectively provided services. Differences between the median equivalent income and the median equivalent GDP percentages are largely the product of the last two factors.

We note that the median equivalent income and median GDP measures of real economic well-being relative to the United States differ by 5 percent or less in ten of the fourteen countries. For these countries, both lenses for viewing real economic well-being give us a roughly comparable picture. We see that there are large discrepancies in Italy and Spain and a significant one for Belgium. The

TABLE C.2 Estimating Real Median Income in Fifteen Countries

Nation	Median Equivalent Income in National Currency	OECD PPP	Median Equivalent Income in U.S. Dollars[a]	Median Equivalent Income as Percentage of U.S. Median Equivalent Income	Percentage of Real U.S. GDP Per Median Equivalent Person
Australia	24,450	1.342	18,219	77.7	79.0
Belgium	764,561	37.832	20,209	77.5	89.4
Canada	30,074	1.190	25,272	90.2	88.7
Denmark	166,949	9.157	18,232	81.5	80.9
Finland	105,868	6.299	16,807	70.1	70.7
France	121,955	6.686	18,240	78.3	79.2
Germany	37,779	2.070	18,251	77.7	79.3
Italy	24,515[b]	1,589.000	15,428	61.4	84.2
Netherlands	37,523	2.183	17,189	75.2	79.6
Norway	203,980	9.370	21,769	86.6	92.3
Spain	1,234,723	109.500	11,276	52.9	69.9
Sweden	168,664	9.809	17,195	67.3	67.8
Switzerland	52,718	2.163	24,375	108.9	98.5
United Kingdom	11,697	0.670	17,458	69.5	69.2
United States	28,005	1.000	28,005	100.0	100.0

Source: Authors' calculations, using data from the Luxembourg Income Study.
a. Result of dividing column one by column two.
b. In thousands.

culprit is probably underreporting of income in the LIS surveys for those countries—that is, underreporting is a greater problem in those countries than in the United States.

We find the opposite situation in Switzerland in that median equivalent income is higher relative to the United States than is equivalent GDP. We do not have a ready explanation for this result, although the combination of lesser inequality in Switzerland compared with the United States and a high level of real income may be the principal factors.

In the other countries the two measures of real income are rather close, with the average discrepancy being less than 2 percent.

POVERTY RATES BASED ON REAL INCOME

We have considered three measures of income: relative equivalent money (and near-cash) income in national currencies, and two alternative definitions of real income; real equivalent GDP per household; and the money income of the first measure converted by OECD PPPs to real U.S. dollars. Using these three measures, we can define poverty lines that allow us to make comparisons across countries:

- One-half the median equivalent income in national currencies (the relative poverty lines used for the analysis in part 1)

- One-half the U.S. median equivalent GDP per household (the poverty line used in the discussions of real income in chapters 2 through 7)

- One-half the U.S. median real equivalent income with each country's currency converted to dollars using OECD PPPs

Poverty rates according to these three definitions are given in figure C.2. By definition, the U.S. poverty rate is the same for all three. As expected, the rates are at least somewhat higher for the other countries when based on median equivalent GDP, reflecting the fact that by this measure the real income in other countries is lower than in the United States. Poverty rates are also higher when based on real dollars.

FIGURE C.2 **Child Poverty Rates According to National and U.S. Standards**

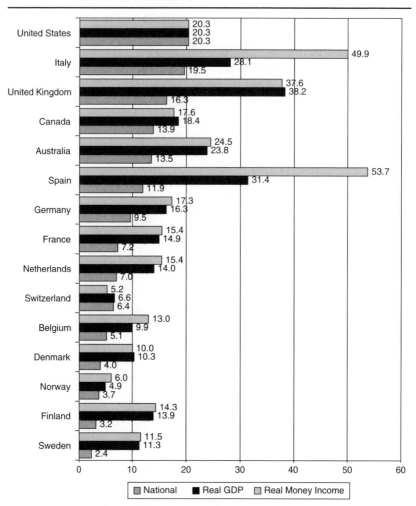

Source: Authors' calculations, using data from the Luxembourg Income Study.

Comparing the rates by these three measures for the six countries with very low relative poverty (6 percent and below), we see that in Switzerland and Norway rates based on real income are not very different from the national relative poverty rates. In the other four, we find rather large proportional increases for the real income rates. The same is true of the three countries with relative national rates between 7 and 10 percent.

We see strong hints of the effect of unmeasured income in the difference between the two real income rates for Spain and Italy. The rates based on the PPP conversions of survey income are twenty points higher than those based on imputed equivalent GDP, suggesting that in those two countries there is much more underreporting of income than in the other thirteen. In the country with the next largest difference, Belgium, we find only a three-point discrepancy.

For this reason, we believe that our conversion of national currency incomes to real dollars of equivalent GDP by the method in table C.1 is less biased than the seemingly more straightforward direct conversion of national currencies to dollars using purchasing power parities in table C.2. If we knew how large a problem underreporting of income was in each country, we would be able to correct for that and expect to have useful results from using the second method as well.

— Appendix D —

Reweighting to Assess the Impact of Demography Versus Income Packaging

I~N~ CHAPTER 3, we investigated the degree to which differences in poverty rates across countries are related to differences in the demographic characteristics of their populations. The technique we used involved reweighting each sample to be comparable demographically to that of the United States, and then similarly reweighting the U.S. sample to be comparable to that of each country. Thus, we used a very simple form of microsimulation to separate the effects of population characteristics from those of economic and social institutions.

Separating one set of forces from another can be accomplished in many ways. The process is most often termed decomposition: one set of forces (demographic, economic, social policy, specific institutions, and so on) is separated from the others and allowed to vary across nations while all other characteristics are held constant. In more elaborate microsimulation it is also possible to impose new characteristics, such as new structures or social policy programs. The new policies can be truly new, or they can involve the imposition of one nation's policy parameters on another nation's population. The Luxembourg Income Study data have been used to carry out both types of exercises (see, for example, Smeeding 1997; Jäntti and Danziger 1994).

Microsimulation methods can be extremely complex. We have chosen the simplest approach by using reweighting. Its advantage is that it is a relatively transparent technique and easy to understand. Whatever disadvantages it has do not seem relevant in our situation since the questions we have sought to address are fairly straightforward: If the United States had the demography of another country, would its poverty rate be as low as in the other country? If another country had the demography of the United States, what would its poverty rate be?

Note that the question of how much difference demography makes in accounting for poverty rate differences among countries involves two issues: How different are demographies from one country to another? And to what extent does the difference in demography between two countries account for any differences in their poverty rates?

For the first question, we can calculate an inequality coefficient. That is, for whatever demographic factors we want to control, we can calculate the extent to which those characteristics are different or the same in any two countries. A simple measure of the inequality of the demographic distributions of two countries is calculated by comparing the percentage distributions of the relevant demographic categories (for example, young parents, old parents, nonparents). We sum the absolute difference between pairs of categories and divide by two. The resulting number tells us what percentage of cases would have to be reassigned to another demographic category to make the two distributions the same. The index varies from 0 for distributions that are identical to 100 for distributions that are mirror images of each other.

For the second question, we need to reweight the sample of a given country to reflect the demography of the comparison country. The first step in reweighting involves constructing a matrix of demographic characteristics that the investigator believes may be important in explaining differences in poverty rates or other income inequality measures. The demographic matrix we used for this simulation by reweighting was constructed with the following dimensions:

- Sex of head

- Number of adults other than head and spouse (zero through three)

- Number of persons in the family with earnings (zero through three)

- Number of children in the family (zero through three)

- Age of head (up to thirty-four years of age; thirty-five to forty-four; forty-five to fifty-four; fifty-five to sixty-four; sixty-five to seventy-four; and over seventy-four)

The matrix has a potential 768 cells, but some of the cells are impossible. For example, it is not possible to have no other adults in the house but also to have three earners. In fact, we find that for the United States, which has the largest sample and therefore is likely to have the most cells, the matrix has some 605 cells. Samples in the other countries are smaller, and we thus find far fewer cells. For example, the matrix for Norway has only 264 cells.

The inequality indices of comparisons of the U.S. percentage distribution over these cells with that for each of the other fourteen countries vary considerably, from a low of 18 to a high of 51. Figure D.1 presents the inequality coefficients for the total populations and for the child population. We note that the two measures are quite similar except in a few cases. The child distributions are quite a bit more unequal than the total distributions in the comparison of the United States with Germany and Denmark. In Switzerland the child distribution is quite a bit more equal than the total.

But these differences are overshadowed by the differences between countries. Italy and Spain have very different demographies from the United States—around 50 percent of Italians and Spaniards would have to be moved to another demographic category to produce equal distributions. Around one-third of persons in Sweden, Belgium, Denmark, Switzerland, and the Netherlands would have to be moved to make the distributions in these countries equal to that of the United States. In these countries reweighting might make a big differences in our poverty measures because the demographics are quite different. In contrast, the inequality coefficient is 18 in Canada and 26 in Finland. In these countries demography would have to have a powerful influence for the reweighting to produce large effects.

To carry out the reweighting, the following steps were required:

1. We calculated the percentage of the total sample of country A in each of the cells represented by the cross-tabulation of the five variables described earlier.

FIGURE D.1 **Difference Between U.S. and Fourteen Other Countries' Demography**

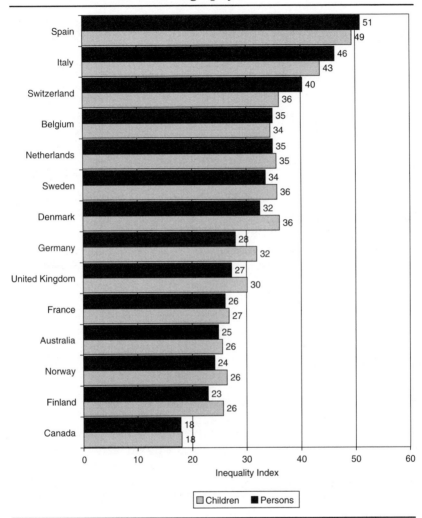

Source: Authors' calculations, using data from the Luxembourg Income Study.

2. Next, we calculated the percentage of persons in country B in each of the cells.

3. To calculate the reweighting ratios, we divided the percentages in country A by the percentages in country B to get a set of ratios.

4. We multiplied these ratios by the percentages in country B to yield the new weights. Using these new weights to calculate a poverty rate produces results based on the assumption that the demography of country B is the same as in country A.

It was necessary to do two reweightings based on two matrices of weights for each of our fifteen countries. The two matrices are necessary because the distribution of children across the various cells of the demographic matrix is not necessarily the same as the distribution of persons.

First, we reweighted the total samples based on the (weighted) number of persons in the sample in order to calculate new medians of net equivalent income with the simulated demographies. Then we made a second matrix based on the (weighted) number of children in order to calculate the effect of the simulated demographies on children's economic well-being. In the remainder of this appendix, we illustrate the method in more detail.

THE UNITED STATES AND NORWAY:
AN EXAMPLE

For this simplified example, we compare the demographies of the United States and Norway. Rather than using the very elaborate set of five variables used earlier, here we use only three variables: sex of the head, age of the head, and the number of children. We categorize age of head as under forty or forty and over, and we consider the number of children from none to three or more. This gives us a matrix with a potential of four times two times two cells—a total of sixteen cells in all.

The first step in calculating the new weights is to calculate the number of cases in each of the sixteen cells. Tables D.1 and D.2 have the results for the total and child samples. In columns 1 and 2 of table D.1, we see the weighted counts for the U.S. total population and the Norwegian total population.[1]

For this example, we produce two aggregate files, one for the United States and one for Norway. Each dataset has four variables: sex of head, age of head, number of children, and weighted count. Thus, the distributions in columns 1 and 2 would be preserved in two small datasets. These datasets are then merged into one. In the resulting file the weighted counts for the United States are contained in one variable and the counts for Norway are in a second variable. If some of the cells were empty in one country but not in the other, that would be reflected in missing values for empty cells.

The next step involves calculating the percentage distribution in each country across the cells of the demographic matrix. These percentages are given in columns 3 and 4 of table D.1. If any of the cells had been empty (missing values), it would have been necessary to recode the missing values to zero in order to calculate the percentage distribution for the country.

Now we can calculate a reweighting multiplier that we can use to generate the income distribution of the United States as if it had the Norwegian demography and the Norwegian income distribution as if it had the demography of the United States. To calculate the United States as Norway, we divide the Norwegian percentage in each cell by the American percentage in the cell. For example, in table D.1 we divide 8.3 percent by 7.9 percent and enter 1.061 as the reweighting multiplier for the cell defined by male head of household, under age forty, with no children.

If any of the cells in the divisor (the United States) are zero, we must provide some small amount in order not to have an error. Cells that are zero in the numerator do not cause trouble. This small amount varies depending on how many cells there are in the matrix, since the minimum percentage in the cells is smaller the more cells there are. We could pick a number that is one-half of the minimum cell percentage and enter it in divisor cells that are zero.

To compute the reweighting factor for Norway as if it had American demography, we reverse the procedure and divide the U.S. percentage in the cell by the Norwegian percentage. In our example in the first row of table D.1, we divide 7.9 by 8.3 to yield a reweighting multiplier of 0.943.

We now have a dataset whose variables are the original counts for each country in each cell, the percentage of cases in each cell,

(*Text continues on page 237.*)

TABLE D.1 Calculation of Total Population Reweights: The United States and Norway

Demographic Characteristics	Weighted Counts		Percentage Distribution		Reweighting Multiplier		New Weights	
	U.S. Distribution	Norway Distribution	U.S. Distribution	Norway Distribution	United States as Norway	Norway as United States	United States as Norway	Norway as United States
Male head of household								
Under forty								
No children	20,732,650	364,025	7.9	8.3	1.061	0.943	21,997,186	343,098
One child	17,148,313	251,377	6.5	5.8	0.886	1.129	15,190,113	283,782
Two children	26,335,442	429,941	10.0	9.8	0.987	1.014	25,980,358	435,817
Three or more children	21,093,839	257,505	8.0	5.9	0.738	1.356	15,560,414	349,076
Forty and over								
No children	67,651,974	1,343,190	25.6	30.7	1.200	0.834	81,165,882	1,119,552
One child	21,730,313	365,854	8.2	8.4	1.017	0.983	22,107,739	359,608
Two children	21,117,619	341,171	8.0	7.8	0.976	1.024	20,616,208	349,469
Three or more children	13,495,517	226,731	5.1	5.2	1.015	0.985	13,700,830	223,333

Female head of household

Under forty								
No children	5,996,616	121,661	2.3	2.8	1.226	0.816	7,351,696	99,236
One child	4,294,305	104,876	1.6	2.4	1.476	0.678	6,337,435	71,065
Two children	5,516,575	70,412	2.1	1.6	0.771	1.297	4,254,818	91,292
Three or more children	6,247,839	25,368	2.4	0.6	0.245	4.076	1,532,954	103,394
Forty and over								
No children	21,479,599	396,414	8.1	9.1	1.115	0.897	23,954,416	355,459
One child	5,484,898	42,657	2.1	1.0	0.470	2.128	2,577,641	90,768
Two children	3,146,061	20,357	1.2	0.5	0.391	2.557	1,230,133	52,063
Three or more children	2,594,537	8,411	1.0	0.2	0.196	5.105	508,276	42,936
Total	264,066,099	4,369,950	100.0	100.0	—	—	264,066,099	4,369,950

Source: Authors' calculations, using data from the Luxembourg Income Study.

TABLE D.2 Calculation of Child Population Reweights: The United States and Norway

Demographic Characteristics	Weighted Counts		Percentage Distribution		Reweighting Multiplier		New Weights	
	U.S. Distribution	Norway Distribution	U.S. Distribution	Norway Distribution	United States as Norway	Norway as United States	United States as Norway	Norway as United States
Male head of household								
Under forty								
One child	5,501,169	85,442	7.8%	8.4%	1.082	0.924	5,953,106	78,955
Two children	12,909,723	214,057	18.3	21.1	1.155	0.866	14,914,303	185,287
Three or more children	12,895,296	157,097	18.3	15.6	0.849	1.178	10,945,605	185,080
Forty and over								
One child	6,208,798	103,715	8.8	10.2	1.164	0.859	7,226,237	89,112
Two children	9,783,303	161,337	13.9	15.9	1.149	0.870	11,241,059	140,415
Three or more children	8,019,154	136,724	11.4	13.5	1.188	0.842	9,526,123	115,095
Female head of household								
Under forty								
One child	1,875,639	51,980	2.7	5.1	1.931	0.518	3,621,657	26,920
Two children	3,386,511	46,046	4.8	4.5	0.947	1.056	3,208,224	48,605
Three or more children	4,584,106	19,148	6.5	1.9	0.291	3.436	1,334,131	65,793
Forty and over								
One child	2,007,580	18,046	2.8	1.8	0.626	1.597	1,257,322	28,814
Two children	1,669,763	12,666	2.4	1.3	0.529	1.892	882,509	23,965
Three or more children	1,700,405	6,188	2.4	0.6	0.254	3.944	431,173	24,405
Total	70,541,447	1,012,446	100.0	100.0			70,541,447	1,012,446

Source: Authors' calculations, using data from the Luxembourg Income Study.

and the reweighting multiplier for each country. We merge this file (defined as a lookup table) with the raw data file for each country in order to define the reweighting multiplier appropriate to each respondent, depending on which cell of the demographic matrix that respondent falls into. It is now possible to adjust each respondent's weight to represent the simulated demography by multiplying his or her weight by the reweighting multiplier for the cell he or she falls in.

We multiply the reweighting multiplier by the individual weights for each case in the survey. That is, in order to simulate a Norwegian demography for the United States, we add 6.1 percent to its weight for each case in that cell. If the dataset is unweighted, we assume an implicit weight of one for each case. Using the new weights for each country, we produce the values in the last two columns of table D.1. One check on the accuracy of the steps to reweight is that the sum of the new weighted counts must equal the sum of the original weighted counts. If they do not, then somewhere along the line an error has crept in, perhaps because we have mishandled the setting of the empty cells to zero or to some small number in the divisor when calculating the reweighting multiplier.

Once we have the percentage distributions for each country, we can calculate an index of the inequality of the demographic distributions. The inequality index for the demographic distributions in table D.1 is 8.0. This is one-half of the sum of the absolute differences between the percentages in each of the cells. It tells us that we would have to reassign 8 percent of the cases in order to make the distributions equal. This inequality index is smaller than any of the indices in figure D.1 because we have a very simplified demographic matrix of only sixteen cells compared with the hundreds of cells in the reweighting used for this study.

With the new weights we can now calculate a new median equivalent income, which will differ by a small or large amount from the actual one depending on how different these percentage distributions are and on how much impact demographic characteristics have on the incomes of persons in the middle of the income distribution. We define a new poverty line as one-half of the simulated median equivalent income.

Table D.2 presents the same information as table D.1 but now for the child population. To develop new child weights, we follow the same procedures as for the total population. First, we calculate the percentage distribution of children in each of the demographic cells. Using these percentages, we calculate new reweighting multipliers and multiply those by the weight of each case in the survey. We check to see that the sum of the new weights is identical to the sum of the original weights. We find that the Norwegian and American child distributions are somewhat less equal than the distributions for the total population given that we have an inequality index of 11.6.

Using these simulated demographic distributions, we are now in a position to make whatever poverty rate tables we wish—or indeed, calculate any other inequality measures. We can follow this method for various subgroups in the population as reported in chapters 6 and 7 to focus more sharply on the effect of demographic variations.

— Notes —

Chapter 1

1. In the United States cohabiting is imputed by the U.S. Census Bureau.
2. This pattern is dramatically different from the one found using the official poverty line, with a steep decline over the years to a little over 10 percent in 1997 and after. The difference reflects the fact that our equivalence scale assumes greater needs of elders compared with those of younger persons and the bunching of elders in the income range between the official poverty line and the LIS line.

Chapter 2

1. We have to assume that the percentage distribution across categories is not significantly different for the median real GDP compared with the mean real GDP. See chapter 11 for a discussion of moving from mean GDP per capita to median GDP per capita.

Chapter 4

1. Unfortunately, imputed rent, part of the definition of family income in the longitudinal datasets, is not in the LIS data, and in this respect the panel income definition is superior to the LIS definition. This difference in definition could have had an important effect on poverty rates, since differences across countries in homeownership presumably have an important effect on differences in economic well-being. In fact, however, these differences turn out to be only very slight.

Chapter 5

1. It can be noted that the correlation of escape odds with a measure of the social democratic versus residualist welfare state regimes—the

Hicks and Kenworthy (2003) variable "progressive liberalism"—is slightly higher than that with left cabinet share (0.87). But because they use information about transfer benefits, a measure of welfare state regimes as a cause of income involves a kind of tautology; one deals with income at a macro level and the other at a micro level. For example, a correlation between poverty rates and the proportion of GDP spent on transfers does not tell us anything new. Therefore, we have preferred to stick with a political measure.

Chapter 6

1. We note that the United States and the United Kingdom have high proportions of children in single-parent families, which tends to reduce the proportion of two-parent children in the lower third, while in Spain and Italy there are very few children in single-parent families and consequently a larger proportion of two-parent children in the lower third.
2. The results here for Italy and Spain are underestimates because of the inclusion of child allowances in earnings.
3. All references to "average" refer to average amounts of the various sources as a percentage of the median equivalent income. Each source is equivalized so that the total of the averages of each source adds to the household's total equivalent income.

Chapter 9

1. Two other papers by Fisher (1993, 1995) provide a history of the development of poverty lines in earlier periods and in other countries.

Chapter 10

1. We might expect respondents in families of four to give the same answer to both questions. In each of the surveys analyzed, about half of them do, with the balance splitting their answers in roughly equal proportions between less and more.
2. We cannot examine the effect of the ages of children since Gallup asks only about the age of the survey respondent. We analyzed Steven Dubnoff's (1985) small dataset to determine whether age of child as well as age of respondent has an effect on MIQ. We found no such effect.
3. Dubnoff (1985) does find that the family size elasticity of public views of needed income is greater the lower the level of income asked

about (from "prosperous" down to "poor"). But analysis of quite similar questions in Rainwater (1974) did not find such an effect.

Chapter 11

1. This convention is also adopted by OECD and the European Community (Townsend 1979; Förster 1994; Hagenaars, de Vos, and Zaidi 1998; Eurostat 1998).
2. In what follows, we use the term "states" to apply to the available regional breakdowns for each of the countries, whether these regions are formally named states or provinces or regions.
3. Canada has only 30.3 million people, and Australia 18.3 million; California, with 32.2 million, has a larger population than Canada. The Australian population is slightly less than that of Texas (19.4 million) and about the same as New York's (18.1 million). Italy and Spain contain 57.4 and 39.6 million persons, respectively. All figures here are for 1997 and are taken from United Nations Development Programme (1999, 197, table 16) and U.S. Census Bureau (1998, 33, table 33).
4. The 8.2-percentage-point difference for New Jersey—21.8 percent of poor children by the state standard versus 13.6 percent by the national standard—translates into a 60.2 percent difference (8.2 divided by 13.6) in figure 13.5.
5. We note that we can accomplish even this level of detail only by combining the large American survey for three years. Results for other countries can only be suggestive given the small size of the surveys.

Appendix D

1. These cell frequencies can be derived in different ways depending on the particular statistical program used. We used the SPSS aggregate procedure to produce a small dataset containing the number of cases in each cell. The cells of this dataset contain either the actual count of cases or the weighted count. (In LIS analyses weights are always used.) If some cells are empty, the aggregate file has fewer cells than the potential number.

References

Adema, William, and Marcel Einerhand. 1998. "The Growing Role of Private Social Benefits." Labor Market and Social Policy occasional paper 32. Paris: Organization for Economic Cooperation and Development (April 17).

Anderson, Elijah. 1999. *Code of the Street: Decency, Violence, and the Moral Life of the Inner City.* New York: W. W. Norton.

Applebaum, Diana Karter. 1977. "The Level of the Poverty Line: A Historical Survey." *Social Service Review* 51(3): 514–23.

Atkinson, Anthony B. 1970. "On the Measurement of Inequality." *Journal of Economic Theory* 2(3, September): 244–63.

Atkinson, Anthony B., Lee Rainwater, and Timothy M. Smeeding. 1995. "Income Distribution in OECD Countries: Evidence from the Luxembourg Income Study (LIS)." Social Policy Studies 18. Paris: Organization for Economic Cooperation and Development (October).

Bradbury, Bruce. 1989. "Family Size Equivalence Scales and Survey Evaluations of Income and Well-being." *Journal of Social Policy* 18(3, July): 383–408.

Bradbury, Bruce, Stephen P. Jenkins, and John Micklewright, eds. 2001. *The Dynamics of Child Poverty in Industrialized Countries.* Cambridge: Cambridge University Press.

Bradley, David, Evelyne Huber, Stephanie Moller, Francois Nielsen, and John Stephens. 2001. "Distribution and Redistribution in Post-Industrial Democracies." Center for Policy Research, Luxembourg Income Study working paper no. 265. Syracuse, N.Y.: Syracuse University (May). Available at: www.lisproject.org/publications/liswps/265.pdf.

Bradshaw, Jonathan. 2001. "Child Poverty Under Labour." In *An End in Sight?: Tackling Child Poverty in the United Kingdom,* edited by Geoff Fimister. London: Child Poverty Action Group.

Bradshaw, Jonathan, and Jun-Rong Chen. 1997. "Poverty in the United Kingdom: A Comparison with Nineteen Other Countries." *Benefits* 18(January): 1–16.

Büchel, Felix, Joachim R. Frick, Peter Krause, and Gerg G. Wagner. 2001. "The Impact of Poverty on Children's School Attendance: Evidence from

West Germany." In *Child Well-Being, Child Poverty, and Child Policy in Modern Nations: What Do We Know?*, edited by Koen Vleminckx and Timothy M. Smeeding. Bristol, Eng.: Policy Press.

Buhmann, Brigitte, Lee Rainwater, Gunther Schmaus, and Timothy M. Smeeding. 1988. "Equivalence Scales, Well-being, Inequality, and Poverty: Sensitivity Estimates Across Ten Countries Using the Luxembourg Income Study (LIS) Database." *Review of Income and Wealth* 34(2, June): 115–42.

Burtless, Gary, and Timothy M. Smeeding. 2001. "The Level, Trend, and Composition of Poverty." In *Understanding Poverty,* edited by Sheldon H. Danziger and Robert H. Haveman. New York and Cambridge, Mass.: Russell Sage Foundation and Harvard University Press.

Chase-Lansdale, P. Lindsay, Robert A. Moffitt, Brenda J. Lohman, Andrew J. Cherlin, Rebekah Levine Coley, Laura D. Pittman, Jennifer Roff, and Elizabeth Votruba-Drzal. 2003. "Mothers' Transitions from Welfare to Work and the Well-being of Preschoolers and Adolescents." *Science* 299(March): 1548–52.

Cherry, Robert, and Max B. Sawicky. 2000. "Giving Tax Credit Where Credit Is Due: A 'Universal Unified Child Credit' That Expands the EITC and Cuts Taxes for Working Families." Briefing paper. Washington, D.C.: Economic Policy Institute (April). Available at: www.cpinet.org/briefingpapers/EITC_BP.pdf.

Citro, Constance F., and Robert T. Michael. 1995. *Measuring Poverty: A New Approach.* Washington, D.C.: National Academies Press. Available at: http://books.nap.edu/books/0309051282/html/index.html.

Coleman, Richard Patrick, Lee Rainwater, and Kent A. McClelland. 1978. *Social Standing in America: New Dimensions of Class.* New York: Basic Books.

Corcoran, Mary. 2002. "Mobility, Persistence, and the Consequences of Poverty for Children: Child and Adult Outcomes." In *Understanding Poverty,* edited by Sheldon H. Danziger and Robert H. Haveman. New York and Cambridge, Mass.: Russell Sage Foundation and Harvard University Press.

Cornell University. College of Human Ecology. N.d. "Cross-National Equivalent File, 1980–2001." Available at: www.human.cornell.edu/pam/gsoep/equivfil.cfm.

Cowell, Frank A. 1978. *Measuring Inequality: Techniques for the Social Sciences.* New York: Halsted Press.

———. 1984. "The Structure of American Income Inequality." *Review of Income and Wealth* 30(3, September): 351–75.

———. 1988. "Poverty Measures, Inequality, and Decomposability." In *Welfare and Efficiency in Public Economics,* edited by Dieter Bös, Manfred Rose, and Christian Seidl. Berlin and New York: Springer-Verlag.

Danziger, Sheldon H. 2001. "After Welfare Reform and an Economic Boom: Why Is Child Poverty Still So Much Higher in the United States Than in Europe?" Paper presented to the Eighth Foundation for International Studies on Social Security (FISS) Conference on Support for Children and Their Parents: Why's, Ways, Effects, and Policy. Sigtuna, Sweden (June).

Davies, Hugh, and Heather Joshi. 2001. "Who Has Borne the Cost of Britain's Children in the 1990s?" In *Child Well-being, Child Poverty, and Child Policy in Modern Nations: What Do We Know?*, edited by Koen Vleminckx and Timothy M. Smeeding. Bristol, Eng.: Policy Press.

Davis, Allison. 1946. "The Motivation of the Underprivileged Worker." In *Industry and Society*, edited by William F. Whyte. New York: McGraw-Hill.

———. 1948. *Social-Class Influences upon Learning*. Cambridge, Mass.: Harvard University Press.

Dubnoff, Steven. 1985. "How Much Income Is Enough?: Measuring Public Judgments." *Public Opinion Quarterly* 49(Fall): 285–99.

Duesenberry, James S. 1949. *Income, Saving, and the Theory of Consumer Behavior*. Cambridge, Mass.: Harvard University Press.

Duncan, Greg J., and Jeanne Brooks-Gunn, eds. 1997a. *The Consequences of Growing up Poor*. New York: Russell Sage Foundation.

———. 1997b. "Income Effects Across the Life Span: Integration and Interpretation." In *The Consequences of Growing up Poor*, edited by Greg J. Duncan and Jeanne Brooks-Gunn. New York: Russell Sage Foundation.

Duncan, Greg J., Wei-Jun J. Yeung, Jeanne Brooks-Gunn, and Judith Smith. 1998. "How Much Does Childhood Poverty Affect the Life Chances of Children?" *American Sociological Review* 63(3, June): 406–23.

Ellwood, David, and Rebecca Blank. 2001. "The Clinton Legacy for America's Poor." Research working paper RWP01–028. Cambridge, Mass.: Harvard University, Kennedy School of Government (July).

Esping-Andersen, Gøsta. 1990. *The Three Worlds of Welfare Capitalism*. Cambridge: Policy Press.

———. 1999. *Social Foundations of Postindustrial Economies*. Oxford: Oxford University Press.

European Commission. 1985. "On Specific Community Action to Combat Poverty (Council Decision of December 19, 1984)." 85/8/EEC. *Official Journal of the European Communities* 2(24).

———. 1989. "Communication from the Commission on Family Policies (COM [89] 363 final)." *Social Europe: Official Journal of the European Communities* 1(94, October 31): 121–29.

———. 2001. "Social Protection Committee Report on Indicators in the Field of Poverty and Social Exclusion." Brussels: European Commission

(October). Available at: europa.eu.int/comm/employment_social/news/2002/jan/report_ind_en.pdf.

Eurostat. 1998. "Analysis of Income Distribution in Thirteen EU Member States." 11. Luxembourg: Eurostat (Statistical Office of the European Communities).

Expert Committee on Family Budget Revisions. 1980. *New American Family Budget Standards.* Madison: University of Wisconsin, Institute for Research on Poverty.

Fisher, Gordon M. 1992. "The Development and History of the Poverty Thresholds." *Social Security Bulletin* 55(4, Winter): 3–14. Available at: www.ssa.gov/history/fisheronpoverty.html#15.

———. 1993. "An Overview of (Unofficial) Poverty Lines in the United States from 1904 to 1965." Poverty Measurement working paper. Washington: U.S. Bureau of the Census.

———. 1995. "Is There Such a Thing as an Absolute Poverty Line over Time?: Evidence from the United States, Britain, Canada, and Australia on the Income Elasticity of the Poverty Line." Poverty Measurement working paper. Washington: U.S. Bureau of the Census. Available at: www.census.gov/hhes/poverty/povmeas/papers/elastap4.html.

Flores, Kimura, Toby Douglas, and Deborah Ellwood. 1998. "The Children's Budget Report: A Detailed Analysis of Spending on Low-Income Children's Programs in Thirteen States." Assessing the New Federalism Series 14. Washington, D.C.: Urban Institute.

Förster, Michael. 1994. "Family Poverty and the Labor Market." Luxembourg Income Study working paper 114. Syracuse, N.Y.: Syracuse University, Maxwell School of Citizenship and Public Affairs, Center for Policy Research (July).

Foster, James, Joel Greer, and Erik Thorbecke. 1984. "A Class of Decomposable Poverty Measures." *Econometrica* 52(3): 761–66.

Gallup Organization. various years. "Gallup Surveys." Roper Center for Public Opinion Research, University of Connecticut, Storrs. www.ropercenter.uconn.edu/.

Goedhart, Theo, Victor Halberstadt, Arie Kapteyn, and Bernard van Praag. 1977. "The Poverty Line: Concept and Measurement." *Journal of Human Resources* 12(4, Fall): 503–20.

Gornick, Janet, and Marcia K. Meyers. 2003. *Families That Work: Policies for Reconciling Parenthood and Employment.* New York: Russell Sage Foundation.

Government of Canada. Social Union. 1999. "National Child Benefit Progress Report: 1999." Ottawa: Government of Canada (May 14). Available at: www.nationalchildbenefit.ca/ncb/NCB-99/toceng.html.

Gregg, Paul, and Stephen Machin. 2001. "Child Experiences, Educational Attainment, and Adult Labor Market Performance." In *Child Well-being,*

Child Poverty, and Child Policy in Modern Nations: What Do We Know?, edited by Koen Vleminckx and Timothy M. Smeeding. Bristol, Eng.: Policy Press.

Hagenaars, Aldi J. M. 1991. "The Definition and Measurement of Poverty." In *Economic Inequality and Poverty: International Perspectives,* edited by Lars Osberg. Armonk, N.Y.: M. E. Sharpe.

Hagenaars, Aldi, Klaas de Vos, and Asgharm Zaidi. 1998. "Patterns of Poverty in Europe." In *The Distribution of Welfare and Household Production: International Perspectives,* edited by Stephen P. Jenkins, Arie Kapteyn, and Bernard M. S. van Praag. Cambridge: Cambridge University Press.

Harrington, Michael. 1962. *The Other America: Poverty in the United States.* New York: Macmillan.

Hauser, Robert M., and Megan M. Sweeney. 1997. "Does Poverty in Adolescence Affect the Life Chances of High School Graduates?" In *Consequences of Growing up Poor,* edited by Greg J. Duncan and Jeanne Brooks-Gunn. New York: Russell Sage Foundation.

Haveman, Robert. 2003. "When Work Alone Is Not Enough." *LaFollette Policy Report* 13(2): 1–15.

Haveman, Robert, and Barbara Wolfe. 1994. *Succeeding Generations: On the Effects of Investments in Children.* New York: Russell Sage Foundation.

Hicks, Alexander, and Lane Kenworthy. 2003. "Varieties of Welfare Capitalism." *Socio-Economic Review* 1(1): 27–61.

Hills, John. 2002. "The Blair Government and Child Poverty: An Extra One Percent for Children in the United Kingdom." Unpublished paper. London School of Economics.

Huber, Evelyne, Charles Ragin, and John D. Stephens. 1997. "Comparative Welfare States Data Set." Data set. Available at: www.lisproject.org/publications/welfaredata/hrscode98.PDF.

Immervoll, Herwig, Holly Sutherland, and Klaas de Vos. 2000. "Child Poverty and Child Benefits in the European Union." EUROMOD working paper EM1/00. Cambridge: Cambridge University Press.

Jäntti, Markus, and Sheldon Danziger. 1994. "Child Poverty in Sweden and the United States: The Effect of Social Transfers and Parental Labor Force Participation." *Industrial and Labor Relations Review* 48(1, October): 48–64.

Johnson, Lyndon B. 1964. "Proposal for a Nationwide War on the Sources of Poverty: Lyndon B. Johnson's Special Message to Congress, March 16, 1964." Reprinted in *Public Papers* of *U.S. Presidents, Lyndon B. Johnson, 1963–1964.* Washington: U.S. Government Printing Office.

Kamerman, Sheila B., and Alfred J. Kahn. 1995. *Starting Right: How America Neglects Its Youngest Children and What We Can Do About It.* New York: Oxford University Press.

———. 1997. *Family Change and Family Policies in Great Britain, Canada, New Zealand, and the United States.* Oxford: Oxford University Press.

———. 2001. "Child and Family Policies in an Era of Social Policy Retrenchment and Restructuring." In *Child Well-Being, Child Poverty, and Child Policy in Modern Nations: What Do We Know?,* edited by Koen Vleminckx and Timothy M. Smeeding. Bristol, Eng.: Policy Press.

Kapteyn, Arie, and Bernard M. S. van Praag. 1976. "A New Approach to the Construction of Family Equivalence Scales." *European Economic Review* 7(4, May): 313–35.

Katz, Michael B. 1986. *In the Shadow of the Poorhouse: A Social History of Welfare in America.* New York: Basic Books.

———. 1989. *The Undeserving Poor: From the War on Poverty to the War on Welfare.* New York: Pantheon.

Kilpatrick, Robert W. 1973. "The Income Elasticity of the Poverty Line." *Review of Economics and Statistics* 55(3, August): 327–32.

Korenman, Sanders, and Jane E. Miller. 1997. "Effects of Long-term Poverty on Physical Health of Children in the National Longitudinal Survey of Youth." In Greg J. Duncan and Jeanne Brooks-Gunn (eds.), *Consequences of Growing Up Poor.* New York: Russell Sage Foundation.

Korpi, Walter. 1980. "Approaches to the Study of Poverty in the United States: Critical Notes from a European Perspective." In *Poverty and Public Policy: An Evaluation of Social Science Research,* edited by Vincent T. Covello. Cambridge, Mass.: Schenkman.

———. 1983. *The Democratic Class Struggle.* London: Routledge and Kegan Paul.

Lancaster, Kelvin. 1971. *Consumer Demand: A New Approach.* New York: Columbia University Press.

Lesthaeghe, Ron J. 2002. "From the Reformation to Multiculturalism: A Political and Cultural Reading of the Demography of the Low Countries." Erasmus Lectures, Harvard University (Spring).

Levenson, Irving. 1978. "Updating Poverty Standards and Program Benefits." *Growth and Change* 9(1, January): 14–22.

Loprest, Pamela. 1999. "How Families That Left Welfare Are Doing: A National Picture." New Federalism: National Survey of America's Families B-1. Washington, D.C.: Urban Institute (August). Available at: newfederalism.urban.org/pdf/anf_b1.pdf.

Meyers, Marcia K., Janet C. Gornick, Laura R. Peck, and Amanda J. Lockshin. 2001. "Public Policies That Support Families with Young Children:

Variation Across U.S. States." In *Child Well-Being, Child Poverty, and Child Policy in Modern Nations: What Do We Know?*, edited by Koen Vleminckx and Timothy M. Smeeding. Bristol, Eng.: Policy Press.

Miller, S. M., and Pamela A. Roby. 1970. *The Future of Inequality*. New York: Basic Books.

Moffitt, Robert. 2002. "From Welfare to Work: What the Evidence Shows." Welfare Reform and Beyond 13. Washington, D.C.: Brookings Institution (January).

Moynihan, Daniel Patrick. 1996. "Opinion: When Principle Is at Issue." *The Washington Post,* August 4, 1996, p. C7.

O'Hare, William, Taynia Mann, Kathryn Porter, and Robert Greenstein. 1990. "Real Life Poverty in America: Where the American Public Would Set the Poverty Line." 90–007. Washington, D.C.: Center on Budget and Policy Priorities (July).

Organization for Economic Cooperation and Development. n.d. "About: Purchasing Power Parities (PPP)." Available at: www.oecd.org/EN/about/0, ,EN-about-513-15-no-no-no-0,00.html.

Ornati, Oscar A. 1966. *Poverty Amid Affluence: A Report on a Research Project Carried out at the New School for Social Research*. New York: Twentieth Century Fund.

Orshansky, Mollie. 1965. "Counting the Poor: Another Look at the Poverty Profile." *Social Security Bulletin* 28(1, January): 3–20.

Osberg, Lars. 2002. "Time, Money, and Inequality in International Perspective." Luxembourg Income Study working paper 334. Syracuse, N.Y.: Syracuse University, Maxwell School of Citizenship and Public Affairs, Center for Policy Research (November).

Palmer, John L., Timothy M. Smeeding, and Barbara Boyle Torrey. 1988. *The Vulnerable*. Washington, D.C.: Urban Institute Press.

Parsons, Talcott, and Niel J. Smelser. 1956. *Economy and Society: A Study in the Integration of Economic and Social Theory*. Glencoe, Ill.: Free Press.

Patterson, James T. 1981. *America's Struggle Against Poverty, 1900–1980*. Cambridge, Mass.: Harvard University Press.

Peattie, Lisa, and Martin Rein. 1983. *Women's Claims*. Oxford: Oxford University Press.

Rabier, Jacques-Rene, and Ronald Inglehart. 2002. *Euro-Barometer 5: Revenues, Satisfaction, and Poverty, May 1976*. Paris/Ann Arbor, Mich.: Institut Français d'Opinion Publique (IFOP)/Inter-University Consortium for Political and Social Research. Available at: www.ispsr.umich.edu:8080/ICPSR-STUDY/07418.xml.

Rainwater, Lee. 1966. "Crucible of Identity: The Negro Lower Class Family." *Daedalus* 95(1, Winter): 176–211.

———. 1969. "The Problem of Lower Class Culture." In *On Understanding Poverty: Perspectives from the Social Sciences,* edited by Daniel Patrick Moynihan and Corinne Saposs Schelling. Perspectives on Poverty Series, vol. 1. New York: Basic Books.

———. 1974. *What Money Buys: Inequality and the Social Meanings of Income.* New York: Basic Books.

———. 1991. "The Problem of Social Exclusion." Human Resources in Europe at the Dawn of the Twenty-first Century. Luxembourg: Eurostat.

———. 1992. "Changing Inequality Structures in Europe: The Challenge to Social Science." In *European Social Science in Transition: Assessment and Outlook,* edited by Meinolf Dierkes and Bernd Biervert. Boulder, Colo.: Westview Press.

Rainwater, Lee. 1994. "Family Equivalence as a Social Construction." In *Standards of Living and Families: Observation and Analysis,* edited by Olivia Ekert-Jaffe. London: John Libby and Company Ltd.

Rainwater, Lee, Martin Rein, and Joseph E. Schwartz. 1986. *Income Packaging in the Welfare State.* Oxford: Oxford University Press.

Rein, Martin. 1970. *Social Policy: Issues of Choice and Change.* New York: Random House.

Riesman, David, and Howard Roseborough. 1960. "Careers and Consumer Behavior." In *A Modern Introduction to the Family,* edited by Norman W. Bell and Ezra F. Vogel. New York: Free Press.

Ross, Katherin. 1999. "Labor Pains: Maternity Leave Policy and the Labor Supply and Economic Vulnerability of Recent Mothers." Ph.D. diss., Syracuse University.

Ruggles, Patricia. 1990. *Drawing the Line: Alternative Poverty Measures and Their Implications for Public Policy.* Washington, D.C.: Urban Institute Press.

Saunders, Peter, and Bruce Bradbury. 1989. "Some Australian Evidence on the Consensual Approach to Poverty Measurement." SPRC discussion paper 14. Sydney: Social Policy Research Centre (July).

Sawicky, Max B., and Robert Cherry. 2001. "Making Work Pay with Tax Reform." Issue brief 173. Washington, D.C.: Economic Policy Institute (December 21). Available at: www.epinet.org/Issuebriefs/ib173/ib173.pdf.

Sen, Amartya Kumar. 1973. *On Economic Inequality.* Oxford: Clarendon Press.

———. 1981. *Poverty and Famines: An Essay on Entitlement and Deprivation.* Oxford: Clarendon Press.

———. 1992. *Inequality Reexamined.* New York and Cambridge, Mass.: Russell Sage Foundation and Harvard University Press.

Skevik, Anne. 1998. "The State-Parent-Child Relationship After Family Break-ups: Child Maintenance in Norway and Great Britain." In *The State of Social Welfare, 1997: International Studies on Social Insurance and Retirement, Employment, Family Policy, and Health Care,* edited by Peter Flora, Philip R. de Jong, Julian Le Grand, and Jun-Young Kim. London: Ashgate.

Skocpol, Theda. 1992. *Protecting Soldiers and Mothers: The Political Origins of Social Policy in the United States.* Cambridge, Mass.: Harvard University Press.

———. 1995. *Social Policy in the United States: Future Possibilities in Historical Perspective.* Princeton, N.J.: Princeton University Press.

Smeeding, Timothy M. 1997. "Poverty in Developed Countries: The Evidence from the Luxembourg Income Study." In *Poverty and Human Development, Human Development Papers 1997.* New York: United Nations Development Programme.

———. 2002. "No Child Left Behind?" *Indicators* 1(3): 6–30. 67.

———. 2003. "Real Standards of Living and Public Support for Children: A Cross-national Comparison." Paper presented at the Bocconi Workshop on Income Distribution and Welfare, Milan, Italy (May 30, 2002). Revised January 2003.

Smeeding, Timothy M., and Lee Rainwater. 2001. "Comparing Living Standards Across Nations: Real Incomes at the Top, the Bottom, and the Middle." LIS working paper 266. Syracuse, N.Y.: Syracuse University, Luxembourg Income Study (May). Available at: www.lisproject.org/publications/liswps266.pdf.

Smeeding, Timothy M., Lee Rainwater, and Gary Burtless. 2001. "United States Poverty in a Cross-national Context." In *Understanding Poverty,* edited by Sheldon H. Danziger and Robert H. Haveman. New York and Cambridge, Mass.: Russell Sage Foundation and Harvard University Press.

Smith, Adam. 1976 [1776]. *An Inquiry into the Nature and Causes of the Wealth of Nations.* In *The Works and Correspondence of Adam Smith,* edited by R. H. Campbell and A. S. Skinner. Oxford: Clarendon.

Smith, Judith R., Jeanne Brooks-Gunn, and Pamela K. Klebanov. 1997. "Consequences of Living in Poverty for Young Children's Cognitive and Verbal Ability and Early School Achievement." In *Consequences of Growing up Poor,* edited by Greg J. Duncan and Jeanne Brooks-Gunn. New York: Russell Sage Foundation.

Summers, Robert, and Alan Heston. 1991. "The Penn World Table (Mark 5): An Expanded Set of International Comparisons, 1950–1988." *Quarterly Journal of Economics* 106(2, May): 327–68.

Townsend, Peter. 1979. *Poverty in the United Kingdom: A Survey of Household Resources and Standards of Living.* Berkeley: University of California Press.

United Kingdom. Department for Education and Skills. 1998. "Meeting the Child Care Challenge." National Child Care Strategy Green Paper. London: Department for Education and Skills (May). Available at: www.dfes.gov.uk/childcare.

United Nations Development Programme. 1999. *Human Development Report 1999: Globalization with a Human Face.* New York: United Nations. Available at: www.hdr.undp.org/reports/global/1999/ln.

U.S. Bureau of the Census. various years. *Consumer Income Reports, 1946–1994.* Series, no. P60. Available at: www.census.gov/prod/www/abs/income.html.

U.S. Department of Commerce. U.S. Bureau of the Census. 1998. *Statistical Abstract of the United States.* Washington: U.S. Government Printing Office. Available at: www.census.gov/prod/www/statistical-abstract-us.html.

———. N.d. *Historical Poverty Tables.* Available at: www.census.gov/hhes/income/histinc/hstpovtb.html.

U.S. Department of Commerce. U.S. Bureau of Economic Analysis. various years. *National Economic Accounts.* Washington: U.S. Government Printing Office.

U.S. Department of Health and Human Services. Office of the Assistant Secretary for Planning and Evaluation. N.d. "Poverty Guidelines, Research, and Measurement." Available at: aspe.hhs.gov/poverty.

Vaughan, Denton R. 1993. "Exploring the Use of the Public's Views to Set Income Poverty Thresholds and Adjust Them over Time." *Social Security Bulletin* 56(2): 22–46.

Walker, Robert, and Michael Wiseman. 2001. "The House That Jack Built." *Milken Institute Review* (fourth quarter): 52–62.

Watts, Harold. 1969. "An Economic Definition of Poverty." In *On Understanding Poverty,* edited by Daniel P. Moynihan. New York: Basic Books.

———. 1980. "Special Panel Suggests Changes in BLS Family Budget Program." *Monthly Labor Review* 103(12, December): 3–10.

Whiteford, Peter. 1985. "A Family's Needs: Equivalence Scales, Poverty, and Social Security." Research paper 27. Canberra, Aust.: Department of Social Security.

Wilensky, Harold L. 2002. *Rich Democracies: Political Economy, Public Policy, and Performance.* Berkeley: University of California Press.

Index

absolute poverty, 7–8, 9, 186

adolescents, economic marginality of, 64, **66**, 67

advance maintenance payments, 124–25

AFDC (Aid to Families with Dependent Children), 6, 184

African Americans, poverty rate of, **31**

after-tax family income, 18

age, of children, 87, 171

age, of household head, 86–87, 167, 168, 169, 170–72. *See also* demographic analysis

age, of survey respondent, and conception of get-along income, 160, **174**

aged persons, poverty of, 26–28, **181**, 182, **190–91**

Aid to Families with Dependent Children (AFDC), 6, 184

Alabama, **191, 192, 198, 203, 209**

Alaska-Hawaii: median income, **191, 192**; number of poor children, **209**; poverty rates, national vs. state standards, **191**, 197, **198**; poverty rate vs. other countries, **203**

Anderson, E., 149

Arizona: median income, **191, 192**; number of poor children, **209**; poverty rates, national vs. state standards, **191**, 197, **198**; poverty rate vs. other countries, **204**

Arkansas: median income, 189, **191, 192**; number of poor children, **209**; poverty rates, national vs. state standards, **191, 198,** 199; poverty rate vs. other countries, **202**

Asian Americans, poverty rate of, **31**

asset income, 93

Australia: family leave, 136; median equivalent income analysis, **193**; population of, 241*n*3; purchasing power parity, 217; regional vs. national analysis, 187–88, **193,** 195, 196, 199, **200, 202–3,** 206–7, 215; social transfer program summary, 105–6, 130. *See also* cross national comparison

Austria, 23, **24, 202**

average (middle-income) class, 32, **33, 35,** 43–45, 79–81

Belgium, 70, 103, 129, **202.** *See also* cross national comparison

blacks, U.S. poverty rate of, **31**

Blair, T., 141

Bradbury, B., 57, 158–59

budget estimation method, 153–54, 178, 179

California: median income, 188, **191, 192**; number of poor children, **209**;

California (*continued*)
  population of, 241*n*3; poverty rates,
  national vs. state standards, **191,**
  197, **198,** 199; poverty rate vs. other
  countries, **204**
Canada: family leave, 136; median
  equivalent income analysis, **193;**
  political control and poverty rates,
  70; population of, 241*n*3; poverty
  measurement, 8; regional vs.
  national analysis, 185, 187–88, **193,**
  195, 196, 199–201, **202,** 206–7, 215;
  social transfer program summary,
  105, 130, 131. *See also* cross
  national comparison
cash assistance, 96, 100–102, 127
Census Bureau (U.S.), 157, 214, 239*n*1
charity, 130
child allowances: in Canada, 105;
  defined as social wage program, 96;
  importance of, 107; in Northern
  European countries, 103, 104;
  single-mother family effects,
  123–24, 129; in Spain, 104;
  two-parent family effects, 97–98
child care assistance, 18, 135–36, 140
child care subsidies, 136
child poverty: vs. elder poverty,
  26–28; overview, 21–26; by race
  and ethnicity, 30–31; research considerations, 2–4; trends, 28–30; U.S.
  vs. European countries, 17
child support, 124–25, 130, 134, 137,
  140
child tax credit, 133
Code of the Street (Anderson), 149
cohabitation, 4, 239*n*1
Colorado-Utah-Nevada: median
  income, **191, 192;** number of poor
  children, **209;** poverty rates,
  national vs. state standards, **191,**
  197, **198;** poverty rate vs. other
  countries, **202**
"Communication from the Commission on Family Policies" (European
  Commission), 135

Connecticut. *See* Rhode Island-
  Connecticut
Consumer Income Series, U.S. Bureau
  of the Census, 157
consumption: and family size, 178,
  179; measurement issues, 169; and
  poverty measurement, 9–10,
  146–47, 152; U.S. vs. other countries, 38–41
continuum of misery or well-being,
  150, 162–65
CPS (Current Population Surveys),
  187, 213
cross national comparison: child
  poverty overview, 21–31; consumption, 38–41; data sources, 2; demographic characteristics, 49–56, 87–89,
  115–17, 228–38; family size, 76–78,
  180–82; income classes, 32–38;
  income packaging, 70–75; median
  equivalent income, **20;** political control, 70, **71;** poverty line determination, 166; real income, 41–48, 216–27;
  at regional vs. national level,
  199–207. *See also* single-mother families; two-parent families
Current Population Surveys (CPS),
  187, 213
Czech Republic, 23, **25**

data sources: cross national comparison, 2; European poverty measures,
  185; GDP analysis, 216–17; purchasing power parity (PPP) measures,
  216–17; regional analysis, 187–88,
  213–15. *See also* Luxembourg
  Income Study (LIS); public opinion
  polling
Davis, A., 149
Delaware-Maryland-Virginia-District of
  Columbia: median income, **190,**
  192; number of poor children, **209;**
  poverty rates, national vs. state standards, **190,** 197, **198;** poverty rate
  vs. other countries, **203**

demographic analysis: data sources, 228; families with and without earners, 53–56; methodology, 49–51, 228–38; observed vs. simulated, 51–52; single-mother families, 115–17; two-parent families, 87–89
Denmark, 102–3, 129, **202**. *See also* cross national comparison
deprivation, 147–48, 149, 162
disability insurance, 103, 128, 140
District of Columbia. *See* Delaware-Maryland-Virginia-District of Columbia
Dubnoff, S., 240*n*2–3
Duesenberry, J., 146

Earned Income Tax Credit (EITC), 106, 133, 138, 139, 140
earnings: as after-tax family income, 18; general patterns, 53–56; importance of, 107–8, 123; in Nordic countries, 102; in Northern European countries, 107; single-mother families, 120–23; two-parent families, 93–95, 102; in U.K., 104. *See also* pretransfer income
ECHP (European Community Household Panel), 185
economically marginal children, longitudinal study of U.S. and Germany, 59–67
economic development, and child poverty rates, 23
economic growth, 1, 48
economic measure of poverty, 9. *See also* poverty line
education, 139–40
EITC (Earned Income Tax Credit), 106, 133, 138, 139, 140
elder poverty, 26–28, **181**, 182, **190–91**
employment: of single mothers, 130, 131; state facilitation of, 133–34; of women, 135, 137
Engel method, 178

equivalence scales: analyses, 170–77; importance of, 177–82; methodological issues, 167–69; research considerations, 169–70
equivalent income: age-of-head effect, 170–72; approaches to, 168–70; by country, **20**; definition of, 168, 180; elasticity of, 168; family size effects, 172–77; importance of, 167; lower third analysis, 36–38, 81–84; overview of, 18–19; percentage net transfers by, 74–75; and poverty measurement, 165, 168, 186; regional analysis, 186, 189, 192, 193, 194
equivalent well-being, 168–69
ethnicity and race, child poverty rates by, 30–31
European Commission, 135, 151
European Community, 8
European Community Household Panel (ECHP), 185
European Council of Ministers, 5
European Union, 5–6, 183–84, 185
existence minimum, 8
Expert Committee on Family Budget Revisions, 154
extreme poverty income class: benefits of analysis, 165; cross national comparison, **35**; definition of, 32; single-mother families, **112**; two-parent families, **80, 81**

factor income, 92, 93
family income. *See* income
family leave, 134, 136–37, 140
family size: and conception of get-along income, 160, **174**; equivalence scales, 167, 168, 169, 172–77; poverty rate impact, 76–78; and single-mother families, 113; trends, 4. *See also* demographic analysis
fathers, earnings of, 94–95
Finland, 102–3, 129, **202**. *See also* cross national comparison

Fisher, G., 8, 156, 240
Florida, **191, 192, 198, 203, 209**
food consumption, cross national
comparison, 40–41
food stamps, 18, 100, 102, 107
Foster, J., 165
France, 103, 129, **202**. *See also* cross
national comparison

Gallop Poll: age of children omission,
240*n*2; age-of-head effects, 171,
172; equivalent income determination, 169; family size effects, 176,
177, **179**; get-along income question, 155, 156, 157, 158; health and
comfort question, 158; minimum
income question, 170, 177; poverty
line definition, 151
GDP (gross domestic product). *See*
gross domestic product (GDP)
gender, and intergenerational inheritance of poverty status, 64–67
Georgia, **191, 192, 198, 203, 209**
German Socio-Economic Panel
(GSOEP), 57–58
Germany: intergenerational inheritance of poverty, 63–67; national
poverty rate, **202**; poverty measurement, 8; poverty persistence, 57–63;
social transfer program summary,
103, 104, 129, 130; tax credits, 139.
See also cross national comparison
get-along income, 155–62, 170, 173,
174
Goedhart, T., 179
government control, and observed
poverty rates, 70
government jobs, 121
government transfers. *See* transfers
Greer, J., 165
gross domestic product (GDP): and
child poverty rates, 23, 26; countries' percentage of real U.S. GDP,
42; cross national comparisons,
40–41; data sources, 216–17; real

income comparisons, 216–23,
225–27
group theory, 147–48
GSOEP (German Socio-Economic
Panel), 57–58

Harrington, M., 7
Hawaii. *See* Alaska-Hawaii
Heston, A., 216
Hicks, A., 239
high-income class, 32, **33, 35**
Hispanics, U.S. poverty rate of, **31**
homeownership, 239*n*1
housing allowances: as after-tax family
income, 18; cross national comparison, 100, 101, 103; single-mother
family effects, 127–28, 129
housing costs, 186
housing expenditures, cross national
comparison, 41
Huber, E., 70
Hungary, 23, **25**

Idaho. *See* Montana-Idaho-Wyoming
IEQ (income evaluation question), 177
Illinois, **190, 192, 198, 204, 208**
imputed rent, 239*n*1
income: categories of, 92; definitions,
70–71, 93; and degree of poverty,
163–64; elasticity of poverty line,
152–59; methodological issues,
68–69, 216–25; minimum standard
of, 8, 19; and poverty line determination, 150–52, 155–57; public opinion of need for, 155–62, 170, 171,
173, **174,** 177, 240*n*2; regional vs.
national analysis, 188–95; and social
standing determination, 148
income classes: and conception of
get-along income, 160–61; definition of, 32; distribution of children
by, 32–34; examples of, 19; and get-
along amount, **174**; lower third
analysis, 36–38, 81–84, 91–92,

110–11; overview, 32–34, **35**; real income by, 41; two-parent families, 79–84

income equivalence. *See* equivalent income

income evaluation question (IEQ), 177

income inequality: cross national comparison, 41–48; equivalence scales, 180–82; and real income measurement, 218, 220; research considerations, 162–63; state-based analysis, 189

income inequality aversion index, 164

income packaging: and family size, 76–78; general analysis of, 70–75; methodological issues, 68–69; political influences, 69–70; U.S. policy recommendation, 140. *See also* single-mother families; two-parent families

income packaging institutions, definition of, 51

income-tested benefits: single-mother families, 126–27, 129, 130, 131; two-parent families, 100–102, 104, 105

Indiana, **190, 192, 198, 202, 208**

inequality, of income. *See* income inequality

inheritance, of poverty status, 63–67

in-kind programs, 100–102, 126–28

Iowa-Nebraska-Kansas: median income, **190, 192**; number of poor children, **208**; poverty rates, national vs. state standards, **190,** 197, **198**; poverty rate vs. other countries, **202**

Ireland, 23, **24**

Israel, 23, **25, 202**

Italy: national poverty rate, **203**; political control and poverty rates, 70; population of, 241*n*3; regional analysis, 187, 188, 195, 196, 201, **205, 206,** 215; social transfer program summary, 130. *See also* cross national comparison

Jenkins, S., 57

jobs, government vs. private-sector, 121

Kahn, A., 136

Kamerman, S., 136

Kansas. *See* Iowa-Nebraska-Kansas

Katz, M., 6

Kentucky, **191, 192, 198, 203, 209**

labor force participation, 130, 131, 134, 135, 137

labor market assistance, 96, 99, 104, 108, 125–26

"Leave No Child Behind" Act, 140

Lesthaeghe, R., 4

LIS (Luxembourg Income Study). *See* Luxembourg Income Study (LIS)

"living wage" laws, 138

longitudinal studies, 57–67

Louisiana: median income, **191, 192**; number of poor children, **209**; poverty rates, national vs. state standards, **191,** 197, **198,** 199; poverty rate vs. other countries, **204**

Luxembourg, 23, **24, 202**

Luxembourg Income Study (LIS): demographic analysis, 228; earnings data, 93; goals of, 211–12; poverty line, 19–20; regional analysis, 187; scope of, 2, 28, 211

Maine-New Hampshire-Vermont: median income, **190, 192**; number of poor children, **208**; poverty rates, national vs. state standards, **190,** 197; poverty rate vs. national rate, **198**; poverty rate vs. other countries, **202**

marginal-income class, 32, **33, 35**

market basket, regional pricing differences, 186

market income, 68. *See also* earnings

marriage, 4
Maryland. *See* Delaware-Maryland-
   Virginia-District of Columbia
Massachusetts: median income, 188,
   190, 192; number of poor children,
   208; poverty rates, national vs. state
   standards, **190**, 197, **198,** 199;
   poverty rate vs. other countries, **204**
maternity payments, 96, 98–99, 135
mean equivalent income, net transfers
   by, 74–75
mean income, vs. median income,
   151–52
means-tested programs: in Australia,
   105–6; in Netherlands, 103–4; two-
   parent family effects, 100–102; in
   U.K., 97, 105; in U.S., 106
median equivalent disposable income,
   187
median equivalent income: in Australia, **193**; in Canada, **193**; by
   country, **20**; in Italy, **194**; as
   poverty measure, 165, 186; in Spain,
   194; U.S. state analysis, 189, **192**
median income, 151–52, 156–57,
   188–95
medical goods and services expenditures, cross national comparison, 41
"Meeting the Child Care Challenge"
   (United Kingdom), 136
men: earnings of fathers, 94–95; intergenerational inheritance of poverty
   status, 64–67
methodology: degrees of poverty,
   162–65; demographic analysis,
   49–51, 228–38; equivalence scales,
   167–69; income category and conception of get-along income,
   160–61; income elasticity of poverty
   line, 154, 157; income sources,
   68–69; real income, 216–25
Michigan, **190, 192, 198, 203, 208**
Micklewright, J., 57
middle-income (average) class, 32, **33,
   35,** 43–45, 79–81

minimum budget estimation, 153–54,
   178, 179
minimum income question (MIQ),
   170, 171, 177, 240n2
minimum income standard, 8, 19
minimum wage, 108, 138
Minnesota: median income, **190, 192**;
   number of poor children, **208**;
   poverty rates, national vs. state standards, **190**, 197, **198**; poverty rate
   vs. other countries, **203**
MIQ (minimum income question),
   170, 171, 177, 240n2
Mississippi: median income, 189, **191,
   192**; number of poor children, **209**;
   poverty rates, national vs. state standards, **191**, 197, **198,** 199; poverty
   rate vs. other countries, **203**
Missouri, **190, 192, 198, 202, 208**
Montana-Idaho-Wyoming: median
   income, **191, 192**; number of poor
   children, **209**; poverty rates,
   national vs. state standards, **191,
   198,** 199; poverty rate vs. other
   countries, **202**
mothers, earnings of, 93–94. *See also*
   single-mother families
Moynihan, D., 6

National Academy of Sciences (U.S.),
   186
national median income standard, lim-
   itations of, 19
national vs. regional-based analysis,
   183–87, **190–91,** 196–99
Native Americans, poverty rate of, **31**
near poverty income class: benefits of
   analysis, 165; cross national comparison, **35**; definition of, 32, 59;
   longitudinal study of U.S. and Germany, 59–61, 62, **65–66**; single-
   mother families, **112**; two-parent
   families, **80,** 81
Nebraska. *See* Iowa-Nebraska-Kansas

Netherlands, 103–4, 129, 139, **202**. *See also* cross national comparison

Nevada. *See* Colorado-Utah-Nevada

New American Family Budget Statistics (Expert Committee on Family Budget Revisions), 153–54

New Hampshire. *See* Maine-New Hampshire-Vermont

New Jersey: median income, 188, 189, **190, 192**; number of poor children, **208**; poverty rates, national vs. state standards, **190**, 197, **198**; poverty rate vs. other countries, **204**

New Mexico: median income, 189, **191, 192**; number of poor children, **209**; poverty rates, national vs. state standards, **191**, 197, **198**, 199; poverty rate vs. other countries, **203**

New York: median income, 188, **190, 192**; number of poor children, **208**; population of, 241*n*3; poverty rates, national vs. state standards, **190**, 197, **198**, 199; poverty rate vs. other countries, **204**

North Carolina: median income, 188, **191, 192**; number of poor children, **209**; poverty rates, national vs. state standards, **191, 198**; poverty rate vs. other countries, **203**

North Dakota-South Dakota: median income, **190, 192**; number of poor children, **208**; poverty rates, national vs. state standards, **190**, 197, **198**; poverty rate vs. other countries, **202**

Norway, 70, 102–3, 129, **202**, 232–38. *See also* cross national comparison

OECD (Organization for Economic Cooperation and Development), 40, 217, 223, 241*n*1

Ohio, **190, 192, 198, 203, 208**

Oklahoma, **191, 192, 198, 203, 209**

Oregon: median income, 188, **191, 192**; number of poor children, **209**; poverty rates, national vs. state standards, **191, 198**; poverty rate vs. other countries, **203**

Organization for Economic Cooperation and Development (OECD), 40, 217, 223, 241*n*1

Ornati, O., 153, 154

Orshansky index, 7

The Other America: Poverty in the United States (Harrington), 7

Pacific Islanders, U.S. poverty rate of, **31**

packaging of income. *See* income packaging

panel studies, 57–67

Panel Study of Income Dynamics (PSID), 57–58

parental insurance programs, 98–99

parental leave, 136–37

paternity payments, 96, 98–99

Pennsylvania, **190, 192, 198, 203, 208**

Penn World Tables (PWT), 216

pension benefits: in Australia, 106; in Nordic countries, 103; single-mother families, 128, 130; in Spain, 104; two-parent families, 95; in U.S., 106

Personal Responsibility and Welfare Reform Act (PRWRA) (1996), 184

Poland, 23, **25**

policy issues : earners vs. non-earner families, 56; earnings of two-parent families, 95; effectiveness measurement, 3; income-tested benefits, 102; U.S. devolution of social assistance to state, 184, 207; U.S. strategy, 1, 132–41

political issues, 69–70, 141

poor income class: cross national comparison, **35**, 45–46, 48; definitions, 32; longitudinal study of U.S.

poor income class (*continued*)
and Germany, 59–67; single-mother families, **112**; two-parent families, **80**
population characteristics. *See* demographic analysis
post-transfer income, 71, 72–73, 89–91, **118**
poverty: American perspectives, 6–7; definition of, 5–6, 7, 32, 183–84; degrees of, 162–65; measurement of, 8–11, 17–20, 145–52, 163, 185–86, 210; persistence of, 57–63; views about living in, 148–49
poverty gap, 131, 163
poverty line: adjustments to, 9; definition of, 18, 183, 186; determination of, 149–52; equivalence factors, 172–73; income elasticity of, 152–59; LIS vs. official U.S., 19–20; research issues, 11; and standard of living, 166; two-earner family effects, 122; of U.S. vs. other countries, 7–8
PPP (purchasing power parity) measures, 39, 40, 216–17, 223–27
preschools, 140
pretransfer income: definition of, 70–71; poverty rates by, 72–73; single-mother families, 117–18, 120–21, 129, 130; two-parent families, 89–91
pricing, of goods, 186
private benefits, 130
private-sector jobs, 121
prosperous income class, 32, **35, 80**
provinces, analysis by. *See* regional analysis
PSID (Panel Study of Income Dynamics), 57–58
public education, 139–40
public opinion polling: age effects, 171–72; elasticities vs. other methods, 177–79; family size effects, 173–77; get-along income question, 155; health and live decently question, 158–59; social equiva-lence scales, 170. *See also* Gallop Poll
public-sector jobs, 121
purchasing power parity (PPP) measures, 39, 40, 216–17, 223–27
PWT (Penn World Tables), 216

quantity budgets, 153–54

race and ethnicity, child poverty rates by, 30–31
Ragin, C., 70
Rainwater, L., 173, 241
real income, 41–48, 84–86, **114**, 115, 216–25
reference group theory, 147–48
regional analysis: cross national comparison, 199–207; data sources, 187–88, 213–15; income differences, 188–95; vs. national analysis, 183–87, **190–91,** 196–99
relative deprivation, 147–48, 149
relative income, of two-parent families, **85**
relative poverty: vs. absolute poverty, 9–11; assumptions about, 166; definitions of, 145–49, 150; local vs. national analysis, 185–87, 225–27; measurement of, 149–52
research considerations: child poverty, 2–4; equivalence scales, 169–70; income inequality, 162–63; social standard of poverty, 11; welfare state regimes, 69–70
Rhode Island-Connecticut: median income, 188, **190, 192**; number of poor children, **208**; poverty rates, national vs. state standards, **190,** 197, **198**; poverty rate vs. other countries, **204**
rich income class, 32, **35**, 42, **43, 80**
Ruggles, P., 156
Russia, 23, **25**

salaries. *See* earnings
Saunders, P., 158–59
self-employment income. *See* earnings
Sen, A., 10–11
sickness payments, 96, 97–98
single-mother families: with additional adult present, 113; child support, 124–25, 130, 134, 137; definition of, 109–10; demographic analysis, 115–17; earnings, 120–23; equivalence factors, 182; family size effects, 113; general patterns, 111–13; income sources, 117–20; labor force participation, 130, 131, 134; lower third analysis, 110–11; proportion of children living in, 109, 110; real vs. relative income analysis, 113–15; social transfer program effects, 123–31
Slovakia, 23, **25**
Smith, A., 145–46
social assistance programs, 95, 96–97, 100–102, 127, 131
social class, 146, 148, 159–62
social equivalence scales, 170
social identity, 5
social measure of poverty, 9–11. *See also* relative poverty
social minimum, 147
social roles, 146
social transfers. *See* transfers
social wage programs, 95–96, 129, 130, 131
societal poverty lines, 11, 149–50
South Carolina, **191, 192, 198, 203, 209**
South Dakota. *See* North Dakota-South Dakota
Spain: national poverty rate, **202**; population of, 241*n*3; regional analysis, 187, 188, 195, 196, 201, **205, 206,** 215; social transfer program summary, 104, 130. *See also* cross national comparison
SSI (Supplemental Security Income), 140

standard of living, 5, 8, 9, 19, 166
standard of poverty, 166
standard package of goods and services, 146
state analysis. *See* regional analysis
state poverty lines, 149–50, 187
Stephens, J., 70
Summers, R., 216
Supplemental Security Income (SSI), 140
surveys. *See* public opinion polling
Sweden: integration of mothers into labor force, 134–35; national poverty rate, **202**; political control and poverty rates, 70; poverty line, 8, 149; purchasing power parity, 217; real income analysis vs. U.S., 45, **47**; social transfer program summary, 102–3, 129. *See also* cross national comparison
Switzerland, 103, 129, 130. *See also* cross national comparison

Taiwan, 23, **25**
TANF (Temporary Assistance to Needy Families), 6, 137, 140, 141, 184
taxation: and income measurement, 70–72; policy, 138–39; reform, 133
tax credits, 18, 106, 133, 138–39, 140
Temporary Assistance to Needy Families (TANF), 6, 137, 140, 141, 184
Tennessee: median income, **191, 192**; number of poor children, **209**; poverty rates, national vs. state standards, **191, 198,** 199; poverty rate vs. other countries, **203**
Texas: median income, 188, **191, 192**; number of poor children, **209**; population of, 241*n*3; poverty rates, national vs. state standards, **191, 198**; poverty rate vs. other countries, **203**
Thorbecke, E., 165
Townsend, P., 147–48

transfer income, 89–91, 92, 117–20
transfers: and income measurement, 18, 70–72, 89–91; poverty rate analysis, 72–75; single-mother families, 123–31; two-parent families, 95–108
two-parent families: age of children, 87; age of household head, 86–87; children living in by country, **78**; demographic analysis, 87–89; earnings, 93–95; employment facilitation policy, 134; income classes, 79–84; income sources, 89–92; poverty-creating effect of, 122–23; real income, 84–86; social transfer program effects, 95–108

unemployment payments: in Australia, 106; in Canada, 105; defined as social wage program, 96; in Northern European countries, 103, 104; single-mother family effects, 125–26, 131; in Spain, 104; two-parent family effects, 99–100; in U.S., 106
United Kingdom: child care programs, 135, 136; child poverty rate trends, 29–30; maternity leave policies, 135; national poverty rate, **203**; policy commitment, 141; political control and poverty rates, 70; poverty line, 149; poverty measurement, 8; social transfer program summary, 104–5, 130; tax credits, 139. *See also* cross national comparison
United States: child care policy, 136; child poverty rates by ethnicity, **31**; child poverty rate trends, 29; demographics vs. Norway, 232–38; family leave, 136; GDP, 217; intergenerational inheritance of poverty, 63–67; median equivalent disposable income, 187; minimum wage legislation, 108; policy strategy, 132–41;

political control and poverty rates, 70; poverty line, 7–8, 19–20, 149, 156, 172–73; poverty persistence, 57–63; real income analysis vs. Sweden, 45, **47**; social transfer program summary, 106–8, 131; state analysis, 187–92, 196–99, **202–4**, 206–9. *See also* cross national comparison
United States National Academy of Sciences, 186
U.S. Bureau of the Census, 157, 214, 239*n*1
U.S. National Accounts, 157
U.S. official poverty line, 7–8, 19–20, 149, 156, 172–73
Utah. *See* Colorado-Utah-Nevada

van Praag, B., 170
Vaughan, D., 10, 156, 157
Vermont. *See* Maine-New Hampshire-Vermont
very rich income class, 32, **35, 80**
Virginia. *See* Delaware-Maryland-Virginia-District of Columbia

wages: minimum wage, 108, 138; of single mothers, 131; social wage programs, 95–96, 129, 130, 131. *See also* earnings
War on Poverty, 1, 7
Washington: median income, 188, **191, 192**; number of poor children, **209**; poverty rates, national vs. state standards, **191, 198**; poverty rate vs. other countries, **203**
Washington, DC. *See* Delaware-Maryland-Virginia-District of Columbia
The Wealth of Nations (Smith), 145–46
welfare reform, 6
welfare state regimes, 69–70
well-being, 150, 162–65, 168–69. *See also* income classes

West Virginia: median income, 189, **190, 192**; number of poor children, **209**; poverty rates, national vs. state standards, **190,** 197, **198**; poverty rate vs. other countries, **203**
Wisconsin, **190, 192, 198, 203, 208**

women: earnings of mothers, 93–94; intergenerational inheritance of poverty status, 64–67. *See also* single-mother families
Wyoming. *See* Montana-Idaho-Wyoming